AFRICAN, AMERICAN

AFRICAN, AMERICAN

FROM TARZAN TO DREAMS FROM MY FATHER—
AFRICA IN THE US IMAGINATION

DAVID PETERSON DEL MAR

ZED
Zed Books
LONDON

African, American: From Tarzan to Dreams from My Father—Africa in the US Imagination was first published in 2017 by Zed Books Ltd, The Foundry, 17 Oval Way, London SE11 5RR, UK.

www.zedbooks.net

Typeset in Haarlemmer by seagulls.net
Printed by CPI Group (UK) Ltd, Croydon, CR0 4YY
Cover design by Alice Marwick
Cover photos used with the permission of Getty Images.

A catalogue record for this book is available from the British Library.

ISBN 978-1-78360-854-6 hb
ISBN 978-1-78360-853-9 pb
ISBN 978-1-78360-855-3 pdf
ISBN 978-1-78360-856-0 epub
ISBN 978-1-78360-857-7 mobi

For Brando Akoto

'Surely I spoke of things I did not understand, things too wonderful for me to know.'

Job 42:3, NIV

CONTENTS

ACKNOWLEDGMENTS

I am particularly indebted to the two scholars who provided exceptionally detailed and perceptive feedback on an early draft of a chapter. A third commented on the revised manuscript. Ken Barlow of Zed Books has been responsive and helpful throughout the process. Wendy del Mar and Daniel Pope provided crucial advice at various stages of the project. Hope Arnold gave the manuscript the benefit of a very close reading near its completion, and Paul Semonin again offered a particularly incisive and generous critique. I am grateful to Taylor & Francis for allowing me to reprint parts of 'At the Heart of Things: Peace Corps Volunteers in Sub-Saharan Africa,' David Peterson del Mar, *African Identities*, reprinted by permission of Taylor & Francis Ltd.

This book's notes are but a faint indication of how heavily I relied on the scholarship of others. Of the many writers who taught me about this book's diverse subjects, I am particularly indebted to: Kwame Anthony Appiah, Algernon Austin, Kenneth M. Cameron, James T. Campbell, Jay Kirk, and Kathryn Mathers.

Since 2010 it has been increasingly difficult to distinguish between this book, my work linking schools in Ghana and the

US through the nonprofit Yo Ghana!, my friendships with Africans in Ghana and the US, and my friendships with Americans who practice the art of friendship as if they were Africans.

As always, my wife and son, Wendy and Peter del Mar, have been supportive and patient. Wendy spent a very formative year in Kenya before I met her; working on this book has helped me to appreciate how Kenyans deepened and shaped her into the woman I am so honored to call my life partner. Peter's courage and resilience continue to astonish me. Muril Helen and Robert Demory, Jon and Lois Peterson, Armand Smith, Lisa and Randy Varga, Kanani and Mike Badnin, Nicole Smith, and Brenda and Ben Fowler have shown and taught me about family loyalty and love. John Goncalves and Barbara Segal, Bill Larremore, Barbara Peterson-O'Hare, Todd Olsen, Wayne Randall, Paul Semonin and Anuncia Escala, Eileen and Mark Summit, Thomas Wright, David Porter and the Old Nicks, and Barbara Peterson-O'Hare, and Oregon Uniting have been like family.

The transformational nature of my first trip to Ghana owed a great deal to my fellow travelers: Bee Jai Repp, Barnabas Omulokoli, Lee Nusich, and Peter and Beth Okantey. Thank you Davina Peterson del Mar Nipaba Brew for your smile. I have been blessed with extraordinarily supportive Chairs in the Portland State University Department of History for the duration of this project: Linda Walton, Tom Luckett, and Tim Garrison. Jeff Brown and Andrea Janda are exemplary departmental organizers, and I am also grateful to T-Rex and the rest of the gang at the PSU Library for keeping a diverse range of books flowing my way.

The administrators, teachers, volunteers, board members, and supporters of Yo Ghana! teach and inspire me beyond measure, particularly: Abdul-Mumuni Abdallah, Joseph Abdulai, Nurideen Abubakari, Susan Addy, Nate Aggrey, Kofi Agorsah, Victoria Agorsah, Daniel Ahama, Lilly Glass Akoto, Kwami Akoto, Sewaah Akoto, Moses Akumey, Nantogma Alhassan, Albert Amoako, Mercy and Rudolph Ampofo, Eric Ananga, Kofi Anane, Bishop Seth Anyomi, Alexa Arnold, Amy Bogran, Gilbert Nipaba Brew, LeeAnn Bronson, Jane Carlton, Sister Mary Divya, Eric Donkoh, Rockson Serlom Dordoe, Daniel Dotse, Francis Dzata, Meghan Eigo, Matthew Essieh, Kankam Mensah Felix, Sarah Florig, Dominic Fordwour, Agbey Gedza, Jeanne Gering, John Goldrick, Rashid Hafisu, Wisdom Havor, Ginny Hoke, Ibrahim Ibrahim, Aaron Jones, Komi Kalevor, Berthy Kpiebaya, Noah Kurzenhauser, Sarah Kutten, Yves Labissiere, Marilyn Lucas, Father Anselmus Mawusi, Dorcas Mensah, Martha Montgomery, Deborah Naugler, Kwame Apoku-Amankwa, Ernest and Regina Opoku-Ansah, Daniel Opong, Rhiannon and Sarah Orizaga, Lizzie Petticrew, Justice Prah, Carolina Ramirez, Lucy Ampate Sarpong, Delaney Sharp, Joshua Siu, Tim Smith, Mike Sparks, Rebecca Summit, Roy Thompson, Harriette Vimegnon, Essan Weah, and Michael Williams. Thank you especially to co-founder Elizabeth Fosler-Jones for your joyful fearlessness. The students and staff of Ashesi University left me astounded at what education and service can look like.

I am grateful to the people of Portland International Church for showing me what God's love looks like, particularly: Pastors Kofi Nelson Owusu and Carol Nzem, along with Saundra Nelson Owusu, Marinus Nzem, and their children; the Kwasi and Elsie Agyapong family; Seth and Regina Asare; Isaya Atonga; the Alex and Beatrice Nkansah family; the Justice and Linda Owusu-Hienno family; the Augustine and Patience Sewor family; Yves and Harriette Vimegnon; Kofi Tweneboah and Margaret Nyarko; Frempong Owusu; James Vandervort; the Edgard and Sanctifiee Luhshima Musafiri family; Kevin Mulohwe; and Willy Musavyi. Thank you Sister Isabel Karnga for your unstinting care and challenges. And dearest Brando: Thank you for showing me what stubborn, abundant love looks like, for sharing your blessed and painful life, and for lighting the path. 'What a joy.'

I am especially thankful to the Friends of History, Portland State University, for their support in creating the book's index.

PREFACE

'AFRICA IN MY HEAD'

In 2006 a seventeen-year-old student who had just spent a summer installing irrigation pipes in Ethiopia asked herself: '"Why Africa?" Why am I not motivated by Iran or something?' She concluded that unlike other parts of the world, Africa's problems were simple. 'I can organize Africa in my head. ...'[1] Sub-Saharan Africa has been so ripe for American quests precisely because we have for so long approached it as an uncomplicated and, above all, passive place. As cultural anthropologist Kathryn Mathers observes, the continent's purported blankness makes it fertile ground for 'Americans' imaginations of self.'[2] Tarzan, America's most famous African, was created by a science-fiction writer who never visited the continent. Darkness has signified the place and its people as savage, heathen, immoral, even sub-human, the foil against which the West defined its superiority. Blackness quickly became a 'symbol of the Negro's baseness and wickedness.'[3] Nineteenth-century Americans devoured stories of

1

the intrepid David Livingstone bringing light to the savage heathens of 'Darkest Africa.' But Africa's dark void could also serve to reveal less flattering self-portraits. In Joseph Conrad's semi-autobiographical *Heart of Darkness*, first published in 1899, dank Africa 'whispered' to Kurtz 'things about himself which he did not know, things of which he had no conception till he took counsel with this great solitude.'[4] Whether revealing western virtue or baseness, passive, abject Africa offered a blank space for white journeys of self-discovery.

Respectable black Americans, fearful of being associated with savage Africa, also treated it as a place apart. Unlike their Caribbean counterparts, they became Creoles well before the American Revolution, creating a hybridized, African-American identity, culture, and society out of traumatized African fragments. By the early nineteenth century, even as slavery spread, black men and women aspiring to economic and social respectability embraced Victorian cultural norms such as temperance and church membership. Frederick Douglas, the distinguished self-made abolitionist and reformer, insisted that America, not Africa, was home. Missionary Alexander Crummell favored resettling black Americans in Africa but described it as a place of 'moral desolation and spiritual ruin.'[5] The former slaves who settled in Liberia during the nineteenth century set themselves apart from native Liberians socially, culturally, economically, and politically.[6]

Black and white Americans viewed black Africa as alien at the twentieth century's turn.

Then Africa became less daunting. European colonization and the associated control of contagious diseases made it safer for outsiders. New technologies quickened international travel and communication. People could get to Africa more easily and were more likely than before to survive there.

But the key to America's rising and enduring interest in Africa was rooted in its own economic, social, and cultural transformations. The nation's per capita GNP tripled between 1897 and 1921 even as most people's work hours fell; there was more time and money than ever before for vacations and entertainment—for having fun. Movies, radios, and record players spread, and by the 1920s the great majority of families owned a car. The average American enjoyed a healthier, more prosperous life than any other people in the history of the world. Prosperity encouraged individualism. The Victorian era had required deferred gratification. The new order touted the installment plan and buying things you did not need because they would make you appear more powerful or sexually desirable; you could buy happiness.[7]

This ethos of consumption, of self-actualization, fostered complex, even contradictory cultural patterns. Certainly hedonism rose and Christian piety declined. Yet life in some respects had become more regimented. Adults were less and less likely to be self-employed as farmers or otherwise; young people spent a greater proportion of their lives in school; and local, state, and federal governments regulated more and more activities and behaviors. A strong masculinist culture developed in reaction to the spread of a society that seemed increasingly androgynous and managed.

America had a long history of quest literature well before the early twentieth century. James Fennimore Cooper's

Leatherstocking in the backwoods, Henry David Thoreau's search for the sublime at Walden Pond and other wild places, Walt Whitman's urban authenticity, Huck Finn's flight from a Christian mother—all of these nineteenth-century authors and figures spoke to a masculine discontent with settled life, a pining for a more engaging and elemental way of living than Victorian America seemed able and willing to provide. Early in the new century, as the gap between masculine independence and American life yawned still wider, Westerns and other stories of harrowing male adventure became ubiquitous.

Masculine individualism has been the nation's True North since early in the twentieth century. An Oregon minister lamented that 'the so called search for happiness' was supplanting 'the old time search for character' by the 1920s.[8] A half-century later sociologist Irene Taviss Thomson contrasted the individualism of the 1920s with the 1970s by observing that modern Americans now conceived of the self 'as an entity apart from society.'[9] The new Imperial Self cut across ideological lines. It was that great icon of modern American conservatism, Ronald Reagan, who proclaimed in his 1985 State of the Union Address: 'There are no constraints on the human mind, no walls around the human spirit, no barriers to our progress except those we ourselves erect.'[10] Reagan's America represented the triumph of the imagination, of Hollywood. A sort of libertarian hedonism prevailed among conservatives, liberals, and radicals alike, a chafing against social norms, from paying one's taxes to living within one's means.[11] Our modern age of narcissism is being capped, in 2016, by the political rise of our biggest narcissist of all, reality-TV star Donald Trump, who promises to 'make American great again' by demanding nothing of us but that we trust in him.[12] The US has led a century-long experiment in shedding shared cultural understandings and social constraints, what George Packer, once a Peace Corp Volunteer in Togo, terms America's 'unwinding.'[13]

For black Americans, too, modern America has generated hope and disillusion. W.E.B. Du Bois and other leading reformers aspired to accomplish full integration into American life. The 1920s brought black culture into white American living rooms through radio and records, and in 1965, one century after the Civil War ended, black Americans at last achieved formal political equality. But racism persisted even as fewer white Americans admitted so, and African-Americans became more pessimistic about their prospects even as those prospects improved. If white searchers have sought meanings in Africa not available in the US, their black counterparts have sought identities that the US has refused to provide.

Africa has seemed like the ideal tableau on which to stage modern masculine American quests, black as well as white. If America was tame, it was wild. If America was white, it was black. If America had become soft and feminized, it was bloody and masculine. If America was alien and hostile, Mother Africa would fold one into her dark bosom. We shall meet a long line of distinguished American men who have sought meaning in Africa since the early twentieth century: Teddy Roosevelt, Marcus Garvey, Edgar Rice Burroughs, Du Bois, George Schuyler, Carl Akeley, Langston Hughes, Martin Johnson, Ernest Hemingway, Richard Wright, Robert Ruark, Saul

Bellow, Peter Beard, Paul Theroux, Stokeley Carmichael, Frank Yerby, Alex Haley, Norman Rush, Michael Crichton, Philip Caputo, George Packer, Barack Obama, and Rick Warren.

But these male narratives have been accompanied and often contested by many distinguished American women: Jean Kenyon Mackenzie, Adelia Akeley, Osa Johnson, Esmelda Robeson, Era Bell Thompson, Kathryn Hulme, Maya Angelou, Martha Gellhorn, Alice Walker, Paule Marshall, Maria Thomas, Barbara Kingsolver, Oprah Winfrey. Women's interpretations of Africa have usually diverged sharply from those of their male counterparts. Marianna Torgovnick points out that modern white men, New Age and otherwise, have associated Africa with codifying the boundaries of masculine selves thought to be at risk in modern America.[14] Modern women, she notes, tend to posit a more oceanic, permeable self. As sociologist Nancy Chodorow pointed out in her seminal *The Reproduction of Mothering*, modern American gender roles have been characterized by men who are striving to individuate and women who are not.[15] Hence white men, especially, have commonly posited and pursued an Africa that forced action and forged manly autonomy. White women, on the other hand, commonly described a highly relational Africa. Black American women have reprised some of these same themes, but often with heightened sensitivity to the vulnerability of their hard-won American identities.

The nature of Americans' quests has depended on what sort of Africa they encountered as well as their own racial and gendered identities. This book is to a large extent a history of how black Africans have impinged on American quests. The closer one approached Africans rather than 'Africa,' the less control one had over one's quests. Visitors such as Teddy Roosevelt or Robert Ruark, uninterested in speaking candidly with black Africans, found what they were looking for. African-Americans and white women were more interested in black Africans and therefore more shaped by them. But Africans have often made themselves heard whether or not Americans have wanted to listen. Black African voices rose in the late 1950s and early 1960s, and white Americans' popular interest and quests in Sub-Saharan Africa declined apace. Africans are again disrupting Americans' African narratives in the twenty-first century, when both American interest in Africa and Africans' stature have crested, creating both more friction and more possibilities than ever before.

African, American is primarily concerned with how race, gender, time and Africans have shaped American quests.

Its chapters are chronological. The first covers the twentieth century up to World War II, when Tarzan and Marcus Garvey galvanized popular interest in Africa for unprecedented numbers of white and black Americans, respectively. Among Americans who actually traveled there, women were much more interested in Africans than men were. The second chapter treats the post-war years, an era in which black African independence movements dampened white and enlivened black American popular interest in the continent. Again, women visitors were much more likely than men to pursue relationships rather than abstractions. The third addresses the 1960s, an intense period of change and conflict in both

Sub-Saharan Africa and the US. The nature of black nationalism in both places underwent profound, often wrenching changes, developments that led to a denouement of white American interest, especially, in Africa. The fourth treats the last three decades of the twentieth century, when popular opinion wrote off the continent and accounts of African quests varied radically depending on the authors' race and gender. Implacable Africa offered a bloody blank slate on which white men inscribed harrowing quests. Other Americans found in Africa shattering but vivifying relationships that deconstructed autonomous American selves. Black Americans also divided over Africa, often along gendered lines. Chapter Five treats how twenty-first century Africans are contesting Americans' growing and diverse African quests at home and abroad.

These chronological boundaries are not absolute, in part because people's lives and work have not always fallen neatly within them. Peter Beard, for example, came to Africa in the late 1950s and kept whining about the loss of his playground straight through into the twenty-first century. Because he became prominent in the 1960s, he is treated most fully in Chapter Three. Likewise, George Schuyler wrote about Africa for half of the twentieth century but is featured in Chapter One because his most extensive descriptions appeared well before World War II and contrast tellingly with the impressions of W.E.B. Du Bois and Langston Hughes.

In a book of wide interpretive and chronological scope it has of course been necessary to choose what to include and to focus on. Throughout this period there is a vast reservoir of material about Africa in popular magazines, though little of it speaks directly to the theme of American quests in Africa. Africa has also been depicted in many popular films. This sort of material tends to appear near the beginning of chapters to provide context. The meat of each chapter consists of extended stories, first-hand accounts of Americans who traveled to and wrote about Africa. There is also quite a bit of fiction, often—but not always—from writers who had spent time in Africa. *African, American* is primarily concerned with widely read stories about American quests in Africa, fictional and nonfictional.

Some of the stories or representations you will encounter here were more exceptional than popular. Americans who traveled to and lived in Sub-Saharan Africa have always represented a small slice of the general populace. Some of these authors, such as Ruark and Haley, have enjoyed wide readership for their nonfiction and fiction alike. But less popular authors, such as Maria Thomas or Gloria Naylor, also have a great deal to tell us about American views of Africa, precisely because their ideas are too complex or too discomfiting to attract as wide a readership as a James Michener. I have paid particularly close attention to writers who expressed through their actual or imagined African quests broader American cultural developments regarding race, gender, identity, even the meaning and purpose of life. Africa has seemed to invite such ruminations.

African, American is a cultural history of American attitudes toward Sub-Saharan Africa that neglects many worthy subjects, including Africans' views of the US and US imperialism in Africa. But I hope a consideration of how a variety of

Americans have felt about Africa, how we have framed our understanding of the place, can be part of a process of both listening to African voices and changing American political and economic policies. I elected to write about American impressions of Sub-Saharan Africa rather than the entire continent because most Americans have, unfortunately, made that distinction.

This book often draws examples from Ghana for two reasons. First, it is a nation that I have visited many times, so I have accumulated many first- and second-hand experiences from there. Second, I am not alone; this small West African nation has long drawn a highly disproportionate number of black and white Americans who have taken an interest in, traveled to, and written about Sub-Saharan Africa.

Zed Books publishes scholarship that promotes international equity and empathy. The argument that Africans have increasingly contested and enriched Americans' African quests certainly has a moral dimension and is the product of personal experience as well as academic reflection, particularly my friendship with Mr. Brando Akoto, the person to whom this book is dedicated. I met Brando a few years after I had first traveled to Ghana, a trip that had certainly triggered the reflexive '[w]e should help them' reaction that historian Curtis Keim describes among his college students.[16] I vividly remember the headmistress who welcomed us into her cramped and humid office, took our measure, and remarked: 'So, what can *you* do for *us*?' But the remark was made so lightly as to suggest both that she did not expect ever to see us again and that the school would do fine in either event. In fact, their many challenges notwithstanding, Ghanaian students, teachers, and administrators commonly exuded a strong sense of earnestness and determination. I wanted to help, but I also wanted to learn more from and about these people who were already confounding my stereotypes about abject Africans.

After a couple of years of trial and error, I became part of a diverse group of friends and teachers on both sides of the Atlantic who constituted a nonprofit: Yo Ghana! The students exchanged letters so that they could learn about each other first-hand; we encouraged the American students to raise some money for the Ghana schools.

Then Brando complicated the mission of Yo Ghana! and my perceptions of Africa by becoming a board member and close friend. I met him not in a muggy Accra school or bright Ghanaian village but rather in prosaic Salem, at the annual Ghana Association of Oregon picnic. He was warm but blunt. Having worked for many years at grassroots development across Ghana, he had a keen appreciation for how easily westerners' eagerness to help could undercut local initiative. When the subject of raising money came up, Brando usually dismissed it. 'Take care of relationships,' he observed, 'and everything else will take care of itself.' His mantra to students in Ghana was pointed: 'Do not beg.' 'You are not poor.' 'You are partners.' Brando suggested that what America most had to offer Ghana was the same thing that I had to offer him: just friendship. As we traveled around Ghana, he kept telling schools that we would not build them a computer lab or buy them a bus, but that decades later we would be back. I had not been prepared to make that sort of commitment; once the words came out of his mouth, I was. Brando had a way of making you feel that you should, and could, do more.

Fifteen months later, after much suffering born with uncommon grace, he died at the age of fifty-one from a rare form of cancer.

Going to Africa has always been a metaphor for Americans, an epic quest to strange lands that inevitably circles back to ourselves. As Princeton University literature professor Wendy Belcher observes, Americans' 'fascination with other cultures often amounts to … what they tell us, through imagined difference, about us.'[17] Brando and many other Africans I met modeled a way of living devoted to tending to people other than oneself. He had far too many commitments in both Ghana and the US to meet, was forever disappointing his innumerable friends. But he would stop to inquire, at some length, into the life plans of a boy selling bananas alongside the road. Nor did he treat our American schools much differently from our Ghanaian ones. Both were full of interesting and dedicated people he enjoyed knowing and working with. That was really, he seemed to believe, all that we had to offer each other. Brando opened up a messy, everyday world of possibilities and vulnerabilities made compelling by the company of the people with whom we share them.

That is the gist of my own African quest. Perhaps it explains *African, American*'s soft spot for encounters characterized by ambiguity and collaboration, more a disruption or undercutting of classic American quests than a fulfillment of them. These quests are likely to 'make the world a smaller place,' as one of our Yo Ghana! letter writers puts it, when complicated and enriched by people such as Brando Akoto.

CHAPTER ONE

'BRIGHTEST AFRICA' IN THE EARLY TWENTIETH CENTURY

Early in the twentieth century Americans found Africa more compelling and inviting than ever before, an interest bound up with their unprecedented prosperity. More people had the wherewithal to undertake long vacations abroad and, more to the point, the spread of comfort prompted Americans to search out, directly or vicariously, more exotic, even dangerous, experiences.

This growing openness to places and activities considered primitive affected black as well as white. Darkness had lost much of its stigma in the early twentieth century; white people sought the sun to darken their complexions. White urbanites showed their sophistication by frequenting jazz joints such as the Cotton Club where African-Americans played and danced to 'jungle music.' Millions more listened to black artists such as Jelly Roll Morton, Bessie Smith, Louis

Armstrong, and Duke Ellington on record players and radios. Black culture offered white Americans a respite from modern strictures: 'pure sensation untouched by self-consciousness and doubt,' as historian Nathan Huggins puts it.[1] Primitivism was now allowed, even encouraged—up to a point. The Harlem Renaissance also represented a shift within black culture, particularly for the young and better educated. Poets such as Langston Hughes embraced African motifs; Josephine Baker headed off for Paris and there became famous for her banana costume. Aspiring black Victorians had kept Africa at arm's length and embraced piety, education, hard work, temperance, and other expressions of self-control. Now black college students, like their white counterparts, were drawn to creativity and spontaneity, characteristics long associated with blackness and with Africa.[2]

Victorian culture had posited rigid distinctions between husband and wife, child and parent, black and white, lower class and middle class. The new ethos invited adults to become more youthful, parents and spouses to become 'pals' with their children and each other, and respectable white people to join their black and working-class counterparts in shedding inhibitions. As historian Cornelia Sears so ably demonstrates, American views of Africa shifted apace, from the Dark Continent motif of the late Victorian era to the Edenic Africa of Teddy Roosevelt and other manly hunters to the Brightest Africa of taxidermist Carl Akeley and film-maker Martin Johnson which predominated by the 1920s and 1930s.[3] This Africa invited masculine searches for transcendent self-actualization. It also created space for women adventurers interested in Africa's people. Black Americans' African quests were more focused on people than animals, but here, too, it was a woman traveler, Esmelda Robeson, who most focused on actual Africans.

AFRICAN VISIONS: EDGAR RICE BURROUGHS AND MARCUS GARVEY

The two most influential interpreters of Africa in America by the 1920s had little in common, save that neither ever set foot on the continent they described so fulsomely. Edgar Rice Burroughs and Marcus Garvey made Africa compelling to white and black Americans, respectively, in ways that no one had done before or has done since.

Burroughs was early into his career as a highly popular if not particularly polished novelist when he started writing a story about a white male raised by the apes of savage Africa. Tarzan quickly spread from a syndicated set of stories in 1912 to a long series of cheap novels to the screen and beyond.[4]

Tarzan blended savagery and civilization without ceding any agency or competency to black Africans. He combined the purported superiorities of the 'white race' (intelligence and morality) with primitive ferocity. Millions of white youth could now imagine themselves at home in Africa without ceasing to be white.[5] West Africa's 'simple native inhabitants' and 'savage tribes' are bit players right from the inaugural *Tarzan of the Apes*, first published in 1912. Animals are more important and virtuous. It is Kala the ape, after all, not a black African, who rescues and nurtures the infant Tarzan after his aristocratic British parents perish. The first group of natives the young Tarzan encounters has the appearance of 'low and bestial brutishness,' and are readily thrown into 'jabbering confusion.' One of them kills Kala. Tarzan reflects: 'these people were more wicked than his own apes.' Tarzan is superior to his black counterparts in every respect. He is stronger, smarter, and, thanks to his racial heritage, innately more civilized.

The first Tarzan film, *Tarzan of the Apes*, 1918, also marginalizes black Africans. The local black villagers are weak and stupid. Tarzan easily throttles Kala's killer, and the villagers '[i]n superstitious awe of the strange white being ... for days made offerings to appease his wrath.' Again, Tarzan's superiority is moral as well as physical. The large, leering black African who carries Jane off clearly intends to rape her. Though upon touching Jane Tarzan is 'thrilled with a new emotion' and 'throbbing pulse-beat,' he heeds her admonition: 'Tarzan is a man, and men do not force the love of women.'

By the 1920s and 1930s Tarzan's Africa had become less savage but remained very racist. He routinely aids animals in distress, such as the deer caught in a hunter's snare in *The New Adventures of Tarzan* of 1938, and he can count on elephants, hippos, chimpanzees, or other charismatic mega-fauna to rescue and nurse him. Jane has become a bit more important. In *Tarzan and His Mate*, from 1934, she fends off a lion and has her own yell. Their Africa has become more bucolic than savage, as shown in several extended underwater swimming scenes, including one in which the censors found Jane's nudity offensive. Indeed, Jane refers to their swimming hole as 'a little Garden of Eden' in *Tarzan Escapes*, 1936. But if Jane's stature rose between the wars, black Africans' did not. Potent villains are either Africans played by white actors, such as Boris Karlof in *Tarzan and the Golden Lion* of 1927, or ruthless Europeans hunting for easy wealth. In *Tarzan Escapes* the expedition leader orders his assistant to check the feet of the black porters for thorns to see if they will be ready to travel in the morning, as if they were brute animals incapable of looking after their own bodies. In *Tarzan Finds a Son*, 1939, 'Boy' is fortunate that monkeys carry him out of the wrecked plane before the 'dreadful savages' arrive. On the eve of World War II, Tarzan's chimpanzees and elephants were still much higher on the evolutionary ladder than its black Africans.

Africa's savageness is central to Tarzan's identity and superiority over other white people; it reflected America's embrace of primitivism as well as the persistence of racism. Jane's father and other educated westerners are impractical and ineffectual, if well intentioned. The second and third installments of Burroughs' Tarzan novels, *The Return of Tarzan* and *The Beasts of Tarzan*, published in 1913 and 1914, respectively, are dominated by Tarzan's battle with Rokov, a Russian who is both more intelligent and more evil than anything Africa can produce. Africa is innocent; it remains a foil to the West. Tarzan expresses a turn to the primitive in American culture, an impulse that historians have traced to respectable white men's growing interest in boxing, football, the outdoors, and the emergence of the western genre of literature early in the twentieth century. Tarzan draws his strength from the jungle's savagery, a strength that makes

17

him both physically but also morally superior to Europeans. If Conrad's Africa reveals western man's evil nature,
Burroughs' Africa redeems it.

Garvey, a charismatic Jamaican immigrant, had a
different sort of African redemption in mind; he was the
person most responsible for prompting African-Americans
to think of black Africa as a home rather than a heathenish
embarrassment. The dark-skinned Garvey grew up in the
middle ranks of a highly stratified Caribbean society that
was even more class than race conscious. Largely self-edu-
cated, it was not until he read Booker T. Washington's paean
to black self-determination, *Up from Slavery*, that Garvey
knew that he would become 'a race leader.'[6] In 1914 he started
what would become the United Negro Improvement Association (UNIA) in Jamaica but was far from famous when he
moved to Harlem two years later, where his oratorical and
promotional skills created a black nationalistic movement of
unprecedented breadth and depth.

Garvey posited Africa as the great social, cultural, and
political fact of 'the Beloved and Scattered Millions of the
Negro Race,' as the wording on the UNIA's membership
certificate put it.[7] The UNIA was not a one-trick pony. It
offered life insurance policies and founded businesses. But
what Garvey was really selling was hope and dignity, and
Africa as a black homeland, and the Black Star Line as a vessel
to that end was central to his program; shares in the Black Star
Line were the organization's biggest money maker. In 1920, at
the first international conference of the Negro peoples of the
world, the audience of 25,000 jumped to its feet and roared

when Garvey uttered these words: 'If the Englishman claims England as his native habitat, and the Frenchman claims France, the time has come for 400 million Negroes to claim Africa as their native land.'[8]

As historian Mary G. Rolinson points out, Garvey's message struck religious, even millennial chords. 'I pray God for the redemption of Africa,' was a common refrain.[9] Emily Christmas Kinch, who had served as an African Methodist Episcopal missionary in Liberia, cited polygamy and witch doctors in urging black American Christians to undertake their special role 'in the salvation of our brothers and sisters in the fatherland,' but she also described Africa as 'a land that flows with milk and honey,' a place 'that would receive you gladly.' 'Africa,' she concluded, 'wants you.' William Henry Moses, a prominent Baptist clergyman, defended Garvey in a speech delivered in New York City in 1923: 'I see a larger day. I see a city of schools and churches,' cities stretching across Africa, and 'this race of mine walking up, hand in hand, American and what not ... having a home together.' 'Under God the hour will come,' he assured his listeners, 'when Ethiopia shall stretch forth her hand unto God and black men shall hold their heads high.'[10] 'Back to Africa' constituted a revitalization impulse in which the cruelties of American racism could be transcended, the clock reset as if the trans-Atlantic transportation of millions of Africans and its brutal, centuries-long aftermath had never occurred.

The actual history of the UNIA in Africa was prosaic and disappointing. The steamship line and plans for emigration to and trade with Africa crumbled, despite the monies invested by thousands of hopeful black Americans. Part of the problem was a lack of coordination with black Africa. 'He talks of Africa,' noted fellow Jamaican-American Claude McKay, 'as if it were a little island in the Caribbean Sea,' not a vast continent of diverse black ethnic groups and polities with their own agendas.[11] When Garvey complimented Africa, he focused on Egypt, rather than West Africa, which, like black American leaders before him, he described as in need of uplift.[12] By 1920 West Africans were complaining of Garvey's presumptuousness in assuming the title of President of the African mega-nation he had posited.[13] The UNIA's effort to get land in Liberia fell apart when President King publicly rebuffed Garvey. The UNIA was left with no Africa to return to.

Yet Garvey's widely publicized 'Back to Africa' program introduced millions of ordinary black Americans to the idea that Africa could be more than a source of shame, that it might constitute a refuge and a home. 'We shall be,' asserted a New Orleans domestic worker, 'a nation respected by the world.'[14]

Black missionaries in Africa in the early twentieth century often continued to set themselves apart from Africans even as they took issue with racist stereotypes. Baptist C.C. Boone in 1927 was often blunt in his assessments of the Congolese, remarking that their 'houses do not amount to much,' that they were 'exceedingly superstitious,' and 'have no standard of right or wrong.' Indeed, he wrote in passing and without comment that the natives referred to him as a 'white man.' Neither *Congo as I Saw It* nor *Liberia as I Knew It*, from 1929, indicated that he made close friends with black Africans, let alone that he felt at home in the Congo or Liberia. But Boone praised black Africans. 'I was never more surprised in my life than to find when I reached Congo, a stable form of government, upheld by the natives themselves,' he remarked. Theft and illegitimate births were rare. In terms of achieving civilization, black Congolese were on the same course as 'the Celts and Barbarians of Europe' not so long ago. His assessments of the natives of Liberia were generally positive.

More liberal, secular-minded black Americans embraced Africa more fulsomely by the 1920s. References to African vistas, jungle beats, and particular groups, such as Zulus, peppered the poetry and songs of the Harlem Renaissance. Black sculptors and painters such as Aaron Douglas featured African motifs. Countee Cullen's 'Heritage' is the most cited example. Its famous first line, 'What is Africa to me,' was followed by enticing images of vitality and innocence, such as 'Strong bronzed men, of regal black' and *'Spicy grove, cinnamon tree.'*[15] The poem suggests Cullen's 'alien-and-exile' approach to Africa, of a lost child wanting to make his way back to an unremembered, exoticized home, an act of self-exploration and self-flight, with Africa serving as 'both opiate and intoxicating whirl.'[16] Africa is abstract, romantic.

Garvey and Burroughs were romantics, too, though they appealed to very different American audiences. Their widely consumed images of Africa shaped the viewpoints of millions of Americans, made both black and white people much more interested in and receptive to the continent than their Victorian counterparts had been. The growing number who went there in the early twentieth century expected magic.

MANLY WHITE MEN IN AFRICA

Before Tarzan there was Teddy Roosevelt. From a child right through his Presidency, the undersized, sickly son of patrician parents honed his body and character into a new, more vigorous model of masculinity by seeking out rugged landscapes and challenges.

Africa seemed tailor-made for Roosevelt, so when the first celebrity-President headed there with son Kermit shortly after leaving office in 1909, it was big news. Newspaper reporters jockeyed with each other for stories on board his ship, and Roosevelt wrote nearly every day while on his year-long journey. *Scribner's* won the bidding war for his account and published fourteen of his articles from October 1909 to September 1910.[17] *African Game Trails* appeared soon after, in 1910.

Roosevelt's African adventure expressed his belief that men of the white American 'race' required continual exposure to danger to avoid going soft. Sensitive to critics who charged him with slaughtering helpless, often endangered, animals, he presented his safari as a scientific expedition to gather specimens for the Natural Museum of History. Indeed, pioneering taxidermist Carl Akeley had played a major role in persuading Roosevelt to go to Africa in the first place. But few puzzled over his primary motive. The middle-aged man who had courted death and danger in the Dakotas and who would identify, before dying, his life's peak experience as killing a Spanish officer on San Juan Hill, the man who brought boxing to the White House, was not headed to Africa for the climate.[18]

Indeed, one of the trip's high points occurred when Roosevelt stood steady in the face of a 'burly and ... savage' lion. Roosevelt 'felt keen delight' when his companion's shot missed the charging beast. Now everything depended on his own nerve: 'he galloped at a great pace, he came on steadily—ears laid back and uttering terrific coughing grunts.' Roosevelt was up to the test. His aim was true, the bullet found its mark on the center of his worthy adversary's chest, and it fell. 'Certainly,' Roosevelt concluded, 'no finer sight could be imagined that that of this great maned lion as he charged.' As they made their way back to camp, night fell: 'the half moon hung high overhead, strange stars shone in the brilliant heavens, and the Southern Cross lay radiant above the sky-line.' Sublime Africa—and Roosevelt—had delivered.

Roosevelt often returned to this theme of Africa's salutary brutality. 'The sentimentalists who prattle about the peaceful life of nature do not realize its utter merciless-ness,' he remarked. Hunting, particularly hunting in a place as dangerous as Africa, returned man to this state of nature, forced him to hone instincts grown flaccid in modern life. Shadowing elephants, for example, in thick vegetation 'made our veins thrill,' as one had to be 'ceaselessly ready for whatever might befall.' *African Game Trails* is suffused with the excite-ment and danger of the hunt; it constitutes another extended illustration of Roosevelt's assertion that western civilized man required at least occasional retreats to harrowing places and activities to maintain his moral as well as physical fitness.

Two other widely read American hunters also published

in the 1910s were cattleman Edgar Beecher Bronson and Stuart Edward White, a prolific writer in the vein of Jack London. White was good friends with Roosevelt, who admired his manly novels and encouraged him to hunt in Africa.[19]

Like Roosevelt, Bronson and White found in East Africa moments that tested and honed their manhood. 'Africa,' White wrote in *The Land of Footprints*, published in 1913, 'is the only country I know of where a man is thoroughly and continuously alive.' Like Roosevelt, Bronson in *In Closed Territory* from 1910 waxed at length of the 'terrors' of walking 'adrift in a sea of elephant grass,' surrounded by unseen carnivores that 'may at any instant catch your wind and be literally upon you,' not to mention the snakes. White repeatedly invoked this sort of danger as the reason for going on safari in the first place. Hunting dangerous animals required the same 'continual alertness' necessarily cultivated by 'the higher animals. And it is good to live these things.' Honorable hunting entailed 'a deliberate seeking of mortal combat,' he explained in 1926, in which both parties risked their lives. The crucible of lion hunting revealed to modern man the answer to a question that might otherwise go begging for a lifetime: was he or was he not a man? Like war, boxing, or football, hunting dangerous game was, literally, a sort of game in which modern men voluntarily placed themselves in situations that required more savagery than civilization. White in 1915 asserted that facing a charging lion at close quarters constituted 'the supreme moment in a hunter's life' because all 'little unessentials are brushed aside' leaving just 'the big primitive idea to fill all a man's mind—kill or be killed.' This primal instinct, heretofore repressed by civilization, suffused the hunter's 'being.'

But if the test of manhood lay in risking one's life against savage animals, then one might conclude that the black Africans who routinely ran more risks, during safari and otherwise, outstripped the great white hunters in this measure of masculinity. Indeed, one of Roosevelt's peak experiences was witnessing a group of Nandi, armed only with spears and defended only by frail shields, encircle a lion and withstand its furious charge before dispatching it with a flurry of spears. It was, Roosevelt concluded, 'a scene of as fierce interest and excitement as I ever hope to see.' But Roosevelt soon parted from the Nandi. They refused to serve simply as beaters for his hunts, and 'I did not care to assist as a mere spectator at any more lion hunts, no matter how exciting.'

Roosevelt had in fact long ago worked out a theory of white supremacy that no amount of Nandi bravery was going to disrupt. He believed that all humans descended from a common ancestor, but that the 'black race,' especially, lagged far behind white Americans and was for the present and foreseeable future unassimilable—though occasional black Americans were fit to hold minor offices.[20] Certainly the cultivation of manly physical courage was necessary to keep the white race or races vigorous, as was the willing-ness of educated white women to bear several children. But success also rested on the cultivation of more civilized virtues that 'childlike savages,' their courage and fertility notwith-standing, were constitutionally unable to muster.

Indeed, every aspect of the safari seemed designed to discount the idea that black Africans could in any way be considered equivalent to white people. Scores of porters carried their masters' equipment for what was, by western standards, a pittance. Roosevelt noted in passing that R.J. Cunninghame, the safari's leader, resorted to putting tags on the 'boys,' since 'we did not know their names and faces.' These anonymous hordes were set apart from white people by their roles, clothing, diet, and sleeping quarters as well as color. White authors invariably emphasized how essential it was to establish and maintain this racist hierarchy. Bronson in 1910 mentioned in passing that he 'had to smash' one of his helpers 'in the nose' for handing him the wrong ammunition, and he prescribed floggings for laziness and insolence. Lest he sound crude, he asked readers to remember 'that the black is of a far coarser fibre than the white man, and, therefore, endures and recovers from punishment and wounds no white man could survive.' In fact the white hunters repeatedly referred to their black employees as animals. They needed to be trained like 'a promising bird dog,' as White put it in 1913. He, especially, emphasized the otherness of black Africans, whom he believed had arrived at a sort of cul-de-sac in their evolution, having reached 'the ultimate highest perfection of adjustment to material and spiritual environment of which they were capable under the influence of their original racial force'—i.e. a state of 'hopeless intellectual darkness.' He encouraged aspiring safari-goers to dispense with sentiment and embrace the management of their 'boys' as part of the adventure: 'This game always seemed to me very fascinating, when played right.' The trick was to use just the right amount of violence, and at the right moment, so as to assure ready and efficient subservience. Minor acts of impertinence required sharp words or blows. Major acts of insubordination, such as running away, entailed having the guilty parties dragged before 'the throne of the canvas chair,' where the white hunter decided upon a suitable number of lashes, delivered by black corporals, or deductions from the porter's pay. As Sears argues, Roosevelt and other American men on safari readily drew from a storehouse of racist tropes of white superiority and dark savagery from the American West and antebellum South.[21]

White's legendary gun bearer, Memba Samba, constituted the greatest threat to his tidy system of racialization; by 1913 he had 'developed into a real friend.' In fact White devoted an entire chapter to him in one of his books. Samba was fearless, tireless, unexcelled in tracking game, utterly and perfectly devoted to the work of finding and assisting with the work of killing dangerous animals. White ended his second book published in 1913 by summing him up as one of the few friends whose 'mere ... existence' made one happy.

White counterbalanced his respect for Samba by continually emphasizing the black man's subservience. In 1913 he recounted overhearing how Samba responded to a safari cook who warned him against going after a wounded lion with just one white man at his side: 'My one white man is enough.' Gun bearer and white hunter 'had become a firm whose business it was to carry out the affairs of a single personality—me.' Samba 'acknowledges the Superman.' At the end of one of their safaris, Mensa followed White for two days rather than returning to his nearby farm and wives. He refused White's attempts to speak to him. He simply 'wanted to see the last of the *bwana* with whom he had journeyed so far,' White remarked in his second 1913 book.

Though he presented himself as a naturalist and eventually a conservationist rather than a hunter, Carl Akeley's Africa much resembled that of White and Roosevelt, whose friendship he treasured. The largely self-taught pioneer of realistic taxidermy spent a total of nearly five years in Africa on five separate safaris stretching from 1896 to 1926, collecting specimens for his wildlife dioramas in the Field Museum of Chicago and then his massive African Hall exhibit in the American Museum of Natural History. Just as Roosevelt pursued the strenuous life to compensate for a childhood of luxury and sickness, a challenging if very different childhood kindled in Akeley a life-long desire to prove himself. His early interest in wild animals and taxidermy provoked the disdain of his peers and the disapproval of his mother and other pious relatives. In rural Wisconsin, such peculiarities burdened young Akeley with a reputation for 'shiftlessness,' according to the 1940 account from his second wife, Mary. These shameful formative years paired with Akeley's sensitivity and brilliance forged a deeply wounded and ambitious man. Risking his life in Africa to further his career came easily to him. It demonstrated his masculinity and justified his calling.

Though professing to 'have found but little enjoyment in shooting any kind of animal' in 1925, Akeley wrote extensively of his hunting exploits. Particularly remarkable was his face-to-face battle with a leopard who gripped his right arm in its powerful jaws, a battle Akeley claimed to have won by pushing a hand down its throat and crushing its ribs with his knees: 'My strength had outlasted hers.'

Such tests of masculine strength and courage swelled Akeley's readership and burnished his reputation among people like Roosevelt, but it was not what kept him coming back to Africa. Rather, in Africa Akeley found his life's passion: capturing its incredible but evanescent beauty, particularly through the use of meticulous taxidermy and dioramas. The title of his widely read *In Brightest Africa*, published in 1925, contained his thesis: Africa was not the dark, forbidding place of Victorian explorers but rather a place of transcendent beauty and joy threatened by the dark 'inroads of civilization.' Rather than bringing light to the darkness, pace Livingston, Akeley aspired to bring Africa's light to America before the stultifying hand of progress snuffed it out.

One of the many ironies in Akeley's vision, his life quest, was that immortalizing Africa's animals required ruthlessly killing so many of them. His diary entries made while in Uganda suggest this tension. In one breath he described a scene of some 700 elephants, 'an impression which somehow seems to make all other African experiences fade away,' a sound 'like that of a mighty wind storm in the forest.' But then the sublime gave way to the ordinary; it was time to shoot some specimens. He got close to 'a young bull' but found it 'not worthwhile.' He crept up on a group of twenty-five 'and for a bit I could see nothing good among them' until 'a good pair of tusks emerged.'[22] Akeley was not unaware of this paradox: his job as a scientist and museum curator seemed to require a cold-blooded assessment or cataloguing of corpses. As the decades passed he seemed to empathize and then identify with the massive animals he killed. His first trip to Mikeno to collect gorilla specimens prompted his realization that 'I was the savage and the aggressor.' When he looked into the face of a young gorilla bleeding out he found 'a heartbreaking expression of piteous pleading. ... He would have come into my arms for comfort,' he wrote in 1925. As Akeley set about the hard work of skinning 'an amiable giant who would do no harm except perhaps in self-defense or in defense of his friends,' he gazed out upon 'the most beautiful view I have ever seen,' a tableau he led an artist back to years later to immortalize in the famous diorama that the gorilla would one day be installed in. Thus began both Akeley's determination to preserve this corner of Africa for gorillas—after he had collected the necessary specimens, of course—and a close, personal identification with what he found to be the most human of animals. Akeley named one of the gorillas after himself, and he created a statue, 'Chrysalis,' that showed a figure resembling a younger Akeley emerging from the body of a gorilla. His Africa was becoming more and more autobiographical and personal.[23]

As the prominent interdisciplinary scholar Donna Haraway points out in *Primate Visions*, the African Hall Akeley sacrificed so much for represents the ethereal, even unreal world that Africa conjured up for him. 'No visitor to a merely physical Africa could see these animals. This is a spiritual vision made possible only by their death and literal re-presentation.'[24] Akeley's relentless desire to get just the right specimen, his dismissal of animals with ordinary flaws as 'not worthwhile,' suggest a desire to transcend the imperfections of life itself. Jay Kirk, in *Kingdom Under Glass*, writes of Akeley's obsessive desire to create an 'asylum from the ravages of decay and oblivion.'[25] In Kirk's deft hands, Akeley's life becomes a cautionary tale of the wages of such single-minded ambition, not least of which was squandering the devotion of the wife who had cast her lot with him when he was just another young man with a big dream, a woman who had tirelessly aided his every project. No mere human being could rival Akeley's African vision.

Black Africans were largely a means to Akeley's end. He nearly beat one to death for carelessness. As one biographer observes, Akeley oscillated between 'respect for the "noble savage" who lived in perfect communion with nature, and arrogant intolerance for him.' He abjured the term 'niggers' in public but not in his diary, even as he seemed to believe that they possessed 'some secret understanding' of nature that eluded him.[26] Like White, Akeley felt very close to his gun bearer and devoted a chapter of *In Brightest Africa* to him. Akeley celebrated Bill's courage, boldness, skill, and resourcefulness. He 'was the best tracker' and 'most keen and alert hunter, black or white, that I had ever known.' Like White, though, it was his black African friend's devotion and loyalty, his willingness to 'go into practically certain death to serve me,' his resemblance to 'a faithful dog' that most touched Akeley. But even Bill could not be allowed to venture across the thick line that white hunters laid down. So when Bill violated 'one of the rules of the game, that a black boy must never shoot without orders unless his master is down and at the mercy of a beast,' Akeley 'wheeled and slapped' him. Realizing that Bill had thought his master's life in danger, Akeley apologized—so far 'as the dignity of a white man would permit.'

Akeley shared much in common with Roosevelt and White. All were accomplished hunters focused on East Africa's animals. They believed in and practiced white racial superiority. Certainly all three found something transcendent in East Africa, some quality they deemed essential for the health of white American men. Africa provided a tableau on which to experience awe while exercising mastery. When Akeley's magisterial African Hall at last opened in 1936, visitors passed by this Roosevelt quotation engraved into the museum's granite walls: '*I want to see you game, boys, I want to see you brave and manly.*'[27]

Ernest Hemingway shared little of Roosevelt's Victorianism and arrived in East Africa a quarter-century later, but the impulses that drew him there were much the same. Freeing himself from a 'still hoping and always praying mother,' Hemingway, too, had sought meaning in warfare and outdoor adventures.[28] By the time of his safari in the mid-1930s, he had already become one of America's great writers and existentialists.

Africa suited Hemingway well. Shortly after arriving, he wrote in 1935, 'I felt at home and where a man feels at home, outside of where he's born, is where he's meant to go.' Like many other 'Lost-Generation' intellectuals, Hemingway believed 'that individuals are cast adrift and left to their own devices to forge their identities and create their personae.'

This destabilization of identity and meaning required a life-long 'process of self-creation,' the continual performance of 'authenticity and honesty,' the work of creating and maintaining a self.[29] In *Green Hills of Africa* and his short stories reflecting on his 1933–1934 safari, Hemingway 'seems primarily concerned with celebrating himself as a white male hunter, with women and black men acting as foils to his self-image.'[30]

American women stood ready and willing to emasculate American men in Hemingway's Africa. In *Green Hills of Africa* Hemingway conflates fame, money, and women as key ingredients that inevitably caused writers (assumed to be male) to go to pot and 'write slop.' This sort of wife is most patently on display in 'The Short Happy Life of Francis Macomber,' published in *The Snows of Kilimanjaro and Other Stories*. Macomber's African safari quickly reveals his true character, shows him to be a bully and a coward. His wife sleeps with the safari leader. But the next day brings a new hunt, and Macomber this time stands his ground when facing a charging rhino and wins the admiration of the manly man who had just cuckolded him. His wife shoots him, though in such a way as to disguise her intent. She had long loathed him as a coward; she cannot abide him as an autonomous, confident man. The misogyny of 'The Snows of Kilimanjaro' is less patent, as the protagonist's wife here seems nurturing, determined to care for the husband who has returned to East Africa to recover a more authentic life. But that is precisely the problem. Helen is like a hyena, feeding off Harry's moral decay. It is her love of comfort that has emasculated him. But unlike the hyena, she wants him alive, on her terms. Harry refers to her as 'this good, this rich bitch, this kindly care-taker and destroyer of his talent.' Harry's good death, then, cheats his wife of her trophy, just as Margaret Macomber had cheated her husband of a manly life.[31]

Hemingway, as we shall see, wrote much differently in and of Africa when he returned in the 1950s. Before the war, though, his misogyny reflected a broadly shared impulse among white men inside and outside of Africa, that the comforts of modern life were antithetical to masculine identity and strength, a strength that could be recaptured or maintained through dangerous encounters with African animals in which black Africans were, at best, loyal help-mates, and white American women were absent or silent.

WHITE WOMEN AND BLACK AFRICANS

Yet white American women did make their way to Africa early in the twentieth century. Several became famous and described an Africa in which relationships with black Africans loomed much larger than they did for their male counterparts.

Delia Akeley seemed a very unlikely African explorer. The ninth child of a rural Catholic family of modest means, she ran away at age thirteen and was married to a barber when she met a young taxidermist eleven years her senior who had grand ambitions. Delia went all in with Carl and for three decades worked unstintingly to further his career. She assisted with his extraordinarily detailed specimens and dioramas and accompanied him on two African expeditions, helping him to track and shoot animals, running the safaris, nursing him through injuries and illnesses.

An intense friendship with an African primate played a key role in making Delia a major African explorer and personality in her own right. While undertaking observations on African wildlife she captured a young monkey and then kept it. So attached did she become to her pet, named J.T., that at the end of the safari she shipped him to New York City, where he spent several years living with the Akeleys until his second attack on Delia finally prompted his removal to a zoo. To what degree this fixation on J.T. was cause or effect of Carl's growing detachment from his wife is difficult to untangle, but as Carl burrowed more deeply into his work, Delia's life, and the couple's apartment, was increasingly ruled by the tempestuous animal. After the separation from J.T. finally came, Delia was 'lost.'[32] She abruptly left for Europe to volunteer as a nurse in World War I, leaving Carl shell-shocked and bitter. After returning she filed for divorce, alleging cruelty, and the reclusive Carl found his name in the newspapers for all the wrong reasons. She then staged her own 1924 African expedition that competed for newspaper space with his. 'Woman to Forget Marital Woe by Fighting African Jungle Beasts—Mrs. Akeley Going Alone to Land Where She Saved Husband, Now Divorced,' read a *New York World* headline.[33] The expedition launched her career as a writer and adventurer in her own right. She outlived Carl by over forty years and passed away with an estate worth $1.5 million in 1970. Not bad for a Catholic girl from Wisconsin who left home at thirteen.

Delia paid obeisance to the great man while suggesting that even before they divorced she was a force in her own right. Her extensive 1933 account of Carl's mauling by an elephant dwelled on her own courage and resourcefulness, virtues that 'without doubt saved his life.' She contrasted Carl's health problems in Africa with her own vigor. 'Owing to the frequency with which Mr. Akeley was a victim of Fever,' she observed, 'the management of our large caravan ... obviously fell upon my shoulders.' Though the Brooklyn Museum of Arts and Sciences in 1924 provided partial funding in return for her collecting some specimens for them, she decided to travel without 'the protection of a white hunter' or guide; she wished to proceed in Africa 'without the help or advice of any one.' Delia had her own ideas about a woman's place in Africa.

Delia was not at first much interested in Africa's people. The Africans in her 1928 biography of J.T. were presented almost wholly in relation to her clever pet. In fact she hired a 'toto' or young boy as J.T.'s servant and delighted in recounting how the monkey often outsmarted the 'boys' of the safari.

She took Africans much more seriously on her independent expedition. She represented the work of collecting museum specimens as a sort of necessary but bothersome prelude to the main event: traversing the Congo and seeking out Pygmy women. She retained a thick line between black Africans and white civilization. 'I honestly tried to view the natives with whom I came in contact as naturally as I viewed the specimens I was collecting,' she wrote with no trace of irony in 1933. She found the Pygmies simple and childlike, with 'standards ... hardly higher than those of wild animals.'

Yet she found much to admire in them. The Pygmies and other groups she met were, as a rule, 'very friendly when they learned that I was a woman traveling without escort through their country.' Her several months among black Africans in the Congo persuaded her that their laziness was something of a virtue when it came to wildlife protection, as unlike 'his white brothers,' he would not 'hunt for the sheer job of killing.' She also took pains to gain 'the friendship of' her black porters, 'my only companions for many weeks,' pointedly contrasting her humane treatment of them with the abuses they had suffered under white men.

Delia Akeley expressed much more interest in black Africans both as a subject of study and as human beings than her husband had.

The second Mrs. Akeley was much different from the first, both before and after her marriage to Carl. Mary Jobe had a master's degree from Columbia University, taught at Hunter College, and had undertaken several demanding expeditions in the Canadian West before meeting and marrying Carl in 1924. This was no teenager fresh off the farm. Unlike Delia, she remained in Carl's shadow after his death, 'becoming "Mrs. Carl Akeley" for the rest of her life,' as Carl's biographer puts it.[34] She repeatedly asserted that her life's work was to continue her husband's legacy, though they had been married for just two years and she had an impressive resume of her own before she had wed.

Like Carl and Delia, Mary emphasized black African's essentially childlike nature. 'All African natives are just overgrown children,' she pronounced in 1929. They lacked foresight, avoided work when they could, came undone over the slightest of injuries.

Like Delia, Mary professed much more interest in Africa's people than her husband did. 'Before coming to Africa,' she wrote in 1929, 'I had imagined that all black boys would look alike to me, but I actually found that they presented as many different physiognomies, statures, and personalities as would a similar number of white people.' It was therefore 'obvious that we of fairer skin are not so far removed in fundamentals from these dark children of the sun.' To be sure, this affection was often rooted in a strong sense of intellectual superiority. Like the great white male hunters, Mary professed herself most deeply touched by her porters' loyalty. They reminded her 'of the only playmate and companion of my early childhood, a collie dog,' who would 'come to me with a look of profound feeling and compassion' when Mary was injured. Her personal attendant, Bob, immediately assumed 'the vigilant attitude of a faithful dog' toward her, she recalled in 1936. Like Delia, her fondest wish seemed to be that black Africans would be protected from rather than integrated into the modern world. But she treated Carl's beloved Bill much more respectfully than her husband did, helping him to start a transport business and covertly sending him a monthly allowance.[35]

Osa Johnson became the best-known white woman explorer of them all before World War II, and like the Akeley women she rose to prominence along with her husband. The Johnsons' African adventures shot them to fame and fortune from the mid-1920s through the 1930s thanks to vivid wildlife films, lectures, books, and articles in the *New York Times Magazine*, *Saturday Evening Post*, *Good Housekeeping*, and *Colliers*, among others. Even after Martin's death in 1937, Osa's star continued to ascend.

Martin Johnson shared Carl Akeley's ambition and focus, but his version was more diffused and less masculinized. He started running away from his Kansas home at a young age and at fourteen wandered for several years in the US and Europe before wrangling his way onto the 1907–1909 Pacific expedition of Jack London, the famous writer. Back in Kansas, Johnson learned he could make money showing the photographs he had taken. He married the fiery sixteen-year-old Osa Leighty, daughter of a railroad brakeman, shortly after she had started performing Polynesian songs and dances as part of his show.

The Johnsons presented themselves as a modern, companionate couple. 'If ever a wife were a partner to a man,' he wrote in *Safari* in 1928, 'it is Osa Johnson.' Indeed, the dedication of his first book, published in 1924, extolled her as 'The Best Pal a Man Ever Had.' Osa in *Safari* described herself as a young bride delighted just to have a handsome husband and a home of her own, that she 'had never wanted to gad about.' But when Martin revealed that he was determined to pursue adventure, she was willing if not eager. They spent several years bouncing around North America and then Europe, steadily improving their shows and saving money for a big trip to the Pacific Islands during which the diminutive Osa 'was captured by the savage man-eaters we were out to film.' By the time of their return, Martin had determined that his future lay 'in preservation of wild life in film form,' and when a promoter urged him to go to Africa, he did not hesitate. Martin repeatedly praised Osa for her willingness to support his unconventional career. Indeed, if Martin was a savvy entrepreneur, Osa was the star of the show. She was pretty and perky, embodied an arresting juxtaposition of violence and femininity, a sort of flapper cum slayer of wild beasts. As the *New York World* observed of *Trailing African Wild Animals*, 'one of the reasons for the film's attractiveness is the presence ... of Mrs. Johnson herself.' 'Her distinctly feminine personality forms a striking contrast with the barbaric and quite evidently dangerous surroundings.'[36] Osa charmed everyone she met in Africa from porters to the wealthy George Eastman, who professed himself smitten by the juxtaposition of her 'pink-silk-dress-little-girlness' and prowess with a gun, she recalled in 1940. Carl Akeley, who had drawn the elderly Eastman to Africa in hopes of persuading him to fund his Great Africa Hall, feared that the Johnsons were using Osa's charms to woo him and his money to their own purposes.

The Johnsons struggled with the tension between educating and entertaining. Martin wrote in 1924 of wanting to create films of Africa that would 'be the whole story of a country, its peoples and its animals,' to somehow capture for armchair adventurers the magic he experienced there. But their appeal and wealth rested on hoary African stereotypes. *Congorilla* of 1932 presumed to debunk the myth of large, savage primates even as advertisements for the film featured drawings of ferocious beasts that anticipated King Kong.[37] Martin wrote of creating films that presented black

Africans as worthy of respect, but the films he actually offered featured the sort of 'racial sight gags and racial put-downs' white audiences expected and responded to.[38] In *Congorilla*, for example, Osa is shown instructing the 'childlike' Pygmies how to dance to 'modern jazz.'

Martin was unusual among white men on safari in that he freely and repeatedly admitted that Osa was much better with a gun than he was. Of course part of this division of labor simply served to free Martin up to focus on what he was most interested in: 'She handled the gun while I cranked the camera,' he remarked in 1928. Handle it she did, twice felling elephants 'at my feet' and a lion 'so close I could touch his mane with my toe.' 'She seems' he concluded, 'to have no nerves.' He recounted in 1924 a day in which he lost face first with an aged Masai man and then Osa for refusing to go lion hunting with them.

Osa, for her part, consistently represented Martin as the leader of their business enterprises and films and continually professed her deep admiration for him. She portrayed herself as emotional, even flighty, and stressed her attention to keeping up her physical appearance even while in Africa. In one film she dispatches two lions then deftly moves back to her housewife duties.

Though Martin repeated the usual stereotypes about black Africans' immaturity and loyalty, he expressed more respect for them than Carl Akeley had. He hoped to make a film about Songo 'the Tale-bearer,' an aged Meru man who served as a sort of traveling newspaper and diplomat, he noted in 1924. He also tempered his criticism of black

Africans with a dash of cultural relativism. He recounted in 1928 complaining to a black African of his odor only to be told that 'to the black man you smell too and very bad.' When in 1924 he characterized 'primitive peoples' as 'immoral,' he prefaced the adjective with this qualifier: 'from my point of view.' Indeed, Martin found a 'savage untouched by civilization' as possessing 'dignity,' a moral integrity lacking in most 'civilized' countries. He claimed to have never beaten any of his many black African servants.

Like the Akeley women, Osa expressed more interest in African people than her husband did, although two of her most extensive treatments of Africans appeared in her two books on African animals. *Jungle Babies* had a chapter on Suku, a boy who lived in the Meru forest 'where the dark people are big, and strong and intelligent' and 'peaceful.' The brief story's dramatic tension comes from Suku's reluctance to become a ruler. His father smooths his passage to this high position in which he would guide his people to 'live in harmony with all beings of the world.' At the end of the decade *Osa Johnson's Jungle Friends* offered a more realistic account in a more modern setting. In 'Story without Words' Osa recounted how she gradually became friends with Lala, a young Somali girl 'as timid as the wild animals' and Bobo, a boy who accompanied her. The pair slowly shared with Osa their harrowing personal history by building a model of their village from sticks, pebbles, nuts, and water. They represented a drought and a slave raid that carried away many people. The young pair then acted out their hard march to their present home. Osa during this long historical rendering also got to know the children's family, who gave the Johnsons a sheep when the explorers departed. The children's father assured them 'that wherever we might chance to travel through the homeland of his people we would find friendship and respect because we had been so kind to him.' In a genre of African travel literature devoted to animals, adventure, and peculiar 'savages,' 'Story Without Words' stands as a rare glimpse into deeper, more somber elements of the actual lives of black Africans.

Martin's unexpected death in 1937 unmoored Osa even as she grew still more popular. She struggled with alcoholism and romantic entanglements. But by 1940 she had a line of stuffed animals, gloves and other outdoor clothing, with fabric known as 'Osafari.' She returned to Africa briefly as a valued consultant for the popular film *Stanley and Livingstone*. The Fashion Academy named her as one of the nation's twelve best-dressed women. *I Married Adventure* rose to the top of the *New York Times* best-seller list for nonfiction and became a Book-of-the-Month selection.[39] Like Delia Akeley before her, Osa Johnson grew out of her deceased husband's shadow, becoming not simply Mrs. Martin Johnson but a celebrity and authority on Africa in her own right.

These three women won a measure of fame during a time in which white male narratives of self-actualization dominated popular literature on Africa. Their role as helpmates to great men gave them a platform from which to describe deeper relationships with Africans than their husbands had pursued.

WHITE MISSIONARIES IN AFRICA

The great majority of Americans who went to Africa in the early twentieth century were missionaries more interested in Africa's people than its animals. Here, too, gender mattered.

The 1880s through World War I was the golden era of American overseas missions. Protestantism resided at the heart of Victorianism, and before the popularization of Freudian psychology, Boasian anthropology, and the horrors of World War I, the great majority of Americans agreed that Christian civilization provided the answer to the world's problems. 'Spiritual imperialism' would root out every evil from cannibalism to poor hygiene. Presbyterians, Methodists, Baptists, and other large American Protestant denominations constructed schools and hospitals as well as churches across the globe. There were of course also many Catholic missionaries and missions, as well as those representing smaller and more conservative Protestant denominations. But mainstream Protestant denominations dominated the field and popular discourse.[40]

Women were at the heart of this movement. By 1910 they constituted the majority of Protestant missionaries—the great majority if one subtracted physicians and ordained men. The Victorian era had defined women as mothers, but middle-class women had steadily expanded their domestic roles far beyond their homes. By the century's turn they could take credit for: ending slavery; closing down innumerable saloons; reforming hospitals, prisons, and insane asylums; founding libraries; and eliminating health problems ranging from public spitting to non-pasteurized milk. Converting millions of heathens in distant lands was a duty they expected to achieve. Overseas missions provided an international stage for particularly bold Christian women, married and single, sustained by the prayers and material support of innumerable women's groups.[41]

Few of these missionaries were cultural relativists. Wilson S. Naylor's 1905 study book on Africa mission work put the matter with typical bluntness: 'African Paganism or Fetishism is a religion of darkness.' Though missionaries occasionally found elements of traditional African cultures to praise—the emphasis on social obligations, for example— the great majority depicted African heathenism as a pit of devilry, superstition, ignorance, suffering, slavery, and brutal exploitation, particularly of women. 'The only thing about a pagan African that need not and cannot be denationalized is his color,' asserted long-time missionary George A. Wilder from Central Africa in 1928.[42]

Unlike the majority of hunters and other white American adventurers, however, the missionaries came to Africa in search of Africans. They stayed for years or even decades, not months, and labored to learn local languages because they believed and asserted, against the arguments of racialists such as White, that black Africans could join the modern, Christian world. 'The African is capable, teachable, and ready to learn,' pronounced Naylor. Albert Helser, who came to Northern Nigeria in the early 1920s, in 1940 quoted an African friend: 'The white people tell us black people what they think we can understand. The black people tell the white people what they think it is good for them to know.' 'Do not fool yourself by thinking that the African is not as good as you are,' he concluded.

American missionaries emphasized the exemplary piety of black African Christians. Naylor remarked that the history of the early Ugandan church featured 'the most sublime faith amid terrible persecution and torture,' a record reminiscent of the New Testament church. Elizabeth Macdonald Wilkinson wrote from Nigeria in 1928 that during her first three months there the only woman she could converse with was a Christian woman whose 'tact and grace' and generosity presented her with a model of Christian humility and power that she despaired of ever matching.[43] Julia Lake Kellersberger in 1936 wrote of a Congolese church constructed by Africans carrying over 40,000 stones for four miles. 'A Christian African is a beautiful character,' remarked a contributor to *The Missionary Review of the World* in 1936.[44] In fact many missionaries seemed more alarmed by the spreading immorality of western civilization in modern Africa than of the influence of witch doctors and other heathen survivals. 'Atheism,' remarked a missionary in 1928, 'does not thrive in Africa except amongst certain of the white population.'[45]

While white American adventurers pointed to their unlettered, dog-like gun bearers as ideal black Africans, white American missionaries countered with James Emman Kwegyir Aggrey, a Gold Coast Methodist who advanced black African education and political rights. Aggrey did undergraduate and extensive graduate work in the US, including the course work for a doctorate at Columbia University, before returning home to lead education efforts there. White American missionaries widely praised him as embodying the ideal mix of humility and intellectualism, African and western traditions. In *Friends of Africa*, a survey of African missions published in 1928, Jean Kenyon Mackenzie, the widely read returned missionary, quoted the former Gold Coast Governor, Sir Gordon Guggisberg: 'Aggrey was the finest interpreter which the present century has produced of the white man to the black, and the black man to the white.' *Men and Women of Far Horizons*, a 1935 compilation from the bulletin of that name, included a piece in which Aggrey traced the natural progression of mission work toward indigenous leadership.[46]

Indeed, by the 1930s missionary publications offered black Africans a direct voice, including the freedom to criticize missionaries and western culture. Some of these black Christians emphasized their abject state before the arrival of missionaries: 'I tell you we were dirty with every kind of dirt, inside and outside.'[47] Others, particularly South Africans, dwelled on themes more discomfiting to white Christians. Donald G.S. M'Timkulu of South Africa, holder of a Fellowship in Race Relations at Yale University, in 1936 criticized modern missionaries for tolerating and practicing racism. South African Bernard Molaba asked in 1936 if the Union Government's 'repressive legislation and color bars originate from God?' Christ, after all, practiced 'a method of love, of peace and of prayer, not of force, domination and punishment.'[48] 'Africans should be taught to govern themselves,' asserted S.S. Tema from Johannesburg a year later. White Christians should respect Africa's 'own peculiar customs' and get their own house in order: 'Africa wants to see Christ in Europe.'[49]

The most widely read American missionary to Africa was a well-educated lay-woman, Jean Kenyon Mackenzie. Born in 1874 to a Presbyterian minister who had emigrated to the US from Scotland, Mackenzie attended the Sorbonne in Paris in her late teens and then the University of California before moving with her parents to New York City. In 1904 she left for a decade at four posts in Kamerun. She returned to the US because of health reasons, but then was prevailed upon to return in 1916 to help broker a peace between the colony's natives and the French government, who had defeated the German colonials. Mackenzie wrote many articles that appeared in the *Atlantic*, *McClure's*, or missionary magazines as well as several books.

Mackenzie believed in the power of Christianity to redeem black Africans, particularly women. 'Polygamy is terrible,' she wrote to her parents shortly after arriving, in a letter later published in *Black Sheep*. 'I had so open a mind about it when I came to Africa—and now I have so many sad thoughts of it.' In *An African Trail*, published in 1917, Mackenzie spoke of the malevolent 'hand' of Africa that inexorably marked the white missionary with fevers, isolation, and other challenges. Africa was 'an unsettled ... evil country,' a 'forest of ignorance,' replete with suffering, particularly for its black natives and most of all for its black women, she remarked in the 1916 book.

Yet Mackenzie repeatedly took issue with the notion that black Africans had been, let alone were, particularly or peculiarly evil. She 'heard with a pang of grief and wonder' educator Mabel Carney's pronouncement 'that she hopes and prays there is no woman on earth more wretched than the primitive African woman.' 'It seems strange,' Mackenzie reflected in 1928, 'to have been eating out of the kettle with the most wretched woman on earth, and to have laughed at her sallies.' The African woman, her innumerable burdens notwithstanding, 'is a potter, a weaver, a diviner in some tribes, a priestess in other tribes,' also a counselor, arbitrator of marriages, even a chief. She dismissed cannibalism, despite or perhaps because 'it seems to possess a peculiar fascination' for white men, by noting in 1917 that it was 'a hidden and a vanishing shame.' 'The cannibals,' she observed in 1924, 'beg you to visit their villages, where they feed you on chicken stewed in peanuts.' Americans interested in African canni- balism should instead ponder the slave trade past and present, or 'our own tribal cruelties, which are mainly developed on the economic side,' she observed in 1928.

In Mackenzie's 1916 telling, Africa's peculiar chal- lenges had made its natives particularly susceptible to the Gospel. Their 'misgivings' over their way of life 'haunt and shake them'; they were ashamed of their 'low estate.' Some reasoned that God had created and then abandoned them, so they had turned to fetishes and lesser spirits to negotiate life's many difficulties. Now, in the early twentieth century, they recognized in Christ a personage resonant with their ancient beliefs. It was as if the Gospel unspooled truths deeply, if unconsciously, hoped for. 'The day when I knew Jesus,' a Bulu told Mackenzie, as she recollected in *African Adventures*, 'it was as if my mother put her hand on me.'[50] For a people accustomed to rigid customs, the Ten Commandments, often rendered as 'bindings,' had a special resonance. Mackenzie in 1917 wrote of a woman who, 'with an almost anguished timidity' presented herself as 'a person of God.' Her husband, with an air of 'affectionate and contemptuous tolerance' remarked that 'she has learned a commandment.' Mackenzie marveled that this little piece of knowledge 'had made that timid black woman bold to speak to the white woman, in the presence of contemptuous men.'

Much of this could be dismissed as propaganda calculated to goose financial support for mission work to abject Africans if Mackenzie had not so often suggested that African Christians were of a superior type. She recounted in 1917 a native who listened to a story of how the pioneering missionary Livingstone grieved the death of a faithful convert and then observed: 'That is good, … Livingstone had a heart like a black man.' A friend, Luanga, told her of how years ago as a child she had served a woman, a solitary Christian in an isolated village, who was killed for refusing the sexual advances of her husband's business partner. It was as if Mackenzie discovered authentic Christianity in darkest Africa. Yet in 1924 she noted that 'many white women … have asked me, looking at me with incredulous eyes: "And do you truly think that they are Christians?"' 'The primitive African,' she declared in 1928, 'is not a soft Christian.' 'When an old woman says to a group of women—"Christ is our husband, let us serve Him" she is not meaning anything less than an entire hardy self-sacrificing service.' Writing of the Bulu in 1917, she noted how so many had 'become for His sake poor, and have laid aside their beautiful and terrible arrogance for the garments of humility,' sacrifices such as surrendering the status of multiple wives or the security of a fetish that had long kept disasters at bay. Racism and ethnocentrism often blinded white outsiders to the depth of African piety, a devotion to Christ that emboldened them to endure painful confessions, ostracism, and beatings. '"Take my yoke upon you," says Christ to the Bulu; and the Bulu bends his neck.'

Working with such people thrilled Mackenzie. She acquired the discipline to accept the challenges her work entailed, the rats, leaky roofs, and bouts of malaria and loneliness. In one letter she chided her parents for worrying over her illnesses: 'You think there should be some sort of special dispensation for your lamb.' She was cheered that she had learned how to present water to visiting women, which her guests interpreted as a hopeful sign 'that I am coming, in spite of my blood, to be something more like a lady.' Mackenzie had, 'at last, in a measure, the passion of what I am doing' and felt 'like the mother of all these poor women.' But her African friends perceived matters differently, for they became 'very sweet and maternal toward me, ... whom they take, ... to be a little girl.' Turning the notion of the white missionary as mother motif on its head, Mackenzie in 1917 recalled 'those black maternal hands upon the hair of lonely white women' and 'kind voices at the end of weary journeys that ask, "What will my child eat tonight?"' 'For such love as these friends give the missionary,' she concluded, 'there is no adequate return but love.' As Hill puts it, Mackenzie described herself not as mother to Africa but 'as the child of Mother Africa.'[51]

Mackenzie never got over Kamerun. Many of her many recollections were rife with 'real longings to be in Africa again,' as Harper puts it.[52] She continued to support and advise mission efforts and wrote about Africa into the 1930s, when illness slowed and then stopped her work. Some premonition of a life outside of Africa came not long before the end of her decade there, as she spoke 'about the things of God' among a group of villagers busy at their work:

> The hands of the women bruising green leaves in wooden troughs and the grinders at the stones were idle. Men laughed with a kind of wonder. One woman flashed with interest behind her mask of purple tattoo and bright beads. Another bridled young thing gazed in a great stillness. I see this thing in my heart like a thing shut in from time and change, and I wish I may never forget it.

Like the British missionary women in Africa described by historian Elizabeth E. Prevost, Mackenzie 'reconfigured' her 'mission work as a medium for religious exchange with African women ... infusing mission Christianity with a dynamic female religiosity ... blurring the sacred and secular, European and African, Christian and non-Christian dimensions of the mission encounter.' The result was 'a feminized and hybridized discourse of spirituality.'[53]

Mackenzie's last book, a 1930 novel that received much critical praise but few readers, reprised her close relationships with African women. Lucy, the protagonist of the *Trader's Wife* is a New England newlywed who determines to follow her husband to West Africa on the eve of the Civil War, where he will continue his work as a trader. She is thoughtless and romantic. Her new home soon breaks her by exposing her to the cruelties of a slave trade she had dismissed while back in the US. She grasps an opportunity to help the slaves to escape, though she relies heavily on her personal slave, Atemba. The novel dwells on the agency of this man, who is seizing his own freedom. But this story is mostly about Lucy's 'spiritual awakening,' her conversion to an engagement with the deep tragedies of a life that heretofore she had skated lightly over.[54]

Friend Ellery Sedgwick, the *Atlantic* editor who so admired the prose of this writer who had challenged his anti-missionary prejudices, remarked at her funeral that she possessed a 'tolerant understanding,' a sympathy 'with the ways of a world she would have liked so much to change.'[55] But as Mackenzie left Africa, forces other than her health were conspiring to ensure that her lyrical hybridization of Victorianism and African women's culture would flicker and then wink out. The professionalization of mission work led away from maternal piety, a trend exacerbated by the shock waves of secularization that hit the western world following the bloody crucible of World War I. American Protestantism suffered twin blows in the 1920s: its disestablishment from high intellectual and academic culture and a split between mainstream churches and more conservative, often self-proclaimed fundamentalists who insisted on the primacy of Biblical authority over ecumenism and of

Christian conversion, narrowly defined, over other forms of Christian service or expression.[56] Mackenzie's *Atlantic Monthly* articles and books were mainstream in the 1910s when, as Hill observes, 'religious and literary audiences ... were not entirely separate.' By 1924 her work fell 'between two stools.'[57] It was insufficiently orthodox for conservative Christians, too religious for the general, increasingly secular reader. Missionaries, like Victorianism, had become passé.

BLACK AMERICANS DISCOVER AFRICA

A quartet of black Americans who came to Sub-Saharan Africa before World War II resembled white missionaries such as Mackenzie by being more interested in the continent's people than its animals. But their varied personal outlooks and political programs led them to radically different conclusions about Africa. The lone woman of the four focused most consistently on black Africans.

W.E.B. Du Bois, a giant in American intellectual life and the history of race relations, had a long, often romantic, relationship with Africa. He played a leading part in the first Pan-African conference and in 1897, as recounted in *Dusk of Dawn*, asserted: 'We believe that the Negro people as a race have a contribution to make to civilization and humanity which no other race can make.' Du Bois consistently urged black Americans, especially, to take Africa seriously for most of the twentieth century; his fidelity to and interest in Pan-Africanism was unrivaled. As Appiah points out, Du Bois' long engagement with the concept of race was personal as well as

political, 'part of the answer to his unending quest to understand who he was himself.'[58] Graduate study in Germany
had brought sustained exposure to theorists such as Herder
who posited that various peoples possessed distinctive folk
characters: hence the title of Du Bois' most enduring book,
The Souls of Black Folk. Du Bois' distinguished career can be
understood as a process of pinning down black and therefore his own identity to its 'real essence,' as he put it in *Dusk
of Dawn*, a personal and intellectual quest in which Africa
played a major part.

Du Bois first visited Africa in 1923 for ostensibly political
purposes. Since the mid-nineteenth century Liberia had been
governed by Americos, descendants of the African-Americans who had colonized it. In a continent awash in European
colonies and white governors and officials, Liberia was, for
Du Bois, a beacon of hope. Its failure would, he believed,
inflict a material and psychological blow to the belief that
black people could run governments and countries. Du Bois,
then, was far more interested in touting Liberia's small ruling
elite than in becoming acquainted with or advocating for the
much larger number of indigenous Africans that the elite
governed. Indeed, he at times used language suggestive of
colonialism: 'Unless Liberia … convinces the great powers
that she is able to stand alone and develop the country and
civilize the natives,' he warned in 1919, 'her territory will
be dis-membered.'[59] Focusing on the government's political
corruption or its exploitation of the disenfranchised indigenous majority would make it even more vulnerable to ruthless
western nations. Hence Du Bois, in the words of historian

Ibrahim Sundiata, 'saw nothing amiss observed nothing amiss' during his stay in Liberia.[60]

DuBois' reaction to Liberia was shaped by his Romanticism as much as by his pragmatism. His extensive accounts of the trip included the names of only a few people, none of whom were indigenous Africans.[61] He was entranced by its atmosphere. 'Africa is vegetation,' he wrote upon returning, and: 'The spell of Africa is upon me.' It was 'a universe of itself and for itself, a thing Different, Immense, Menacing, Alluring.'[62] Du Bois at times sounded like Carl Akeley.

George Schuyler was the perfect man to dispute Du Bois' account of Liberia. Though born to parents of means in upstate New York, he lacked Du Bois' social and educational advantages and had spent some years at or near the bottom of New York City society before becoming America's most influential black journalist. Schuyler became known as the 'Negro Mencken,' for he was just as devoted to debunking as H.L. Mencken, the outrageous editor of *The American Mercury*, was. In fact America's leading contrarian published much of Schuyler's work and became godparent to his daughter. Though Schuyler loved to skewer racists, he was an equal opportunity satirist. 'George got up in the morning,' observed historian John Henrik Clarke, 'waited to see which way the world was turning, then struck out in the opposite direction.'[63] Given Schuyler's irascibility and hardscrabble route to prosperity, he was bound to poke at 'Dr. Shakespeare Agamemnon Beard,' as he dubbed the patrician Du Bois. He was pleased to accept the offer from George Palmer Putnam, powerful publisher of the *New York*

Evening Post, to investigate charges that Liberia's elite was selling native Africans to work on Spanish plantations. In the process of debunking Pan-Africanism, Schuyler would become the first black foreign correspondent for a large newspaper. His harrowing trip eventually resulted in six widely published newspaper articles and the first novel by a black American set in Africa. He also managed, as he likely intended, to nettle Du Bois.

Schuyler's differences with Du Bois were intellectual as well as temperamental. He had little patience for black nationalism as a political or cultural program. Black Americans should focus their energies on improving their lot in America rather than positing some sort of cosmic racial identity. 'The Aframerican,' he asserted in 1926 in the Nation, 'is merely a lampblacked Anglo-Saxon.' After three hundred years away from Africa, he had become, '[a]side from his color, ... just plain American.'[64] Hence he had married his white wife, Josephine Cogdell, he recalled in 1966, because she 'saw Negroes as I saw whites, as individuals.' Schuyler saved his sharpest darts for Garvey, a 'Black Napoleon' adroitly separating countless black 'washerwomen, porters, maids, and other hard-working people' from their hard-earned cash.[65]

Liberia confirmed Schuyler's low opinion of Pan-Africanism. It was divided into mutually antagonistic ethnic groups, Monrovia was 'repugnant and depressing,' its Americo-Liberian leadership corrupt and exploitive. His newspaper articles and 1931 novel, *Slaves Today*, described officials demanding slave labor from villages, whipping uncooperative chiefs, and seizing girls as concubines. Liberia's 'proud motto' was: 'The Love of Liberty Brought Us Here.' '[B]ut the aborigines find little liberty under their Negro masters.'[66]

Though Schuyler was more concerned with revealing injustices and misplaced pieties than in studying native Liberians, he depicted indigenous Africans and Africa positively. Schuyler described enchanting African dances, clean and well-ordered villages that contrasted with Monrovia's moral and physical squalor and superstitious but honorable villagers who were superior to their greedy, lazy, and immoral overlords.

But though Schuyler took up the cause of Liberia's native peoples that Du Bois had elided, his perspective remained resolutely American. When an elite woman in his novel who had been to a black college in the US objects to her powerful Liberian husband keeping concubines, he remarks that she 'had too much American in her.' This woman's ancestors, Schuyler explains in his 1931 novel, had left Maryland for Liberia 'to establish in Africa a replica of America.' But it had been 'they, and especially their descendants,' who 'had been conquered by Africa. One by one they had adopted the worst habits and customs of the aborigines they exploited and despised.' Indeed, the elite had sunk far below their native subalterns. But Schuyler clearly believed that their ancestors never should have left America, the true promised land, in the first place. The best part of Schuyler's Liberia was Firestone's rubber plantation, the American island of order and justice, and if he often found the native Liberians to be admirable, he seemed to take little personal interest in them. They were primitives.

Du Bois was predictably outraged by depictions of Liberia so contrary to his own, so apt to provoke further western meddling in Liberian affairs and increased pessimism over black people's capacity to rule themselves. As before, he argued that Liberia's leaders had been plagued by western exploitation and interference to the point that few options for political and economic viability remained: 'there was only one thing that Liberia had left, and that was her native labor.' Schuyler was of course unmoved by this logic. 'Right is right and wrong is wrong, Dr. Du Bois,' Schuyler countered in a letter to *The Crisis*, the National Association for the Advancement of Colored Persons periodical edited by Du Bois. 'I am sorry,' he concluded, 'that you permitted your belligerent and commendable Nego-philism to warm your vision in the case of the Liberian racketeers.'[67]

Schuyler and Du Bois were not finished with Africa. Schuyler seemed to reverse course later in the 1930s in his serialized fiction, which championed a Pan-Africanist effort to protect Ethiopia and the rest of Africa from white colonialism and hegemony. But Schuyler wrote under pen names to distance himself from these lucrative works. Their popularity left him 'greatly amused,' he wrote, for it was 'hokum and hack work of the purest vein ... deliberately' shot full of 'as much race chauvinism and sheer improbability ... as my fertile imagination could conjure.' Its popularity 'vindicates my low opinion of the human race.'[68] By the time he again visited Africa between 1958 and 1961 Schuyler's anti-Communism overshadowed his other impulses, and he wrote off the young nations as 'hapless aggregations,' 'international retardates' unprepared for independence or to resist Communist machinations.[69] After leaving the NAACP, Du Bois retained his focus on Pan-Africanism and increasingly ran afoul of the very anti-Communist movement that Schuyler so enthusiastically participated in. He left America for good in 1961 to settle in Ghana as a guest of President Kwame Nkrumah and passed away there as a hero in 1963. Schuyler's star continued to decline in the 1960s, when he turned his vitriolic pen on Martin Luther King, Jr. and the Civil Rights Movement. Today Du Bois is much admired, Schuyler nearly forgotten. But their earlier battle over how Liberia in particular and Africa in general ought to be understood vis-à-vis African-American life foreshadowed many later debates.

Schuyler and Du Bois were arguing about the politics of Liberia. Langston Hughes was drawn to Africa for much more personal reasons. His first published verse, 'The Negro Speaks of Rivers,' appeared in 1921 while he was still in his teens and referenced the Middle East and Africa: 'I built my hut near the Congo and it lulled me to sleep.'[70] Hughes entered Columbia University in 1920 and felt at home among the young artists of the burgeoning Harlem Renaissance more interested in self-development than in lucrative careers or racial uplift. At age twenty-one he signed up as a merchant seaman aboard a freighter bound for Africa and threw his books overboard. He would be learning from life—and Africa. 'When I saw the dust-green hills in the sunlight,' he later recalled, 'something took hold of me inside. My Africa, Motherland of the Negro peoples! And me a Negro! Africa! The real thing, to be touched and seen, not merely read about in a book.'[71]

But Africa did not recognize this lost son, Hughes recounted in his 1940 memoir. West Africans laughed out loud when he asserted: 'I am a Negro, too.' 'You, white man! You, white man!' they retorted to the light-brown American. Hughes was repeatedly made to feel as if he were an interloper rather than a brother. In Nigeria he hoped to see a 'Ju-Ju' ceremony, '[w]hite man never go see Ju-Ju,' he was told. Hughes' time in Africa taught him much about colonialism and racism, and it sparked a long-lived interest in Africa. But it also made it clear to him that Africa was not exactly home.

His post-Africa poems on Africa expressed less romance, more alienation than before. In 'Black Seed' black diasporans are: 'Driven before an alien wind, / Scattered like seed.'[72] But Hughes remained engaged with Africa.[73]

Eslanda Goode Robeson enjoyed Africa much more than Hughes had. The wife of Paul Robeson, the iconic African-American actor, intellectual, and activist who located African-American creativity in Africa, Eslanda was a well-read radical in her own right.[74] In London she studied anthropology and met many African students and noted that white academics often slighted black Africans' intellectual capacity. The 1936 trip would allow her to 'meet and study and talk with my people on their home ground,' plus enable their eight-year-old child to at last 'see a black world, ... a black continent,' as she related in her 1945 memoir. As her biographer puts it, Eslanda's trip was a 'personal quest' long hoped for.[75]

Eslanda came to Africa with an agenda, but it was flexible and collaborative. The anthropological research, part of her studies at the London School of Economics, entailed observing and talking with black Africans, people she regarded as 'my people' and was eager to expose her young son to. Though as light-skinned as Hughes, she soon felt at home. The black residents of Johannesburg reminded her of 'Lenox Avenue in Harlem on a summer Sunday afternoon,' she recalled in her memoir. An elderly woman in Uganda remarked of Pauli: 'That boy belongs to us—see his mouth, eyes, nose, the shape of head—pure African.' Esmelda was also judged to have African features, 'especially my spirit.' The black South Africans she spoke with 'make me feel humble and respectful.' The children 'spoke beautiful English.' Their hospitality was peerless, their patience with racism long. 'One gets the feeling that they have confidence in the decency and dignity of human beings in general,' believed wrongs would be righted if they could simply 'bring the facts' of what greedy white Africans were doing 'to the attention of other white men.'

She did her academic research among the Botoro, near Kampala, and liked them very much. She learned to eat with her fingers, worked at the language, seemed to take an interest in every aspect of their culture and particularly in the 'delightful, intelligent, companionable' women. Among the Botoro, as elsewhere in Africa, Esmelda sought out friendships with Africans, approaching them as individuals rather than as types. Her Africa, then, was, as film historian Charles Musser notes, 'a world inhabited and cultivated by people,' people who taught her 'a great deal about the very important business of living,' how to get things done with a poise and deliberateness that Europeans often conflated with lassi-tude.[76] Eslanda was much less impressed by the Europeans she met, most of whom had a low opinion of black Africans. The thesis of her book, really, lay in the last sentence of a postscript written in 1944, eight years after she left Africa: *'Africans are people.'*

Esmelda remained interested in Africans. She returned in 1946, to the Congo, and met 'scads of interesting people,' particularly reformers.[77] Late in 1958 she arrived in freshly independent Ghana for the All-African Peoples Conference; she and Paul had known President Nkrumah back in their London days, before he became a great leader, and she was a strong supporter of his ideas about Pan-African socialism and the African personality. Though she did not move to Africa permanently or become an academic specialist on Africa, a sense of solidarity with Africans forged during her 1936 trip continued to inform her life and her politics.

Black Americans of the early twentieth century took black Africans much more seriously than their Victorian ancestors or most of their white contemporaries did. Du Bois and Schuyler, to be sure, were primarily interested in how Liberia confirmed their political and intellectual preconcep-tions. Hughes and Robeson came to Africa looking to become acquainted with Africans. The latter seemed much more satisfied with those interactions than the former did; Hughes anticipated a sense of brotherhood that eluded him. Robeson was pleasantly surprised by the congruence between black Africa and black America, but her primary purpose was to demonstrate black Africans' full humanity, a task that made her more receptive and flexible than were her black male counterparts.

Of the dozen or so Americans who authored accounts of visits to Africa examined in this chapter, Robeson and Mackenzie were the most engaged with black African people and the least interested in personal visions or quests. Roosevelt and White sought to stage harrowing moments in which to test and demonstrate their masculine character. Carl Akeley and Martin Johnson were fixated on reproducing East Africa's magical landscapes and megafauna, a task that their three wives loyally assisted in and extended to include African people. Du Bois and Schuyler focused on black Africans in the abstract, as props for their opposing programs of identity formation. Gender and race constituted fundamental, if not determinative, variables in how Americans approached and experienced Sub-Saharan Africa.

Time also mattered. Africa became less fearsome in the 1920s and 1930s as the US became more secular and Brightest Africa images championed by the Akeleys and the Johnsons shouldered aside more savage motifs even in Tarzan films. Black Africans also slowly emerged in both popular and first-hand accounts.

As Africans began to make themselves heard, they described an Africa much different from the one sketched by the great majority of white visitors. Mackenzie presented compelling African people. Black South Africans in the *Missionary Review of the World* criticized the savage, unchristian spirit of white racists. Like Robeson, academic Charles Coulter found in the 1930s that Central Africans both recognized and resented the systemic racial discrimination that blighted their lives and prospects. The several hundred natives he surveyed were virtually unanimous in reporting 'that the white man had no respect for the native, regarded him as inferior, and "treated him like a dog."'[78] The great white hunters had in fact often likened black Africans to dogs; black Africans both noted and resented the comparison.

The veil of abject loyalty that black safari hands assumed as part of their work occasionally slipped. Whites present at Carl Akeley's death were disturbed and puzzled by the reaction of his beloved Bill, the gun bearer and tracker whose dog-like devotion Carl Akeley so cherished and remarked upon. Immediately after Akeley died Bill recounted the day his master had hit him. Referring to himself as Gikungu, the name Akeley found too difficult to pronounce, he angrily insisted on telling and re-telling how Akeley had slapped him for saving the great man's life. It was an awkward episode for Akeley's colleagues. Was Gikungu grieving over or raging at Akeley's corpse?[79]

After World War II, Americans black and white, male and female, would arrive in Africa with somewhat different sensibilities and expectations from their early twentieth-century counterparts. They would find Africa—and Africans—much changed.

CHAPTER TWO

POST-WAR AMERICA AND THE 'NEW AFRICA'

Traditionalists and liberals alike treat the post-war years as a conservative era. Anti-Communism expressed a widely shared belief in the need for conformity and a celebration of American abundance by people who had toiled through the privations of the world's longest depression and bloodiest war, fifteen years of deferred gratification and uncertainty. Post-war Americans embraced stability and domesticity. There were many more automobiles, high schools, and record players than ever before—and money to spend.

But this very expansion of consumption and leisure prompted what historian Alan Petigny characterizes as a 'permissive turn.' Widely read authors such as child-rearing expert Benjamin Spock and psychologist Carl Rogers articulated a highly optimistic view of human nature and potential. 'The turn inward,' Petigny summarizes, 'took the individual further away from the goal of self-mastery and closer to the Romantic ideal of being unrepressed and unencumbered.'[1] Religious beliefs became less dogmatic and demanding even as church membership swelled. Hence President Eisenhower spent the 'National Day of Prayer' he proclaimed fishing, golfing, and playing cards.

This ethos of pleasure seeking affected men more than women. The leading post-war rebels were white males: James Dean, Elvis Presley, the Beats. 'All woman wants is security,' warned Hugh Hefner's *Playboy*. 'And she's perfectly willing to crush man's adventurous, freedom-loving spirit to get it.'[2] Women's discontent was expressed more obliquely, focused more on their husbands' shortcomings than on the institution of marriage. There was a sort of perverse symmetry between the regrets of husbands and wives: many of the former seemed to desire more freedom from marriage; most of the latter wished for more committed husbands, deeper relationships.[3]

If white America was largely focused on enjoying the good life after the war, black America was still trying to achieve it. African-Americans made modest gains in employment and education but had a lower cultural profile than during the Harlem Renaissance of the 1920s. The leading black organizations of the post-war years devoted themselves to civil rights, to integration, and by the mid-1950s this movement had become powerful.

More white Americans took racism seriously. Nazism in particular and the war more generally discredited white supremacy, at least outside the South. Race became the 'American Dilemma' to growing numbers of white people.

World War II also accelerated Sub-Saharan African independence movements. By the mid-1950s it was obvious that colonialism's days in Africa were numbered, and much sooner than most white observers had anticipated. Africa therefore became a key theater in the Cold War between the West and the Soviet Union. US leaders worried that it might pass from colonialism to communism. This eventuality—and hence Africa—could not be ignored.

Americans uninterested in geopolitics had diverse reactions to black Africa's emergence. Mainstream accounts strove to accommodate this new, black-led Africa while still positing picturesque, savage Africa as a foil to modern America. White women, as before the war, focused on relationships with rural Africans. The black popular press was delighted by the emergence of black Africa, but three leading black Americans who traveled there had very different reactions. By the mid-1950s, black Africa impinged more than ever before on diverse Americans' African quests.

THE RISE AND FALL OF WHITE AMERICA'S AFRICAN GOLDEN AGE

Coverage of Africa in the popular press and popular movies reached unprecedented heights early in the 1950s. Africa was occasionally savage, more commonly picturesque, and always receptive to white American quests. Then black African independence movements intruded.

Popular magazines served up to post-war Americans an Africa that was exotic but innocuous. The thesis of the

National Geographic's 'Carefree People of the Cameroons,' published in 1947, lay in its title. The fifteen pages of photographs featured many topless women, a long-established feature of the magazine's treatment of 'primitive,' dark-skinned people, and scantily clad men going about their work and their rituals. 'After the Ball Is Over … A Girl Must Rest' was the caption for a young woman sitting on the ground after a ceremonial dance.[4] 'Hollywood Safari' condensed by the *Reader's Digest* from *Collier's*, described the 1949 filming of *King Solomon's Mines* in Eastern and Central Africa. Masai dances ended 'in a frothing hysteria' or with 'eight-foot spears … singing right and left' that sent cameramen scrambling for cover. But no harm was done. Africans were like fascinating overgrown children. The leading African actor, Kimusi, was 'an enchanting rogue' whose threatened departure was avoided by the promise of six cows when the filming was completed, a prospect that left Kimusi 'as happy as a starlet with a new fur coat.'[5]

Optimism for Africa rested on its willingness to follow western patterns. A 1948 *Reader's Digest* article on Liberia identified the Goodyear Rubber Company as its most progressive force. Its vast plantations offered high wages, good homes, schools, and medical care.[6] 'The Conqueror of the Congo' in the *Saturday Evening Post* was a warm portrait of American missionary William Alexander Deans. Since 'the African is an image of his particular white man,' it followed that 'where the white man is haughty, the black man is sullen. Where the white man is brutal, the black man is stupid.'[7] Since Deans was a good man, so were the black

Africans he ministered to. W.R. Moore in the *National Geographic* repeatedly juxtaposed white progress and black primitiveness in articles such as 'White Magic in the Belgian Congo.'[8] Extensive pieces by Elsie May Bell Grosvenor, who had traveled across much of Africa with her husband, the President of the National Geographic Society, sounded the same note. Though the first was entitled 'Safari through Changing Africa,' the photographs, especially, emphasized the traditional and the peculiar, and Africa's progress was white driven: 'Invariably we were impressed by the work British colonial governments are doing,' most of it 'devoted to improving the status, not of the English settlers but of the Africans.'[9]

Life approached black African politics more seriously and sympathetically than did the *Reader's Digest*, *Saturday Evening Post*, or *National Geographic*. A 1949 piece described the new South Africa's government's racial politics as 'extremist.'[10] A year later, 'South Africa and its Problems' described apartheid as 'an unabashed outbreak of racialism and nationalism' and included an excerpt from Alan Paton, the white anti-apartheid activist whose *Cry, the Beloved Country* had appeared just a few years before. It featured a very affecting photograph that filled nearly an entire page: a three-year-old black girl looking through a barbed-wire fence from her 'bleak, filthy slum.'[11]

But these stories were illustrated by more hackneyed images. Though the text of the piece on South African riots underscored white culpability, the lead photograph was of a black man with a fiendish grin hurling a rock. The caption described his body as 'a study of rhythmic rage.'[12]

Life maintained its paradoxical coverage of Africa into the 1950s. A black African was on the cover of a May 1953 issue devoted to 'Africa: A Continent in Ferment.'[13] But he had exotic ornaments and hair. No sign of the new Africa here. Pages juxtaposed traditional dancers with modern buildings, canoes with automobiles and air travel. The issue's longer stories dwelled on 'timeless' Africa: 'Lost Peaks and Big Game' focused on the animals of Albert Park in the Congo, and 'Black Africa' depicted Africans who 'still live in a jungle twilight of the primitive past.'[14]

That most famous African of all, Tarzan, still offered America an Africa in which a great white man remained firmly in control.

As before, the post-war Tarzan has it both ways. He is both the strongest man in the jungle and civilized. He is clean-cut, honest, hard-working, moral, decisive, powerful in every way, a sort of younger and more athletic version of President Eisenhower, the sort of man that Americans liked to imagine themselves to be. He lives in a split-level suburban house in the sky run by a domesticated wife (Jane) and populated by an earnest son (Boy) and clownish family pet (Cheta). The post-war Tarzan and Jane are beautiful and shapely; their patches of clothing reveal more than they conceal. But theirs is a domestic, highly consensual sexuality. There are flowers to pluck and a swimming pool. In fact the surrounding jungle is a sort of Edenic, giant backyard, full of friendly, pet-like animals. Tarzan is a kind-hearted zookeeper, not the savage carnivore of Burroughs' fiction. He loves the jungle and opposes greedy poachers and miners much like post-war suburbanites criticized hunting and unfettered development.

The post-war Tarzan remains unconcerned with black Africans. His cul-de-sac is racially segregated. There are no black servants or side-kicks.

In fact many of the more prominent African "natives" are light-skinned. The good king in *Tarzan and the Huntress* of 1947 is played by a Mexican-born actor. The beautiful women in the Edenic city of eternal youth in *Tarzan's Magic Fountain* from 1949 have very light skin and long, flowing hair, whereas dark-skinned people inhabit a squalid town. The sirens of *Tarzan and the Slave Girl* of 1950 include Hungarian-born Eva Gabor. In general, the more important and civilized the native, the lighter her or his skin. The leading villains are white, often European.

The natives played by dark-skinned people inspire neither fear nor respect. The Lykopo of *Tarzan and the She Devil*, 1953, are easily captured and controlled by evil white men. As Tarzan fights to free them they watch passively. Returned to their homes, the grateful Lykopo assure him that they can now defend themselves. But they are soon recaptured and must again be rescued. *In Tarzan and the Slave Girl* a black porter panics and falls off a bridge right after a white villain tells him, 'don't look down, you fool.' A particularly telling scene in *Tarzan's Savage Fury*, of 1952, has black natives using boys as human bait for crocodile hunting: they tie a rope around a boy, have him splash about to draw a crocodile's attention, then reel him into shore to draw the unwitting crocodile into their trap. Tarzan watches without comment until a white boy who has been raised in the jungle (soon to be Tarzan's adoptive son) is in danger of being attacked when the rope snags. Tarzan kills the crocodile, lectures the half dozen or so adults ('no use boys for bait!'), and then easily routs them when they take offense. Black Africans' flaccid incompetence is a constant foil for Tarzan's muscular and moral strength.

More serious post-war films represented a manly, less suburban Africa, but one in which black Africans remained marginal.

The early 1950s marked the acme of Hollywood's interest in Africa. By Kenneth M. Cameron's meticulous count in *Africa on Film*, US movies of the continent numbered twenty-four in the 1930s, thirty-six in the 1940s, and fifty-seven in the 1950s—before precipitously declining.[15] Many of these films, furthermore, were big productions, with Hollywood's leading directors, actors, and actresses. Several of them won large audiences and critical acclaim. Africa is central to their plot and popularity; it removes the distractions of modern civilization so that white protagonists cannot help but confront their true natures.

Hollywood's post-war Africa is dangerous. The aptly entitled *Savage Splendor* of 1949 spelled out its thesis in the opening scene's voiceover: 'The "Dark Continent" they call it. Land of shadowed mystery and ancient menace, and yet it blazes with light and color.' The movie offered the closest approximation so far of going on safari without leaving home, an adventure filled with dangerous animals and exotic natives, though its narrator referred to its plains as 'endless, brooding, unpeopled.'[16] Likewise, the great white hunter of

King Solomon's Mines of 1950 seems delighted that in Africa he could 'die at any time' from disease, natives, or animals. Here, 'man is just meat.'

As it had before the war, these renderings of Africa presented white men with a chance to be men. Hollywood offered Hemingway's *The Macomber Affair* and *The Snows of Kilimanjaro* in 1947 and 1952, respectively, both starring Gregory Peck. The screenplays are less stark and misogynistic than the original stories. But Africa remains the white man's antidote to modernity. Likewise, *Bwana Devil* of 1952 follows the transformation of an aimless alcoholic into a man obsessed with killing the lions terrorizing his work force. He at last succeeds and becomes fully a man.

Not every man—or woman—passes the Africa test. *Mogambo*, 1953, features four characters whose lives quickly and dramatically intersect in Africa. Victor Marswell (Clark Gable), the supremely capable but solitary safari leader, eventually gives himself to Eloise Kelly (Ava Gardner), a street-smart, big-hearted broad who wanders into Africa by accident. Kelly cannot tell a rhino from a kangaroo, but Africa reveals her sunny nature and good heart. Baby animals cavort with her. The appearance of a cheetah in her tent surprises but does not unnerve her. Linda Nordley (Grace Kelly), in contrast, professes a great love for Africa: 'Oh, it's so exciting and thrilling.' But she is both drawn to and appalled by Africa's violence, of hippos fighting, a lion dragging away its prey. When Marswell saves her from a black panther, this wife of a clueless professor begins a sexual pursuit of the great white hunter. Passions containable elsewhere quickly explode

75

here. 'Africa,' notes film historian Tag Gallagher, 'brings out the unconsciousness of the characters.'[17] Africa is unable to liberate the repressed Linda and her educated husband, but it is perfect for Victor and Kelly.

Black Africans are bit players in these journeys of white self-discovery. All of the above films include dark-skinned natives, some in large numbers—'lean, muscular, sometimes dangerous-looking Africans,' as Cameron puts it, very different Africans, indeed, from the listless or light-skinned villagers of the Tarzan movies.[18] But very few of these impressive physical specimens utter more than an occasional line. In *Mogambo* Marswell is always the most capable man in every situation, knows the animals best, speaks native languages fluently, and is far more courageous and decisive than Africa's black men. When he and the Nordleys advance on the gorillas, the natives run away in fright. Like Tarzan, he is more African than the Africans. Black Africans spend much of their time singing and dancing, they are an inferior part of the exotic scenery.

The African Queen, a 1951 Hollywood blockbuster directed by John Ford and starring Katherine Hepburn and Humphrey Bogart, is a particularly strong example of the salience of Africa's landscape and the near invisibility of its people. This juxtaposition appears from the outset, when the wonderful sounds of the jungle contrast with the discordant, unnatural singing of black Africans at a Methodist mission church. Then Charlie arrives on his little steamboat, the *African Queen*, and the childlike natives are easily diverted by the prospect of capturing his discarded cigar. Indeed, Charlie mentions that his black crew ('boys') deserted as soon as they heard that there were German troops in the vicinity, 'moaning and rolling their eyes.' Black Africans then vanish save for brief gigs as incompetent marksmen in a German fort and as background characters on a German ship. At the heart of the film are just Charlie and Rose on a dream-like river. Cut off from everything but each other and this Eden, Charlie discovers his courage, Rose a passion for danger and Charlie. They are 'an Adam and Eve uniquely mated in an aboriginal garden'—but without the aborigines.[19] Rose begins the journey primly dressed and nicely scrubbed, and when Charlie counters her lecture on the evils of alcohol by claiming that his attachment to strong drink is only 'natural,' she has a ready retort: 'Nature, Mr. Olnutt, is what we are put in this world to rise above.' But Rose, who cultivated European roses in her mission garden, is soon embracing African nature. Her sensuality is first awakened when she bathes in the river, a sort of secular baptism. (Life imitated art in that Hepburn found the water in her hotel bathtub to be 'like honey. It is the most spectacular water.'[20]) Shooting some rapids leaves her marveling that a 'mere physical experience' could 'be so stimulating.' They then share their first kiss. The next morning brings beautiful jungle vistas and wondrous sounds. Remarks the unpoetic Charlie: 'The more I look at this place, the prettier it gets.' Rose's body and clothing become more soiled and tattered as her African journey and Charlie's admiration soften her.

The movie's premise and plot demand the erasure of black Africans. When Rose espies a beautiful flower overhanging the river she exclaims that 'perhaps no one' has ever seen it before, 'that it might not even have a name.' Yet filming was commonly interrupted by the inconvenient appearance of African canoes on this well-traveled transportation artery.[21] It was hard work keeping the Africans out of *The African Queen*.

Africa's land also dwarfs its native peoples in *Untamed*, which appeared in 1955. The film features a female protagonist, Katie, who is immediately enthralled by the South African landscape: 'It's like the end of the world—or the beginning' she remarks on her first view of the coast. Katie and her first husband, who soon dies, join a group of trekkers who head north in much the same way as Hollywood depicted American settlers headed west. They ford a river, circle their wagons, fight off the natives (Zulus), and are overjoyed to arrive at their new home, a fertile valley with a river running through it. Katie asks her new husband, her life's true love: 'How much is mine?' He replies: 'As much as you can cover on a horse in a half a day.' She then spurs her horse into a mad gallop and flies across the land. 'This is where we'll spend our lives, Paul,' she tells him. 'This is our place. Home.' Paul's political duties and other difficulties intercede, but by the movie's end they have been reunited and are again in a wagon, headed '[b]ack to the land,' into the setting sun.

Untamed has more black characters than most films set in Africa through the mid-1950s. Paul has a trusted black African assistant or servant who ends up saving his life. Zulu warriors are depicted in a drawn-out battle scene, and respect is offered for their courage and determination. But this warfare seems to have no relationship to white occupation of their land, which has presumably been lying there, vacant and unappreciated, awaiting Katie's arrival.[22]

In all of these films, Africa is a passive tableau for the dreams of white Americans. By the mid-1950s, however, it had become tricky to ignore the emergence of black-led movements for independence and economic developments. It became more and more difficult to posit an Africa without Africans.

Even the conservative *Reader's Digest* at first expressed more hope than pessimism about Africa's emergence. It featured the work of John Gunther, who had published the latest of his continental overviews: *Inside Africa*.[23] As the scholar David Apter pointed out, the book was flawed by Gunther's heavy reliance 'on officialdom or Westernized leaders' and tendency to present indigenous cultures as 'ebullient, nationalistic, and imbued with a lusty irrationalism.'[24] But his first *Reader's Digest* piece answered 'yes' to the question posed in its title: 'Is the White Man Finished in Africa?'[25] The West could support black Africa—or risk losing it to the Communists. Gunther's article on South Africa emphasized the failings of 'unmitigated white supremacy,' a system that had created 'in some respects the ugliest government I have ever encountered in the free world.'[26] The emerging black nations inspired much more hope than dread. Nigeria's people, for example, 'are committed enough to education and modernization to keep' them from '"going back to the tribes."'[27] Uganda's 'prevailing tone and atmosphere' was 'reformist, humanitarian and New Dealish.'[28] Other *Reader's Digest* writers perceived commonalities between black African independence and American history. A piece condensed from the *New York Times Magazine* characterized Ghana's Nkrumah as a 'religious man' and 'practical politician' who was 'almost certain to keep ... clear of the Communists.'[29] A year later, in 1958, the *Reader's Digest* published a version of 'I Saw the New Africa' from the *Saturday Evening Post* stressing the parallels between emerging black Africa and '[t]he spirit of our 1776.'[30]

The more liberal *Life* magazine was bullish on the new Africa, particularly Ghana. A long piece by Robert Wallace even complimented its past: the once mighty Asante Empire, which he characterized as 'nonliterate but not properly "primitive."'[31] A photo essay upon Ghana's independence a year later entitled 'Proof of Progress' featured a modern supermarket, new housing, and Vice President Richard Nixon embracing a chief.[32] Other photographs showcased the nation's university and legislative hall and distinguished visitors, including Dr. Martin Luther King and Ralph Bunche. President Nkrumah's 1958 visit to the US elicited photographs of his meetings with President Eisenhower and Vice President Nixon and characterized him as 'a symbol of levelheaded African nationalism.'[33]

But popular magazines continued to evoke old Africa even in the midst of black independence movements.

Photographer Emil Schulthess dwelled on the Africa of 'early ... Genesis' in his 1958 *Life* article.[34] Robert Coughlan's two-part series on African independence at the decade's close asserted that the continent was shifting from 'the Stone Age into the modern world,' but seemed more interested in the former than the latter. The second opened with dawn in a village, 'Africa as it millennially was and still is.'[35]

As anthropologist Catherine A. Lutz and sociologist Jane L. Collins point out, *National Geographic*, a magazine pitched to more educated Americans, dwelled on innocuous exoticism.[36] Most of the images in staff member W. Robert Moore's 'Progress and Pageantry in Changing Nigeria' focused on the timeless rather than the modern: traditional 'Helter-skelter Adobe Houses'; naked women with shaved heads pounding grain; painted herdsmen.[37] A journey into Nigeria and French Cameroon on the cusp of independence aspired '[t]o record the human images of Africa before primitive tribal ways could be blurred by the movement of progress.'[38]

Popular magazines paid their respects to Africa's 'winds of change' but preferred hackneyed images. The same tension between respecting modern Africa while indulging in more popular clichés characterized American film in the late 1950s.

Tarzan is still superior to black Africans. In *Tarzan and the Lost Safari* of 1957 the Opar are a 'bad' tribe who wish to sacrifice the white survivors of a plane wreck to their gods. Luckily for these survivors, the Opar are not very bright. One Opar is done in by the bite of a poisonous spider, which Tarzan had warned his own party about—and had spotted from several yards away. The Opar, however, does not even notice that he has been bitten. In *Tarzan's Greatest Adventure* black Africans disappear altogether after the opening scenes, as the movie turns to the great showdown between two powerful white men.

But other Tarzan films of the late 1950s depict black Africans as potent or heroic. *Tarzan's Fight for Life*, 1958, features Futa, an evil, scheming witch doctor played by James

Edwards, a noted African-American actor, the most significant and powerful black figure, villainous or not, yet to appear.
His demise, moreover, paves the way for a young prince who
accepts western science, a chief who will lead his people into
a bright future free from superstition. The film even features
a speech by Jane that hints at cultural and moral relativism:
'No one is completely wrong ... The Nagasu tribe with all of
their superstitions and a thousand years of strange beliefs,
they think that they're right.' Jane still believes in civilization, in bringing 'light into darkness.' But earlier Tarzan films
were not invested enough in their African subjects to even
raise such questions, let alone to offer up any explanations for
why Africans might reasonably prefer their own traditions.
Tarzan the Magnificent, from 1960, puts still more emphasis
on interracial friendships. Tarzan's most loyal and respected
helper is not an animal or Jane or a white traveler, but Tate,
the black first mate to a murdered white captain who 'treated
me like a friend.' The least likable and most cowardly man in
Tarzan's party is a racist white man who is confounded when
Tate risks his life for him. Tarzan has become a medium for
racial sensitivity.

Other Hollywood films also paid more attention and
respect to black Africans as the 1950s progressed, even as
they continued to feature white characters' self-actualization in Africa. *The Nun's Story* of 1959, for which Audrey
Hepburn received an Academy Award nomination, features
a French nun who is most at home in the Congo. Unlike the
best-selling book by Kathryn Hulme on which the film was
based, black Congolese have little bearing on the plot. But

if Africans are in the background, they are also depicted as people of dignity, working in a semi-urban setting rather than devoting every waking moment to drumming and dancing in the jungle, and they are capable of reflection and change.

The Roots of Heaven, 1958, based on the book of the same name by popular French writer Romain Gary, exhibits this same tendency to incorporate black African characters in the harrowing quests of white existentialists. The film hinges on a quixotic character, Morel, whose devotion to saving elephants in particular and nature in general attracts fellow travelers similarly traumatized by the modern West. Morel's epiphany flowered in a Nazi prisoner of war camp, where he realized that elephants were the perfect image of freedom. Minna, the film's second most important character, is also a refugee from the war, forced by the Germans into one of their 'dolls' houses' to service their soldiers. Morel's evocation of the elephants' suffering and humanities' need for friendship draws her in: 'I know about suffering.' Major Forsyth (played by Errol Flynn) bears a different scar from the war, for he is the lone survivor of a company of paratroopers he commanded. He alone talked upon being captured, so survives as a self-loathing alcoholic whose only friend is a Toto, a Mexican jumping bean tormented by 'a little worm inside him' that 'tries to eat its way out and of course this makes Toto try to jump out of his skin,' much like his owner reacts to his memories of the war. Joining Morel to protect the elephants eventually provides Forsyth with the opposite of what the war bequeathed him: a brave death for a noble cause. Africa and its elephants offer these casualties of war and refugees from modernity a second chance at meaning and significance.

And what of French Equatorial Africa's many black Africans? They fall into two categories. Most notable is Watari, a French-educated black nationalist who joins Morel for strictly utilitarian reasons, hoping that Morel's critique of the colonial administration will redound to the nationalists' benefit. But Watari is a more modern and therefore more corrupt man than Morel, whom he betrays for the promise of guns. In fact Watari's leading assistant complains that the elephants crossing a road and delaying their truck are a nuisance that interfere with the work of building 'a modern country.' Africa's black nationalists resemble the modern West in choosing human and material progress over elephants and nature; they are squandering their continent's precious natural birthrights for a mess of modern pottage. It is the simple, unpretentious Africans who repeatedly respond with warmth to Morel and his cause, though none of these supporters get many lines. Only modern white people, the detritus spat out by the most ruthless war in history, can appreciate and articulate what Africa has to offer.[39]

Something of Value, 1957, goes much further in depicting Africa from the point of view of a black nationalist and is that rare film that is more nuanced and racially progressive than the book on which it was based, Robert Ruark's novel of the same title.[40] As in the book, Peter (Rock Hudson) and Kimani (Sidney Poitier) grow up as brothers but end up on opposite sides of the Mau Mau struggle in Kenya after World War II. Cameron is certainly correct in pointing out that the film's treatment of the two is hardly equivalent: Peter's family life is rendered much more fully and sympathetically than Kimani's, and the Mau Mau are depicted as exotic and savage.[41] But Mau Mau leaders have a lot of time on screen to make some compelling arguments. Kimani is much more likeable in the film than he is in the book, and Peter tries to rescue rather than kill him. 'The come-to-Jesus ending is just plain bad,' remarked the patently racist Ruark. Liberal Hollywood was not going to have Hudson throttle Poitier. The ultimate villains in the piece are racist whites. The Mau Maus are the logical end of colonialism's racist cruelties, and Poitier's character offers up his life instead of resisting to the end, a choice which 'discourages black action while encouraging white compassion.'[42]

But *Something of Value* was not the commercial success that its makers had predicted. The racist book was much more popular than the sensitive film. White American filmmakers and other broadly liberal opinion makers were sympathetic to the idea of black rights at home and abroad by the mid-1950s and adjusted their treatments accordingly. But those adjustments both cost them audience share and were more often than not half-hearted. Black African agency was difficult for mainstream American culture to accommodate.

WHITE MEN'S SELF-ACTUALIZATION IN CHANGING AFRICA

The rise of black Africa also complicated the quests of white men traveling in and writing novels of Africa in the 1950s.

This is most clearly illustrated by the life and work of the largely forgotten Ruark, America's leading interpreter of Africa for a decade. Ernest Hemingway, whom Ruark much admired and imitated, also visited Africa in the 1950s, but wrote very differently about it than he had two decades before. Saul Bellow, well into his distinguished career as a leading American novelist, offered a very different type of white male protagonist in Africa at the decade's close.

Storm and Echo, a 1948 novel from a much lesser-known writer, Frederick Prokosch, suggested that American intellectuals still viewed Africa through a Conrad-esque lens. Prokosch penned his doctoral dissertation on Chaucer before becoming a prolific professional writer who pursued highly idiosyncratic themes. His fiction, he remarked in 1945, attempts 'to detect a universal and lasting pattern in each contemporary situation; … and above all, never to forget that man is now as always a terrifying animal who can be clearly perceived only through the cooperating powers of compassion, fearlessness, and love.'[43] Such virtues were best forged under extraordinary circumstances in places such as Asia and the Congo, where 'the civilized surfaces are sloughed off.'[44] *Storm and Echo* is a highly symbolic quest across Central Africa in search of a place, Mount Nagala, which may or may not exist, and the Kurtz-like white explorer who may or may not live there.

Prokosch's Africa is neatly divided between white seekers and passive black helpers. His American protagonist is joined by three European scientists who 'have lost their faith in reason' and a group of black porters 'submerged in an atavistic swamp of instinct.'[45]

Storm and Echo's seekers confront a string of horrific, pornographic African landscapes. One village is full of pathetic, deformed, and diseased sufferers. Another is populated wholly by the children of the king, all other males having been castrated. 'The whole kingdom was drowned in incest,' the royal hospital awash in a 'tangle of bodies … coiled in the darkness.' Another village consists of thieves with 'the eyes of cocaine addicts.' A fourth is 'a miracle of squalor … to look through the doorways was like peering into the abdomen of a corpse.' The children looked as if they were 'looking for a little grave to rest in.'

Prokosch's Africans are hardly human, always unfathomable. The group's 'hideously ugly' guide, Oudangé, follows the protagonist to the end of his quest because he has no choice: '"The black man," he said softly, "accepts everything. We are resigned. In this world the white man is our master. We suffer. We obey. It is the will of the gods.."' Africans throughout the book are creatures of nature: sexual, violent, superstitious, and, ultimately, passive—but also ineluctable. One of the Europeans explains: '"They sulk. They begin to lie. They glide back into their watery depths, like amphibians, and disappear."' As one critic puts it, Prokosch's primitives, be they Asian, Latin American, or African, mingle 'a dark, superstitious ignorance with some show of intuitive wisdom,' for they must embody 'all the things which our civilized hearts yearn for.' It is 'an artistic anthropology,' but also a highly racialized one.[46]

Prokosch required a formless Africa. The protagonist is there to encounter 'the inner darkness; the uncontrollable.

Call it nature if you wish. Or call it instinct. Call it unreason. Call it evil. Call it the devil. I long to see it face to face. I long to recognize it and touch it. And finally free myself of it.' Prokosch creates an Africa in which 'there is no such thing as happiness … or lucidity, or reason.' Africans must be 'haphazard splinters of a huge and amorphous, tormented mass of mankind' because that, according to Prokosch, is the human condition, a fact that western man, clothed in reason and progress, has contrived to forget. Wisdom and truth cannot be found until these chimeras are stripped away. *Storm and Echo* is a quest narrative in which western pilgrims 'have escaped from the modern "civilized" world to an elemental one.' They have 'met *life*' in Africa.[47]

Much better known and more accessible to American readers was the work of Ruark, already a prominent newspaper columnist and magazine writer when he went on the first of many Kenyan safaris in 1951. Four years later his fictional account of the Mau Mau rebellion *Something of Value* (1955), made him rich and famous. It reached sales of over 120,000 in hard-bound copies alone, and the film rights set a record for a novel.[48] A very large proportion of Americans who read something about Africa in the 1950s got much if not most of their information from Ruark.

East Africa offered Ruark a second chance at childhood. Like Hemingway, he had chafed against a strong mother. 'We declared war on each other as soon as I was able to walk,' he recalled, adding that she 'would have made a good lesbian.'[49] He began hunting at a young age and 'had early fallen under the spell of Mr. Burroughs and his *Tarzan*' and other accounts of Africa until, he recalled in 1953, 'it seemed I would bust a gusset if I didn't get to see jungles and lions and cannibals someday.' Travel across the Pacific Ocean in World War II and great success as a syndicated columnist and magazine writer did not dull this desire. He led a dissolute life in New York City, a 'steaming, sweating, raucous, stinking, overcrowded asphalt purgatory.' East Africa brought rebirth. Living outdoors, rising and retiring early, and risking his life against wild animals began to heal modernity's wounds. As he left the bush and headed toward home he felt 'the way I felt when the Japs quit and the war was over ... All the excitement and the dangerous security of war were finished. Now it would be work and civilian frustration and complication again.' These feelings did not pass: 'as soon as I can afford it I'm going home again to Africa. I'm not sleeping well in New York.' Africa, ultimately, was about life itself, a place 'to meet God.'[50]

Black Africans threatened Ruark's dream. He called *Something of Value*, his best-selling 1955 novel, a fictionalized but balanced piece of reportage; he was simply presenting the facts of a bloody conflict through the lives of two young Kenyans, one white (Peter) and one black (Kimani), who grew up together as friends but are divided by the Mau Mau conflict. But Peter and other white characters are rendered much more fully and sympathetically than Kimani and other black characters are. Both commit savage acts, to be sure, and the war against the Mau Mau seems to dehumanize Peter. But the atrocities give him nightmares. He is, at heart, a gentle, admirable, and capable man, a character in fact patterned after the white safari guide that Ruark so esteemed, a man accomplished at killing animals but who would wreck his automobile to keep from running over a nest of baby birds. Kimani is brutal by nature. After fornicating with a prostitute, he tosses money at her, calls her a 'whore,' and remarks: 'If you have given me a disease I shall come back someday and twist your neck.' Ruark makes some empathetic gestures toward black Kenya in arguing that Europeans changed black Africa too quickly, leaving them between two worlds: 'We educated them and made them want things and took away their old securities and then didn't give them any other securities to replace what we'd taken.' But this critique of rapid social change dovetails too neatly with his own nostalgia for a colonial Kenya in which black Africans remain in the bush and out of positions of authority.

Like Roosevelt, White, and Carl Akeley before him, he found the black 'boys' who accompanied him on safari infinitely more likeable and noble than black intellectuals and politicians. 'The best man I ever met' was 'a Nandi boy, about twenty-eight years old, who was my gunbearer.'[51] Kidogo was brave, hard-working, humble, and trusted Ruark with his life. He fitted with Ruark's view of what Kenya should remain: an alternative to the modern world. Ruark hated the Mau Mau for the same reason that he hated educated Africans: they wanted to change a place that he liked just the way it was. As he admitted in 1955: 'When the Mau Mau invaded the Africa I knew, I experienced an anger that, I suspect, was first based on selfishness, because my Paradise was spoiled.'[52] In Africa, notes a biographer, 'he stepped back into a time remembered from his childhood—where men were men, women stayed in the kitchen and the blacks knew their place.'[53]

By the early 1960s, Ruark perceived that his Africa was slipping away. *Uhuru*, the Swahili word for independence, was published in 1962 and focused on the dreary prospect of a black-ruled Kenya, which would in fact arrive the following year. Ruark explained in the preface what 'Uhuru' meant to various groups of black East Africans: 'slothful ease' for many; 'endless flocks of lovely useless cattle,' for nomads; 'an absence of game wardens' for ivory poachers; 'a sea of honey beer' and harems for alcoholics and womanizers, respectively; 'the white man's magically rich and loamy land' for peasants; and 'a licence to rob and steal, to kill without punishment and to flout rules of decent human behaviour with reckless impunity' for 'the wilfully lawless.' And that apparently covered it; every black East African who looked forward to independence was a knave or a fool. For white Africans 'who love the land, who were born on the land,' Uhuru meant 'the destruction of a created beauty selflessly performed as a labour of love.' Uhuru distorts not only the lives of white Africans and the pleasant world they have lovingly labored to create. It also distorts black Africans, who are noble only in their original state.

This is most obvious in the character of Stephen Ndegwa, an ambitious black politician who even with 'my white friends, my India partners, Moslem and Hindi, my vari-coloured wives and my several houses' still only feels 'keenly alive' when back home in the red dirt of his simple farm, 'the true black man's Kenya.' As the faithful gun bearer puts it to his 'Bwana,' men like Ndegwa are, at heart, 'ashamed of themselves, like monkeys who have put on a man's hat but realize that they are still monkeys.' Ruark's black Africans are happiest when they are serving white hunters or living simple lives in villages.

Dermott is Ruark's usual white protagonist, a great white hunter who is a bit too brutal but nonetheless noble because he represents and defends a precious, colonial way of life that he fears is doomed. He identifies black Africans such as Ndegwa as the culprits, 'the city slickers and their detribal-ized wenches,' the 'union officials and small politicians,' as well as the spineless British politicians who defer to them.

Ruark was prophetic about his own future in black East Africa. Kenya banned him for his racist writings. A piece published in the *Saturday Evening Post* on his last hunt in Kenya had the protagonist, an old white hunter, stalking an aged elephant. 'When the old bull fell with a mighty crash, much of what I loved best of the old Africa died with him.' Ruark and Selby, his famous guide, were not optimistic about Kenya's prospects under black rule. Ruark gives Selby the last word on the beautiful place they so loved: 'It's a pity we don't own it any more, isn't it?'[54]

Meanwhile, Ruark's inspiration, Hemingway, had made a sort of private peace with black Africa. By the time he finally returned in 1953, a trip funded by *Look*, a photograph-based magazine, he was more fully prepared than before to discard western norms, for 'opening up the borders of the self rather than protecting them.'[55]

To be sure, Hemingway's brief text and the photographs in *Look* revisited well-worn clichés. The cover had him dead center, with a black African man behind him, in the shadows. Inside were images of a calm and commanding Hemingway posing with a leopard he had just killed, standing firm against a charging rhino, and parrying the blows of a much younger black African boxer. Hemingway's page-long essay spent little ink on any African save Philip Percival, his 'white hunter.'[56]

But Hemingway's private writings—a blending of memoir, meditation, and fiction—revealed a man who had become much more modest and receptive than during his earlier safari. As before, Africa provided a foil: 'I had been a fool not to have stayed on in Africa and instead had gone back to America where I had killed my homesickness for Africa in different ways,' he remarked in *Under Kilimanjaro*, eventually published in 2005. But he now came as an initiate, with much to learn. 'There were very many things I did not know,' he wrote in the book's third paragraph. 'There were more every day.' They 'were in another man's country,' after all. He and his wife, Mary, took pains to show respect to black Africans in his camp; they never 'called a man a boy.' Hemingway realized that Africa was not really home, that he was an outsider who must learn from black Africans to become an insider.

Hemingway wondered if whiteness had become a liability to rather than a prerequisite for African self-actu-alization. 'It always seemed stupid to be white in Africa,' he wrote. Hemingway hoped he was dark enough to be taken as 'half caste,' and while his wife was away took a Kamba 'fiancé' into his tent, shaved his head, dyed his clothes as the Masai did, and went out to hunt in the middle of the night unclothed, with a spear, all of which suggested a mingling of 'actual tribal customs with his own romantic notions of primitivism.' Mary, who had evidently tolerated the African mistress, drew the line when it came to earrings: 'The fiction that having your ears pierced will make you a Kamba is an evasion of the reality, which is that you are not and never can be anything but an honorary Kamba, and it is out of harmony with your best character which is that of a wise, thoughtful, realistic adult white American male.'[57] But upon Mary's return, they blurred their gender identities and sexual behaviors so that Mary 'came to me as something quite new and outside all tribal law,' as recounted in her 1976 memoir. Africa was 'a space of transgression as well as of self-exploration,' as English professor Suzanne del Gizzo observes. The two expressions were part of the same impulse. Embracing primitive Africa and criticizing the modern West was an attempt 'to recover elements of his own personality repressed by that same domineering culture.'[58]

America was ready neither for Hemingway's gender transgressions nor his new version of Africa. *Under Kilimanjaro* and *True at First Light*, a more heavily edited version of his journal, were not published until long after his death. The widely read and viewed *Look* piece, replete with photographs and text representing 'a reassuring narrative of a Westerner's visit to East Africa,' was examined by millions in the 1950s, as were his earlier, more racist works.[59]

A story featuring a white male quester who made some accommodations to modern black Africa reached a large audience at the decade's close. Saul Bellow had been a critic of modern America's penchant for absolute freedom since his first novel, *Dangling Man*, appeared in 1944. Fifteen years later, in 1959, *Henderson the Rain King* nearly won the Pulitzer Prize and constituted both a critique and sophisticated articulation of white American men's African quests. Henderson constituted '[a] direct parody of the Hemingway stoic or narcissist,' 'the Hemingway hero.' 'Its African setting,' literary scholar Gloria L. Cronin adds, 'is an attempt at mocking the inward psychic journeys of a generation of modern questers.'[60] But for all that, this is also a novel in which a troubled American man self-actualizes in an Africa with consequential African characters.

Henderson is an unlikely protagonist. His body and personality are outsized, baroque. This wealthy pig farmer has grand ambitions and intentions yet seems fated to quarrel with and alienate everyone he meets and loves. Behind his bluster lies 'a disturbance in my heart, a voice that spoke … *I want, I want, I want!* … every afternoon'—but would never say a thing more. Henderson is tortured by frantic but dimly understood desires. Matters come to a head when an elderly neighbor woman overhears one of his rages and drops dead from the stress. Henderson, the anti-hero, reflects: 'I should do something,' and of course that means going to Africa. But three weeks of lounging around Hemingway-esque scenery bores him, so he and a native named Romilayu head into the bush—first by jeep and then on foot—for he is 'kind of on a quest.'

Africans complicate and enrich this quest. Henderson's first contacts reprise and lampoon the usual tropes: the simple and kind villagers of Arnewi provoke him to feel 'that living among such people might change a man for the better.'

But he of course overreaches. Determined to eliminate frogs, this enchanted paradise's one blemish, Henderson manages to destroy their pond and is expelled. He and his loyal guide then travel on and live among a very different set of people, the Wariri, whose abundant corpses suggest another hoary African theme. Henderson again distinguishes himself, this time by moving a massive stone idol, and is proclaimed the 'Rain King.' But some of the leaders dislike and distrust both Henderson and the ruler who befriends him. King Dahfu proves to be more than Henderson's equal. The western-educated monarch studies scientific texts that leave Henderson baffled and compels Henderson to become courageous. The other major African character in the novel is Romilayu, the pious servant who always seems wiser than the white man he serves. Consider his reaction to Henderson's explanation of the American need for quests:

> 'I can swear to you, Romilayu, there are guys exactly like me in India and in China and South America and all over the place. Just before I left home I saw an interview in the paper with a piano teacher from Muncie who became a Buddhist monk in Burma. You see, that's what I mean. I am a high-spirited-kind of guy. And it's the destiny of my generation of Americans to go out in the world and try to find the wisdom of life. It just is. Why the hell do you think I'm out here, anyway?'
> 'I don't know, sah.'
> 'I wouldn't agree to the death of my soul.'
> 'Me Methdous, sah.'

The blundering Henderson relies heavily on the patience and good sense of black Africans.

Henderson the Rain King, then, is not simply ironic. As Cronin argues, Bellow does not oppose out of hand 'the anthropological search through primitive cultures for truths lost to Western civilization,' but rather the more extreme and naïve expressions of this impulse, a project that reflects the 'irresponsible unbounded romantic individualism ... at the heart of the pain and disappointment in life itself which scar modern literature.'[61] So even as Bellow pokes fun at Hemingway's trope of Africa as the place for disaffected white men to be transformed, his own protagonist requires an African setting for his own untidy achievement of self-actualization. Africa provides the 'difficult discipline needed for renewal,' the respite 'from the complex superficialities of twentieth-century American life' required 'to achieve personal wholeness.'[62] It is evidently Henderson's vulnerability, so unlike the flawless great white hunters of Ruark's prose, that earns for Henderson a happy ending to his transformative African safari. Cronin cites Henderson's prayer as evidence of his (restrained) optimism:

> 'Oh, you ... Something,' I said, 'you Something because of whom there is not Nothing. Help me to do Thy will. Take off my stupid sins. Untrammel me. Heavenly Father, open up my dumb heart and for Christ's sake preserve me from unreal things. Oh, Thou who tookest me from pigs, let me not be killed over lions. And forgive my crimes and nonsense and let me return to Lily and the kids.'[63]

Bellow's God hears and answers such abject prayers.

Henderson the Rain King is the exception that proves the rule, a well-received novel that incorporates major black African characters and a bumbling white protagonist. Its nuanced version of the white man's American quest would not resurface for another quarter-century.

BLACK AMERICANS AND THE NEW BLACK AFRICA

Black America's view of Africa was in many respects the converse of white America's. It became much deeper and more enthusiastic as black African independence movements and states emerged, though black Americans who spent time in Africa had more diverse reactions.

A few leading African Americans remained or became drawn to Africa after World War II. Du Bois continued to advocate Pan-Africanism. Paul Robeson took a leading role in bringing more than 15,000 people together in a Council on African Affairs meeting in New York City in 1946 that called for the decolonization of the continent, and he posited Africa as the source of African-American creativity.[64]

But most Black Americans expressed little interest in Africa through the early 1950s. Du Bois and Robeson were repeatedly frustrated that fear of being considered soft on Communism blunted mainstream black editors' criticism of colonialism and US foreign policy.[65] Wariness of being associated with savage black Africa continued to shape how most black Americans approached the continent. The epithet 'ABC' ('Africa's Blackest Child' could start a fight in some black neighborhoods.[66]

Ebony, founded in 1945 by John H. Johnson and widely read among black America's growing middle class, at first approached Africa gingerly. Patterned after *Life*, each issue was filled with photographs of and stories about successful African Americans. 'We wanted,' Johnson later recalled in his 1989 memoir, 'to emphasize the positive aspects of Black life,' stories that white writers and publications seldom told.

An editorial entitled 'A Future in America, Not Africa' laid out a position that the magazine repeatedly reiterated. The occasion was the centennial of Liberia's founding by 'a hardened band of stout-hearted American pioneers—white as well as colored—who had hacked a bit of civilization out of the wild jungle.' But the piece criticized the nation's 'little bureaucratic clique' and urged black Americans to remain at home in 'what is unquestionably the greatest nation in the world.' Fragments of Marcus Garvey's UNIA and its '"back-to-Africa" movement' were 'looked upon by most intelligent Negroes as a crack-pot hangover from the past.'[67]

Yet *Ebony* eagerly reported the signs of black African progress that popular white magazines ignored. 'Africa's New Medicine Men' detailed not the sort of exotic practices so popular in *National Geographic* but rather how black West African doctors trained at African medical schools were 'tackling longtime scourges like sleeping sickness, leprosy and malaria with up-to-date scientific methods' and gaining the trust of less-educated residents.[68] Five years later, a headline proclaimed: 'U.S. Negroes Changing their Opinion of Africa Cousins.' The emergence of modern doctors and well-educated leaders such as 'Nkrumah and other pipe-smoking, cultivated African leaders' were beginning to shoulder aside the 'witch doctors' who 'still rattle bones over cholera victims and stick thorns in images of people they do not like too well.'[69] A year later the magazine celebrated the accomplishments of Bishop Bowers, a black clergyman in Ghana who spoke fluent French, German, Italian, Greek, and Latin and played the organ.[70]

Unlike white writers who sought in Africa a respite from or alternative to the West, *Ebony* celebrated African traditions which meshed with modernity. 'African Influence on Fashion' illustrated how western designers, white as well as black, drew on African styles of clothing and grooming. 'The $60-and-up turbans of Lilly Dache and John Frederics and the feathered bonnets of Sally Victor, the top trio among American hat designers, bear a striking resemblance to the festive headgear of East African tribes.'[71] A year later, in 1949, the magazine presented highly stylized sculptures and paintings from Nigeria and dwelled on the accomplishments of their creator, young Ben Enbwonwu, who had won the respect of European patrons.[72] *Ebony's* black Africa participated in and enriched modernity rather than providing a respite from or foil to it.

Ebony supported black independence movements much more forcefully than white magazines did. South Africa received frequent criticism. Their black shanty-towns were 'The World's Worst Slums.'[73] An editorial, also from 1947, criticized the US and Great Britain for so often shielding South Africa from criticism in the United Nations.[74] *Ebony* soon broadened its treatment of African politics. A 1949 article on the production of chocolate by 'industrious Negro cocoa farmers of West Africa' remarked that the British were 'smacking their lips over the sweet profits reaped' by their control of an industry built on the backs of black farmers.[75] 'All Africa Stirring with Native Cries for Self-Rule' appeared two years later.[76] Nor did the apparent failures or atrocities of African nationalists much worry the magazine's writers. The editorial 'How to Stop the Mau Mau' pointed out that Europe's pillaging of Africa made such violence 'inevitable.' 'With their backs against the wall, they have struck out blindly at their white oppressors in the only way they know.' The British were making a bad situation worse by 'fighting terror with terror' rather than undertaking necessary reforms. British protestations that black Africans were incapable of self-government 'is the English version of the American phrase which cautions that the Negro "just ain't ready."' The comparison was a telling one. African colonialism was not simply cruel and exploitive. It also asserted or implied that black-skinned people across the globe were not fully human. But black Africa 'had going civilizations before the British Empire was founded.' Many of its people, to be sure, remained 'primitive,' but: 'Africa is awakening from a long sleep.'[77] Africa was not home for the growing black bourgeois that *Ebony* represented and spoke to. But neither was it the exotic refuge from modernity of white magazines.

The same African developments that complicated white America's projection of its desires and fantasies upon the 'Dark Continent' electrified black Americans. Several black newspapers had correspondents in Africa by the late 1950s, and a 1957 survey found that black Americans were about eight times more likely to express an interest in Africa than were their white counterparts.[78] A 1957 editorial in the *Pittsburgh Courier* observed on the occasion of Ghana's independence that the young black nation's 'contributions, ... to peace, to art, to industry, to government, will be regarded by American Negroes as symbols of their own worth and potential.' Nkrumah, who had earned a doctorate at Lincoln University in the US, drew huge crowds of black Americans in New York and Chicago when he visited a year later. 'Harlem Hails Ghanaian Leader as Returning Hero,' read one headline.[79] Kenya's Tom Mboya spoke to large crowds at Howard University and elsewhere.[80]

Africa loomed especially large in the work of one of black America's leading writers, Lorraine Hansberry. Born in Chicago to prosperous parents who hosted Du Bois and Hughes, among other luminaries, Hansberry was also the niece of Leo Hansberry, the prominent Howard University professor of African Studies who impressed on his gifted niece black Africa's numerous and overlooked accomplishments. She had met many visiting black Africans, studied African history with Du Bois, and wrote several magazine articles on Africa before turning to drama. Her best-known work, *A Raisin in the Sun*, which premiered on Broadway in 1959 and appeared as a film two years later, features a Nigerian character, Asagai, critical to its plot. Asagai brings to the Younger family some of Africa's material culture, its dress and music, and he prompts Beneatha, to whom he is attracted, to talk about Africa's historical developments in

such fields as metallurgy and surgery, material straight out
of Hansberry's academic studies. But Asagai also offers the
beleaguered black family its best shot at survival. When
Beneatha expresses her sense of hopelessness over her
brother, Walter, squandering their father's insurance money,
funds that were to pay for her college tuition, he suggests
to her that her family's future, like Africa's, is not a circle
of pointless suffering but rather 'simply a long line' whose
end 'we cannot see.' The answer to the difficulties and paradoxes of struggling to advance, for individuals and nations,
can only be lived out through hope and determination, as
Beneatha's mother did when she trusted the family's treasure
to her feckless son. Asagai ends by inviting Beneatha 'home'
to Nigeria: 'Three hundred years later the African prince
rose up out of the seas and swept the maiden back across
the middle passage over which her ancestors had come.'
It will be as if 'you have only been away for a day.' But the
larger implication of Asagai's vision is not what it portends
for Beneatha, but rather her brother, Walter, who overhears
the Nigerian's speech. Walter had been planning to accept a
bribe from a white man in return for not moving into a white
neighborhood. Talk of Africa prompts Walter to remember
his family's heritage, particularly his father's pride. Hansberry would treat Africa much more fully and explicitly
in *Les Blancs*, her anti-colonialist drama set in Kenya that
was first presented in 1970, five years after her death. But
it is Asagai and *A Raisin in the Sun* which best capture the
gathering sense among black American intellectuals and
others that their freedom and possibilities were bound up

somehow with black Africa's, a sort of deep Afrocentrism that black American novelists such as Toni Morrison would later express.[81]

Ebony also drew closer to Africa in the later 1950s. Its celebration of the new Africa peaked with Ghana's independence celebration of 1957. The magazine sent several representatives to the event, including publisher Johnson, who reported that the young nation's 'ability to accept her triumph in a spirit of moderation and restraint' signified its 'maturity.' For Johnson and his wife, Eunice, Ghana's '[m]odern buildings, new schools and universities, comfortable homes and luxurious hotels belied the old belief that Africa is a backward continent.'[82] Nkrumah and President Eisenhower graced the first page of an article detailing the former's 1958 visit to the US. An editorial marked the appearance of Basil Davidson's *The Lost Cities of Africa*, a book which illustrated 'the "unity of Africa with the peoples of the rest of the world"'—that Africa was not a place apart, after all.[83] Editor Era Bell Thompson's article on independent Ghana quoted an African who remarked: 'Freedom is not new to us. … My people ruled long before the British, the Danes, or the Portuguese.'[84]

During the 1950s, then, mainstream black American depictions of Africa followed the opposite trajectory from white American ones. Always more interested in Africa's people than its animals, and sensitive to perceptions that those people might reflect badly on them, the rise of modern black Africa provoked interest and pride among black Americans even as it confounded the white ones.

As Stanford historian James T. Campbell points out in *Middle Passages*, his excellent account of African Americans in Africa, it is a neat coincidence that the travel accounts of a leading black man and woman of African American letters, Richard Wright and Era Bell Thompson, were published within days of each other in September 1954.[85] Wright had vaulted to fame in 1940 with the publication of *Native Son*, the path-breaking novel of black realism. Five years later he produced another best-seller: *Black Boy*, his autobiography. Fame and fortune did not reconcile Wright to life in the US; he moved to Paris in 1947. Thompson's career developed more slowly. She became associate and managing editor at *Ebony* in 1947 and 1953 respectively, the first black woman to edit a mass-market American magazine, and her own coming of age story *American Daughter*, appeared one year after *Black Boy*. Wright and Thompson differed profoundly in how they approached, experienced, and interpreted both America and Africa. Certainly some of those differences could be laid at the feet of their political and philosophical differences. Wright, a former member of the Communist Party, mixed a prickly personality with idealized political programs. Thompson's default outlook was sunny and liberal; she expected and celebrated incremental improvements. As with their white counterparts, gender also strongly informed their outlooks.

Wright's brutal Southern childhood left deep, life-long wounds. He recounted his father's abandonment, his mother's illnesses, poverty, deeply entrenched racism, his grandmother's religious fanaticism and intolerance, and a stint in an orphanage. Wright was from a young age bright,

curious, and defiant; his Southern childhood both radical-
ized and scarred him. But his radicalism was much more
political than cultural. Margaret Walker, who met Wright
after he came north to Chicago, in 1927, characterized him
as 'a Pan-African Black Nationalist with a Western world-
view' whose intellectual 'teachers and master-models were all
white.'[86] Wright's iconic 1945 account of his childhood, *Black
Boy*, spelled out his sense of alienation from the black mores
that the Harlem Renaissance had so often idealized: 'When I
brooded upon the cultural barrenness of black life, I wondered
if clean, positive tenderness, love, honor, loyalty, and the
capacity to remember were native with man.' For Wright, the
problem with Euro-American racism was not that it ignored
or denigrated African and African-American culture; rather,
it sought to deny black people its blessings, tried to keep its
cultural bounty to itself. His life pivoted when he got his hands
on a library card that moved him from the stiflingly provincial
black community to the boundless world of white literature.

Like Hemingway, whom he admired, Ruark, and so many
other white male novelists, Wright was at heart an American
individualist, a restless rebel. 'I'm a rootless man,' he
proclaimed near his death, in *White Man, Listen!*, published
in 1957. 'I do not hanker after, and seem not to need, as many
emotional attachments, sustaining roots, or idealistic allegiances as most people.' Like Hemingway and Ruark, Wright
was particularly ambivalent over women.

In retrospect, then, Wright was very unlikely to be
impressed by West Africa, his enthusiasm for Africa in
the abstract notwithstanding. Though Wright championed

freedom for black people, he did so through a highly Euro-centric, masculinist, egocentric lens. He was a 'rationalist,' a person 'of the West,' as he often put it.[87]

Wright was put off by Ghanaian culture before he even left Europe. While visiting London and George Padmore, the radical West Indian intellectual facilitating his trip, Wright was disturbed to learn that a visiting chief was shielded from the sun by a large umbrella for religious reasons. Padmore laughed at Wright's incredulousness and advised: 'Keep calm. … It's all part of a vast, complex philosophy of life.'[88] He was further alarmed when the highly educated Joe Appiah, Nkrumah's personal representative in Great Britain, confirmed that he believed in ghosts. Appiah, who was about to marry an English woman from a prominent family, practiced the sort of cosmopolitanism that their son, Kwame Anthony Appiah, would one day publicize in academic circles. But Wright was no cosmopolitan.

Wright sailed for Ghana, he recounted in *Black Power*, published in 1954, wondering whether or not there would 'be something of "me" down there in Africa'—and soon concluded that there was not. 'Ten minutes' into his bus ride from the port 'was enough to make Africa flood upon me so quickly that my mind was a blur and could not grasp it all.' The succession of 'mud villages' dizzied him: 'The kaleidoscope of sea, jungle, nudity, mud huts, and crowded market places induced in me a conflict deeper than I was aware of; a protest against what I saw seized me.' The 'unsettled feeling engendered by the strangeness of a completely different order of life' grew stronger and stronger. A particularly vivid example occurred when he followed the sounds of drums to a funeral dance. The dancers' vacant faces and languid movements disturbed him, and he was asked to leave. 'I had understood nothing,' he concluded. 'I was black and they were black, but my blackness did not help me.' Near the end of his stay he happened upon a wild funeral. 'I don't know if those painted men with their long knives were successful in scaring away the dead man's spirit or not; all I know is that they sure scared the hell out of me.' When J.D. Danquah, a leading intellectual and politician, assured Wright that if he stayed long enough in Africa he'd '*feel* your race,' Wright replied: 'I doubt that.' He had planned to stay four to six months but barely lasted two and a half.

Wright reacted so strongly to Ghana in part because it was too familiar and familial. Campbell notes that Wright's fixation on and repugnance for African women's breasts echoed his childhood nightmare of being trapped beneath pendulous 'white bags, like the full udders of cows' that threatened 'to fall and drench me with some horrible liquid.' This disgust for breasts suggests his longstanding 'conflicted relationship with female sexuality,' the blending of 'desire but also fear and loathing, along with an acute sense of vulner-ability.'[89] Hence he fled back to Accra the day after 'a tall handsome woman' propositioned him at the second funeral that he happened upon. Other scenes reminded him of the black childhood he had worked so hard to escape. 'Snakelike, veering dances' triggered memories of 'store-front churches' and other places of worship he had despised as a child: 'this African dance today was as astonishing and dumbfounding to me as it had been when I'd seen it in America.' Literature professor Manthia Diawara posits that Wright 'sees himself' in such spectacles, 'and he cannot handle it.'[90] Appiah, the cosmopolitan son of the man whose belief in ghosts so unnerved Wright, remarks that Wright's persistent racialization of Ghanaians betrayed his fear that the black continent 'reflects badly on *him*.'[91] Ghana exacerbated Wright's fear that blackness connoted femininity, irrationality, inferiority, the very forces he had worked so hard to extricate and separate himself from. He even dressed as if he were on a sort of safari, complete with pith helmet and cameras.

Wright was soon heaping the same sort of scorn on black Africa that he so often inflicted on black America. The continent 'might well be mankind's queerest laboratory. Here instinct ruled and flowered.' The climate itself created torpor. Rust soon covered all the metal in his toiletries: 'What could last here? Suppose the Gold Coast was cut off from the Western world, for say, ten years? Would not the material level of existence be reduced to that which existed before the coming of the white man?' Away from British influence, in the countryside, villagers were 'static': 'There is not enough foundation to this jungle life to develop a hard and durable ego,' leaving '[t]he tribal mind' fixated on 'images, not concepts; personalities, not abstractions; movement, not form; dreams, not reality.' In a later essay, written after Ghana had achieved complete independence in 1957, he asked: 'can the African drive out of himself that religious weakness that enabled the European to enter his land so easily and remain there as master for centuries? Can the

African get *Africanism* out of Africa?' Wright's Africa was blighted by its own essence.

Thompson's approach to Africa, like Wright's, was rooted in her childhood, temperament, and gender. She grew up in Iowa and North Dakota, where black people were rare and racism less acute than in the South of Wright's childhood. Though she recounted many instances of prejudice, she never seemed to fear for her life, and she and her family had close white friends. Thompson's 1946 memoir, *American Daughter*, repeatedly emphasized the sort of hybridity Appiah would later champion. Her brothers spoke 'Negrowegian.' When she returned to Mandan upon her father's death, '[t]he whole town rallied around me.' Upon arriving in Chicago she was nurtured by Mary McDowell, the legendary white social worker, who 'restored my self-confidence, confirmed my ideals, told me no obstacle was too great.' Chicago at last afforded Thompson the opportunity to make many black friends. But she continued to find inspiration in America's melting pot. Her first big job was working for the federal government as an employment service interviewer, where she talked with people of every imaginable background, including many who 'ain't never seen no cullud folks workin' in offices before.' But 'I like them all' and found that '[f]or every bad one there are twenty good ones.' Thompson clearly agreed with how an employer summed her up: 'a real American girl.'[92]

Thompson was certainly a determined individualist; she overcame the double onus of her race and sex to achieve great things in a highly competitive profession, and she stayed single and childless. But Thompson's identity was much more social and collaborative than Wright's. She was proud to be from North Dakota and presented herself as a product of, rather than a refugee from, her family, the communities in which she had lived, and, finally, the US itself, the same entities that Wright fled from. Thompson 'sees herself as a part of a larger American family,' notes scholar of black Atlantic literature Joanne M. Braxton.[93] Most of her professional life was spent editing, a highly collaborative activity that entailed improving the work of others rather than polishing a solitary or transcendent vision, in contrast to Wright's lonely existential quest for significance and meaning. Thompson describes herself as nested within layers of warm, sustaining relationships.

Thompson had learned early to be wary of Africa. The texts and films of her childhood depicted it 'as a mysterious land full of dense jungle growths and wild animals, of ignorance and danger,' she recalled in her 1954 travel account, *Africa: Land of My Fathers*. Through the 1920s and 1930s she, 'like most American Negroes, … was … busy shedding my African heritage and fighting for my rights as an American citizen. … Had anyone called me an African I would have been indignant.'

But after World War II she became intrigued. When *Ebony* and Doubleday, the prominent publisher, offered to sponsor a three-month tour of eighteen countries, she decided to go:

My African safari was prompted by the same desire that prompts other Americans to return to Europe and Asia to visit their 'Old Country,' or that of their parents or grandparents. I, too, wanted to return to the land of my forefathers, to see if it is as dark and hopeless as it has been painted and to find out how it would receive a prodigal daughter who had not been home for three hundred years.

For Thompson, then, the stakes of going to Africa were lower than for Wright. She was more open-minded, more curious. Thompson, furthermore, had made a place for herself, socially and cognitively, in Chicago and America, respectively; she claimed both a black and an American identity.

The two writers' personalities and approaches to Africa are neatly illustrated by their relationships with Nkrumah. Wright expected to advise Nkrumah, whom he had met in the US years before. Just three days after arriving, in a rare burst of optimism, he was pondering how he and other black radical intellectuals might settle in Accra to guide Nkrumah and the young nation: 'I can see radiating out from this land an organization devoted full time to redeeming the blacks of this world.' 'All my life I've asked for this,' he added.[94] But Wright soon concluded that Nkrumah distrusted him and had demagogic tendencies. In fact before leaving the Gold Coast Wright went to the American counsel with a four-page report accusing Nkrumah and his political party of being 'Communist minded,' reporting that Nkrumah slept under a large portrait of Lenin.[95] Yet Wright still hoped to influence the man who was well on his way to becoming Ghana's founding father. *Black Power* closed with a long and blunt open letter of advice on how to avoid the machinations of the West. Like Wright's later entreaties to Nkrumah, it went unanswered.[96]

Thompson's relationship with Nkrumah was more congenial. She had been offered the opportunity to collaborate in the great leader's autobiography. She pronounced herself too busy to do so, but volunteered to help organize the project. Unlike Wright, who wished to advise Nkrumah, Thompson assisted him. She did not like everything about the great leader. In their first meeting she detected in him a 'cold, calculating calmness ... beneath the boyish charm' that made her 'glad that I was not his enemy.' But they remained on good terms. Four years later she returned and wrote an article for *Ebony* defending Nkrumah from charges that he was becoming a tyrant.[97]

Thompson was much slower to judge black Africans than Wright was. She admitted that her first impression, in Liberia, 'was negative.' The lack of clothing, the 'foul-smelling shops,' 'ragged' men, the pervasive and 'obvious poverty' offended her sensibilities. She gradually discerned, however, both warmth and progress. When a man criticized black Americans for not doing more to help black Africans, 'I remarked that here in the Gold Coast the African seemed to be doing pretty well without our help.'

Africa: Land of My Fathers affirmed Thompson's fundamental American identity, but this identity was dynamic and inclusive. To be sure, Africa revealed the difference between African Americans and Africans. But it was Africa's relatively small number of whites who made her most feel and take pride in her broader American identity. White officials and the governments they ran were annoying in West Africa, patently xenophobic and segregationist in East and particularly South Africa. She regularly sought out black Africans for evidence on what it was like to live, year after year, under such oppression. Unlike Wright, who saved his strongest criticism for black Africans, Thompson regularly excoriated white African officials and regimes and offered black Africans a platform to do the same. Her trip allowed her to get to know her African cousins and their struggles, Africa's impressive civilizations, and to realize and celebrate 'my black heritage.' But: 'Africa, the land of my fathers, is not my home. ... I owe my loyalty and my allegiance to but one flag. I have but one country.'[98] Thompson continued to boost Sub-Saharan Africa without completely identifying with it during many subsequent trips.[99]

Another prominent African American woman who regularly visited Africa was much more negative. Philippa Schuyler, the brilliant bi-racial daughter of iconoclastic journalist George Schuyler, started touring Sub-Saharan Africa in 1955 as a concert pianist and routinely criticized both Africa and black Africans in her private letters, highly autobiographical novel *Adventures in Black and White*, and 1962 account of recent events in the Congo. In her first visit, recounted in her 1960 memoir, she pronounced Ethiopia's facilities poor and its officials incompetent. Subsequent visits sounded the same notes. She liked Nkrumah, but the African who most impressed her seemed to be Albert Schweitzer, the transplanted European. She nearly married the famous Nigerian painter Ben Enwonwu before pulling out and representing him as a clueless egotist.[100]

Black Africans and blackness in general seemed to rattle the light-skinned Schuyler, whose mother was Jewish. Her powerful parents, cosmopolitan New York, and her own precocious musical and intellectual skills had insulated her from racism well into her remarkable childhood. Her mother and father had hoped that their daughter's undeniable brilliance would help to destroy racism by showing its absurdity. But she was more comfortable in Europe and Asia than in Africa. Latin America's fluid racial system intrigued her. There, as her able biographer, Kathryn Talalay puts it, she 'was accorded the privileges of a beautiful mulatto.' Indeed, by 1961 she had persuaded herself that 'I HAVE NO RELATIONS TO AFRICA AT ALL,' that 'I am Malay-American Indian—and European!' Changing her name to Felipa Monterro y Schuyler, she ordered her proud father to excise her from the book he was writing on black Americans' accomplishments. Her newspaper articles and 1962 book on the Congo asserted that the nation and the continent required more, not less colonization. In 1963 President Nkrumah accused her of betraying the trust that he and other black Africans had bestowed upon her.[101]

Philippa seemed to be becoming a racist. 'Just live around Africa for a while,' she wrote to her mother in 1962, 'and you get rid of any kind of nonsense that all … races … have the same capacities.' She aborted a pregnancy in 1965 in part because the father was African. Talalay notes that at the time of her death as a war correspondent in Vietnam, Schuyler was expressing more solidarity with African Americans, and had become more sensitive to the level of white American racism toward all people deemed not white.[102] But it is telling that this cognitive breakthrough came in Asia, not Africa.

Schuyler was an outlier. But Wright's disillusionment with and Thompson's arm's-length acceptance of Africa suggests that the continent was often easier for black Americans to embrace in the abstract than in person, a painful experience that would often repeat itself in the next decade.

FOUR WHITE WOMEN AND THE MINGLING OF SELVES

If black Americans might perceive in Africa a home and white American men continued to imagine and seek a primitive Africa on which to forge their manhood, white American women would seem to be out of place, out of their depth. Cameron observes that Hollywood films often portrayed Africa as a 'punishment' for them, a place to learn 'that they are too inept to deal with the world without men.'[103] As we have seen, that was not always the case. Rose has more of a backbone than Charlie does, Kelly is ignorant of but hardly intimidated by Africa, and Katia and the South Africa she loves are the leading 'untamed' figures of the movie of that name. But all of these spirited women are figures of male imaginations, of male writers, directors, and producers, men who much more commonly featured male than female protagonists.

The handful of white women who visited and wrote about Sub-Saharan Africa in the 1950s seemed to be much more content with it than their male and black counterparts were. These women and their protagonists commonly blurred the boundaries of their selves, mingling their life's purpose with black Africans.

Quaker Louise Stinetorf was a missionary in Palestine for two years and visited Africa several times. She began writing about Sub-Saharan Africa in 1945. Her first novel, *White Witch Doctor*, appeared in 1950, sold very well, and was made into a movie. A second Africa novel, *Beyond the Hungry Country*, followed in 1954.

White Witch Doctor features deep interracial friendships. Its middle-aged protagonist, Ellen Burton, goes to the Congo as a nurse and is immediately struck by people's kindness and 'inherent courtesy.' She meets an old, indefatigable woman missionary doctor who is loved by and loves the black Africans among whom she works, a woman who respects witch doctors and believes in conveying Christianity by example. She describes natives with brutal superstitions and practices and Pygmies who live a sort of 'animal existence.' But Africa's 'most somber shadows' came not from its dark-skinned residents but from 'the enlightened civilization of my fair-skinned brothers,' the many whites who at every opportunity malign, cheat, and exploit black Africans. Burton's closest friend is Aganza, a middle-aged African woman. Aganza becomes a splendid nurse and medical trainer who studies English medical books without losing her native wisdom. When Burton is at last too frail to carry on, she realizes that her quarter-century in the Congo had been 'my only years of personal fulfillment,' that she is 'not going home' to Indiana, but rather is leaving home. Aganza gives her a precious and unexpected going-away present, a bundle of peanuts, a gift that 'is a mark of the greatest love and respect for one woman to so honor another's mother.' Burton resolves to go to her mother's grave to tell her 'of this wonderful old black woman who so loved and honored her for the daughter she had borne.'

Stinetorf developed this theme of cross-cultural friendship more fully still in Beyond the Hungry Country. Here again the author's protagonist is a woman, Laura, who begins her life in Africa as the child of missionaries, who was 'born under a trailside bush' and is known by villagers as 'The-Little-Black-Inside-White-Outside-Mama.' Going to the US for college does not change this. She feels more at home in Africa than America.

Laura's opposite number is aloof from and disliked by Africans. The pretty missionary, Esther Grove, was popular and nice enough in America and on board ship. But once deposited in Africa she immediately betrays that she is, in the words of Laura's wise father, 'frightened all the time and in flight from something all the time.' She soon dies in childbirth after alienating the villagers, and Laura soon marries Esther's patient and likeable widower. As in the era's Hollywood films, Africa reveals white visitors' true nature, but in Stinetorf's stories it is Africa's people, not its landscape, that tears away white facades and breaks open American selves.

Beyond the Hungry Country is remarkable for its dogged portrayal and acceptance of African practices that the great majority of its readers must have considered barbaric and brutal. 'Raw, primitive Africa must be seen to be believed, must be lived with to be respected, must be understood by the sensitive heart to be loved,' Laura admonishes. She notices that her husband often winces at the smell of black bodies covered in oils that prevented sunburn, chafing, ulcers, lice, and scabies. He 'judged cleanliness like a white man, more often by his nose than by reason.' Laura is herself shocked when the village chief admits her to a sacred building which houses several skulls. But he explains that the Fan believe that great intelligence continues to reside inside of the heads of these men 'of very great ability.' They at last reach the skull of a white man who even 'understood and respected the laws and customs of black men,' the skull of her very own father. Laura realizes that her father would have found 'this strange honor done him by a tribe of the people he loved' a sort of 'enshrinement.' Rather than reflexively associating skull-keeping with head hunting or other savage tropes, she perceives in the practice an ingenious 'method of forcing sober reflection.'

Like her father before her, Laura believes that western and African cultures can inform each other. She is critical of infanticide, slavery, and treating women as if they were cattle. But she realizes that these practices have persisted not out of some inherent savagery but because they seem logical to their practitioners. Laura also believes strongly that cultural change must be respectful and reciprocal. The black Africans are at least as intelligent and wise as their western counterparts. She is therefore pleased when her husband accepts castigation from the chief. 'I had never heard a black man talk in this fashion to a white man'; but Jimmy whispers to her: 'Be quiet. We are beyond the domination of white men. Our color is without prestige here. And we can learn from him.

119

We can learn much from him.' To be sure, the village's fields can be made more productive, social relations less violent, and Laura is devastated when the adolescent she had rescued and raised dies during his initiation because, as a village woman explains, he was a 'pot ... too frail for the fire.' But even as she vows that night to 'take the cruelty out' of the initiation rites, she will also seek to 'preserve what is good.' And there is much that is good.

Perhaps the book's culmination comes in her husband's last hours. As she sees life ebbing from him, she goes to the village's little Christian sanctuary to beg God to spare him. As time passes she slowly becomes aware that '[t]he church was full of people all on their knees,' all praying with her, and she realized that God has, through these people, given her 'the strength and the courage' to survive her husband's imminent death. As with Jean Kenyon Mackenzie a half-century before, assumptions of who is modeling Christianity to whom are subverted.

The companion who never deserts Laura through her losses is the elderly Maa Koo, a native woman who raised her and who guides her through the death of her husband and the birth of their son. 'What would I have done, what kind of person would I have become without that little old hag, that wrinkled bundle of selfless, almost divine wisdom helping to shape my character, standing between me and stubborn self-will and crippling ignorance at every stage of my life?' Africa's women are much stronger than they seem, and in Stinetorf's Africa white women blossom in a way that they could not back in America.

Stinetorf develops an African character even more fully in her third novel: *Elephant Outlaw*, a children's book published in 1956. Her narrator, Rickey, is a white boy growing up in Kenya whose parents adopt an African boy who has been discarded by his village as having lost his soul. Young Bady aspires to restore his soul through a brave act. The two boys set out to find a destructive rogue elephant. Rickey believes that he has lined up the perfect soft spot in his rifle's sight to kill Old Mutesa when Bady inexplicably throws off his aim by several inches. The apparent mistake proves fortuitous; scar tissue had covered up the spot Rickey had aimed at: 'the spirits that were friendly to Bady … had aimed the weapon. Tembo was Bady's kill!' As in Stinetorf's adult fiction, indigenous Africans are depicted as more capable and wise than white people are, and beliefs that appear to be savage and cruel are redeemable; Bady's hunting accomplishments restore him to full standing with his people. In fact Rickey also becomes a man while the two are away from civilization; among the Pygmies he solves an engineering problem and is rewarded with a belt that 'is the highest honor they can pay you … their badge of manhood.' Like Stinetorf's white women protagonists, Rickey blends cultures. That night he resolves to collapse the sides of a game pit that the Pygmies had constructed so that animals do not fall in and starve to death. When he explains 'it is a fetish of mine that I must never leave behind any trap for animals I am not coming back to kill,' the pit is quickly rendered innocuous by the work of many Pygmy hands. He and the Pygmies respect each other's sensibilities, their fetishes.

As in white American men's fiction, Africa challenges Stinetorf's protagonists to push beyond imagined limits. But these limits are collective and cultural rather than solitary and physical, and black Africans are necessary partners, not passive helpers, in achieving them.

Kathryn Hulme's *The Nun's Story*, a best-selling novel published in 1956, depicts a more solitary quest, but one informed by Africa and Africans. Hulme's well-educated Belgian protagonist, Sister Luke, goes to Africa for essentially the opposite reason of prototypical white, male protagonists: she imagines that it will be the ideal place to lose herself: 'It will be so much easier out there to remember that I am nothing.' Sister Luke is in search not of self-actualization, but self-immolation. Africa does not cooperate.

As with so many other protagonists, Africa betrays Sister Luke's deeper self—which is not compatible with a pious 'life of sacrifice and self-abnegation ... a life against nature.' The Congo becomes 'a passionate obsession' that she must conceal from herself and others as she studies tropical medicine. Africa speaks to Sister Luke's hunger to be useful and esteemed, eventually chokes out her determination to detach, to achieve perfect humility.

Black Congolese are central to Sister Luke's spiritual pilgrimage. She is consistently kind to them, at once recognizes their agency, both their subtle resistance to the more racist sisters and their keen intelligence. She trains her black assistants to take over more and more nursing duties and makes her chief assistant a supervisor. News of her respectful acts spreads, drawing praise that serves to undermine the very humility that she had come to the Congo to cultivate.

White women's nonfiction also described the profound impact of black Africans on white American women. Anne Eisner Putnam, a Jewish-American artist, left New York City for the Belgian Congo in 1946, having fallen in love with an anthropologist, Patrick Putnam, who had lived among the Mbuti Pygmies since 1930. She became one of a succession of wives to the charismatic Patrick, who had a psychological breakdown and passed away in 1953. Anne returned to the US to promote her popular book on life with the Pygmies in 1954, then went back to the Congo to do a piece for *National Geographic* later in the decade. She soon came back to the US for good, in part because she sensed that the Congo was about to enter into a convulsive phase in which even the most respected white people would be anachronistic.

Madami: My Eight Years of Adventure with the Congo Pigmies, published in 1954, was a somewhat idealized account of Putnam's eight years in the Congo. She obscured the details of her unconventional marriage. More importantly, the ghost writer who constructed the book based on letters from and interviews with the dyslexic artist largely ignored her demands that the Pygmies be presented sans sentimental and colonial clichés.

Anne's affection and respect for the Pygmies, and other Africans, nevertheless came through. *Madami* described Anne's quest 'to find honest, unspoiled people to paint, ... subjects as real and as untouched by civilization as any on earth.' The Pygmies did not disappoint, for their village 'was

123

like a small corner of paradise.' But Putnam both recognized her subjects' moral complexity and was willing to learn from them. Most of all, Anne respected the Pygmies' practical and honest approach to life. 'They are real, genuine and gracious ... I never saw a neurotic pigmy.' Like Stinetorf's protagonists, Anne found herself adopting many Pygmy beliefs as her own, such as fear of the Esamba, a spirit which brought death to anyone who even looked upon it. Some elements of Pygmy life repelled her, such as violent rituals. But, pace Stinetorf, she both perceived parallel cruelties in western culture and struggled to discern the rituals' purpose. As Geary points out, she presented 'the Mbuti as people with life histories, hopes, and aspirations.'[104] Anne's art, minimalist ink drawings and watercolors focused on the ordinary features of Pygmy life, suggested a people more dignified than exotic.[105]

Anne trod the line between befriending the Pygmies and realizing that she could never become one. For example, when a hunt failed, the men concluded that they needed to change the net's scent by cutting their tongues and spitting on it. When they invited her to participate, she could not help but think of how their mouths were full of 'yaws, syphilis, tuberculosis and ... other maladies.' Rather than be shown a coward, she agreed, but her friend, Molé, smiled and pretended to remember that 'Madami is a woman,' so: 'Nothing must be done that would keep her from talking.' But the knowledge that the white woman was willing to contribute her blood to their ritual increased their regard for her. Anne in some respects became part of the community. When a grandmother asked her to raise a baby whose mother had died, she complied, and felt a tremendous sense of responsibility. But she returned the child to the grandmother after nursing him through polio; though 'hating to lose him,' she knew 'that his only chance at true happiness rested in a normal life as a pigmy.' Putnam participated deeply in Pygmy life without presuming to have become one.

Elizabeth Bowne came to Africa under very different circumstances but also drew great strength from the relationships she formed there. As first described in her 1955 *Saturday Evening Post* story, 'My Husband Crashed in the Jungle,' Bowne was drawn to Liberia after the plane of her husband, a commercial pilot, had crashed near a remote village in 1951, killing everyone on board.[106]

Bowne found comfort only among black Liberians. No one in the US was able to touch the ache that her husband's death had left. Friends and family members seemed to think that she needed to move on with her life, particularly since she was pregnant. But her son's birth brought no sense of resolution, and Bowne at last determined that she needed to go to the crash site to try to make sense of the tragedy. The great-granddaughter of a Georgia plantation and slave owner, Bowne recalled in her 1961 memoir that she at first 'had no desire to accept' black people 'on an equal social basis.' She found black Liberians alien, even repulsive. But she received from them a succession of favors. When the vehicle she was traveling in broke down in a 'quiet stagnant village' a kindly old woman 'shuffled across the road' and gave her 'a bottle of tepid Coca-Cola' for which she would accept no payment. Nor would the 'burly wild man … nude to the waist' who drove her. The villagers where she stayed sensed that she was more sympathetic to them than were the missionaries. A servant slipped her a smile. A girl showed off her simple home. When a troubled young mother raised by the missionaries confided in Bowne that she felt caught between the two cultures and offered Bowne her baby to hold, the white woman, 'who had never held a Negro baby' reflexively 'flinched.' But she continued to soften. When the elderly Ma walked her about the village and explained the many changes they had weathered, Bowne was struck by Ma's capacity to 'reconcile her instincts as a native' with her Christian conversion and was drawn by her 'graciousness, her humble pride.' Ma, for her part, sensing Bowne's grief, promised to keep her husband's 'grave neat for you, long as I live.'

The villagers accomplished what none of her white family, friends, or the missionaries were able to do. They accepted and shared her grief and showed her a way forward. Three girls went with her to weed the grave, and while Bowne wept, they sang a hymn of consolation.

Bowne realized that these kind and resilient people had absorbed many tragedies of their own. One poor girl, living apart from her mother and blind father, was determined 'to be nurse or teacher. My people need much.' Flumo, a former Christian leader, was expelled from the church when his wife's illness drove him to take a second wife to care for her, and he was childless, the worst calamity that could befall an African man: 'but I find peace with God. You, you will find peace, too.' At last Allison, a Nigerian teacher at the mission school, took Bowne on the long walk to the site of the plane crash.

She gained a sense of closure not merely because she stood on the spot where his body lay, but also because she learned that the villagers defied their chief in moving the corpses from the crash site. 'We cry for folks everywhere,' they explained. Bowne realized that she had been drawn to this village 'not to find where or how Frank died,' but 'to find a better way to live with others.' She found among these black Liberians both 'a deeper suffering' than her own and a capacity to overcome 'self-pity,' to 'express self-dignity' through love for others.

Where white American men found diversion or adventure, their female counterparts encountered human warmth and insight. Black Africans moved from background to foreground in white American women's African quests.

The distance between a feminine Africa characterized by interracial sociality and the much more individualistic version favored by white American men can be measured by the degree to which such men shifted the content and message of white women's stories when they took over their telling.

The film *White Witch Doctor*, released in 1953, confounded Stinetorf's book by elevating a marginal white male character to the center and relegating black Africans to the periphery. The screenplay, written by two men, and directed by Henry Hathaway, veteran of many John Wayne Westerns, features two white protagonists: Ellen, the nurse who wants to help Africans (Susan Hayward), and Lonnie (Robert Mitchum), a tough, jaded safari leader. Black Africans are exotic and superstitious, mostly good-hearted, and the film uses their innocence as a foil to underscore white people's greed. The film features a head servant, Jack, who uses his wits and sacrifices his life to help thwart the film's villain, a white man who is determined to brush aside Africans to get their gold. But although the film offers arguably Hollywood's most sympathetic and least racialized rendering of black African culture and characters to date, they are much more marginal than they were in Stinetorf's novel. Ellen resolves her crisis not through friendships with Africans, but through sacrificing for them—and falling in love with a great white hunter. White men displace black women at the story's center and Ellen's life.

The Nun's Story of 1959, written by Robert Anderson and directed by Fred Zinnemann, is more true to the original than *The White Doctor* had been. But it shifts Sister Luke's focus from black Africans to a white male, the secular, work-obsessed Dr. Fortunati.

Eisner Putnam lamented the many changes that her editor at Prentice-Hall made to *Madami*, from almost every page of the manuscript to the dust jacket: 'I see the word naked appearing two times, which from any point of view except cheapness seems to be in the height of poor taste.' To her editor's argument that readers expected and liked African clichés, she retorted: 'you also add that people are interested in my life because it is not a cliché. Therefore I do not understand why the thing shouldn't be consistent all the way through and we can admit that the book doesn't need to have the usual clichés such as Darkest Africa, steaming jungles.'[107] Since so few of Eisner Putnam's suggestions or demands were instituted, the book as published only partially captured her warm respect for the Congolese that her art continues to reflect.

The more public rendering of these white women's stories moved them into the masculinist platitudes that mainstream America expected from Sub-Saharan Africa. The women authors were biased. They seldom referred to the emerging Africa celebrated by *Ebony*. They were looking for the wisdom and friendship of primitive people, foils to modern life rather than participants in it. But, as before the war, women took a much deeper interest in those people than did their male counterparts.

The new Africa provoked diverse American reactions. White popular culture paid its outward respects while featuring images and stories resonant with a more timeless Africa in which white male protagonists, pace Tarzan and Ruark, still commanded center stage. White men still looked to Africa for adventures not to be found in America. White women found there the deeply satisfying relationships that had eluded them back home. They immersed themselves in those cultures and societies and formed intense friendships, exercises in hybridity which required blending rather than fortifying their selves, their identities. Black Americans expressed much more enthusiasm for the rise of black Africa, though three prominent visitors expressed reservations or even hostility.

Mainstream white America cautiously supported black independence; even Tarzan became more respectful of black Africans. But America's most widely read interpreter of Africa perceived the new Africa as a disaster for American adventurers like himself. Black America was euphoric about the rise of black Africa. But its leading man of letters felt profoundly out of place in and unimpressed by it.

Africa in the 1960s would prove to be still more difficult to bend to American quests.

CHAPTER THREE

FROM POLITICAL TO PERSONAL: WHITE AND BLACK AMERICA CONFRONT A TRANSFORMED CONTINENT

Africa seemed on the cusp of great things at the outset of the 1960s. Most European colonies had or would shortly become black nations, a development that attracted a great deal of notice in the US and pride among members of the African diaspora. The decade closed, however, with a horrific and, for many Americans, confusing civil war in Nigeria that claimed millions of victims, a punctuation mark to a decade in which the promise of the new Africa lost much of its luster.

America, like Africa, went through a sort of rise and decline in the 1960s, and race was at the center of it. The Civil Rights Movement early in the 1960s galvanized many white as well as black Americans. It crested in a series of landmark pieces of legislation in the mid-1960s that at last, a century after the Civil War, brought black Americans into full citizenship. The Civil Rights Movement inspired other reforms. President Johnson oversaw a great expansion of the welfare state that halved the poverty rate and dramatically expanded education. Activists and reformers questioned hierarchical relationships in institutions ranging from the family to the university and staged a mass movement against the Vietnam War. 'The Sixties' would become a sort of catch-all phrase for an interrelated set of movements championing individual rights and potential.

But America fragmented in the 1960s. The Civil Rights Movement splintered and lost white support. It had begun with a highly idealistic, non-violent, and integrationist ethos, what George D. Kelsey, a theology professor who made a big impression on Dr. Martin Luther King at Morehouse College, called a striving for 'the good of all.'[1] By 1965, however, the Black Power Movement expressed a desire to separate from white America. That year also saw the first of a series of riots by African Americans in Watts and elsewhere. The media focused on extreme rhetoric and acts that appalled the 'Silent Majority' so expertly managed by Richard Nixon in his 1968 presidential bid. In 1963 white adults blamed whites rather than blacks for the disadvantages confronting black people by a ratio of more than two to one. Five years later the ratio was more than reversed.[2] In 1965 about a third of the American public identified 'Civil Rights' as the nation's leading problem. Three years later they were twice as likely to name 'Social Disorder.'[3]

Meanwhile, the white counter-culture was becoming more atomized and depoliticized. This was partly a matter of disillusionment spawned by a succession of political assassinations, the persistence of the Vietnam War, and the election of Nixon. But it also reflected the nation's long and deepening commitment to more personal quests. 'The disparity between emotional individualism and collective rhetoric of community' had become unsustainable for many by mid-decade.[4] Young white radicals moved from causes associated with others (civil rights) to ones that largely affected themselves (the draft) to more cultural and personalized concerns ('do your own thing').[5]

Historian Wilson Jeremiah Moses' characterization of Black Power applies to the nation as a whole: 'political separatism and cultural assimilationism.'[6] Black radicals rejected integration with mainstream America, but their assertion of individual and particular rather than broadly shared identities and rights were as American as apple pie. America's increasingly disparate parts, white and black, shared a commitment to expressive individualism, which in turn led to political atomization and withdrawal. By the decade's close, privately pursued dreams and quests had shouldered aside both Dr. King's Beloved Community and President Johnson's Great Society.

America's coming apart in the 1960s was not conducive to Americans' African quests. Militant black Americans were usually disappointed by black African states and people. White Americans felt increasingly ill at ease in a continent that had become less malleable to their political and personal purposes. Coming to terms with the new Africa required leaps of empathy at odds with the decade's tenor.

RETURN OF THE BLACK AFRICAN SAVAGE IN THE WHITE AMERICAN MIND

American popular opinion of Africa plummeted in the 1960s. 'Darkness beckons ceaselessly' intoned *Life*.[7] *Time*, which had waxed optimistic about Africa's future late in the 1950s, observed in 1966 that 'heroic independence leaders' had 'frittered away their mandates in a binge of nepotism, incompetence, tribalism, petty tyranny or greedy corruption while their countries rotted in anarchy and squalor.'[8] By mid-decade, that view had long been a consensus.

The Congo was Exhibit A of black Africa's failings. *Life*'s 'Harvest of Anarchy in the Congo' explained that the young nation's armies were fighting 'among themselves, seemingly without fully knowing why' and contrasted black African misery and incompetence with western efficiency and compassion.[9] A week later it dismissed the recently executed Lumumba as an ineffectual Communist. An article from the close of 1961 recalled that within a day of independence, 'wild tribesmen began fighting each other,' including 'savage and even cannibalistic tribes.'[10] The Congo generated even more attention when white residents were attacked in 1964. An editorial, 'Congo: Savagery Has No Excuse,' asserted that the young nation had descended into 'blood lust, witchcraft and racism.'[11] The *Digest* published one of the most sensationalistic accounts of the Congo War in 1965: an extensive excerpt from David Reed's *The Stanleyville Massacre* painted a picture 'of tribal bloodlust run wild, of nuns, missionaries and American consular officers held at the mercy of primitive Africans.' The piece maintained this unrelenting tone throughout its many pages, dwelling particularly on images of black savagery toward saintly white people who 'had come to the Congo only to help.' 'We shall make fetishes with the hearts of the Americans and the Belgians, and we shall dress ourselves in their skins,' Congolese soldiers threatened. '"We're going to eat you," a soldier shouted.'[12]

Indeed, if journalist John Gunther's ethnocentric liberal optimism had represented the *Reader's Digest*'s view of Africa in the mid-1950s, a decade later that role had been usurped by Reed's pervasive pessimism. 'Africa's Man of Mystery,' promised a balanced account of Jomo Kenyatta but dwelled on his exoticism and closed by remarking that 'all the departed Mau Mau generals—some of them cannibals, most of them murderers, all of them savages'—must 'be grinning hugely' in anticipation of a Kenya led by Kenyatta.[13] Black Africa was always backward, often brutal. 'Africa's River of Mystery' elided signs of modernity and dwelled on savage exoticism. On Bamako 'rooftops, flocks of vultures sit waiting patiently for something to die.' The cliff dwellings of the Dogon featured caves where the alert tourist may find 'a human skull … staring back,' at him or her, and 'bits of human hair blow along the ground.'[14] Reed seemed determined to debunk years of articles touting Africa's promise.

Saturday Evening Post editor and renowned journalist Stewart Alsop concurred with Reed in the early 1960s in a

major set of articles based on his travels in Africa. He opened
by recounting 'some of the more startling and bizarre side-
lights on African politics,' such as the president jailed for
'selling his mother-in-law into slavery' or the government
official who hated white men because some had troubled his
father 'for eating a small child in a vain attempt to regain his
youth.'[15] Alsop repeatedly returned to the theme of otherness, of Africa as wholly alien. The second article opened
with three immediate and 'essentially correct' impressions
about the continent: 'vastness', 'sameness', and 'emptiness'.
'Tropical Africa is, in fact, generally inhospitable to human
life. That fact explains a lot.' No wonder Alsop found himself
'wondering what these people are really like, what really
goes on in their heads, behind the big white smiles.' On long
drives through the jungle, surrounded by a 'tangle of shrubs
and vines and trees, … you begin to feel that behind that high
jungle wall there are things you don't understand, and never
will.'[16] Above all, Africa and Africans were inscrutable. This
was the Africa of Conrad—except that Alsop's white men
were innocent.

In fact these popular magazines started rehabilitating
the reputation of colonialism almost immediately after its
retreat. The *Reader's Digest*'s 'Don't Decry Colonialism!'
presented the views of a Kenyan Englishman who remarked
that his countrymen had 'ejected the Arab slavers, stopped the
wars, attacked smallpox and sleeping sickness, and induced
white men to settle the country.'[17] A year later the *Reader's
Digest* asserted that the 'savage terror' sweeping across
Angola, still a Portuguese colony, represented no 'national-

istic uprising,' as liberal Americans claimed, but rather 'an explosion of tribalism and fetishism among people' duped by Communism. Portuguese colonialism, though imperfect, was humane and progressive.[18] An article from *The Atlantic Monthly* urged readers to reconsider South Africa's negative reputation, to appreciate not only its staunch anti-Communist credentials but also its impressive record in educating black children and achieving 'the highest per-capita income of all the black races in Africa.' Much remained to be done by white South Africans. But: 'In the end they will do right.' Meanwhile Americans should 'lower our voices' and 'give them a little more time.'[19] 'Long Live Imperialism' read the title of a 1965 *Saturday Evening Post* article.[20]

The only good people depicted in most articles were white. During 1964–1965 *Life* published stories on: white American women hitchhiking across the Sahara; a story about Hemingway and Africa by science fiction writer Ray Bradbury; and two pieces, including a cover story, on Albert Schweitzer. The *Saturday Evening Post* offered up the adventures of three white men who ballooned their way around East Africa, courting danger as they photographed wild animals. Black Africans were safely in the background, usually as servants. One photograph featured the ubiquitous Masai, who had concluded that the ballooners 'were gods.'[21]

More often, the dwindling number of articles on Africa presented a timeless continent. The *Reader's Digest*'s 'Africa's Garden of Eden' detailed the natural wonders of Tanganyika's Ngorongoro Crater, which 'has belonged for eons to the beasts.' A Masai eventually appeared, but the reader was assured that he 'could be Neolithic man returning, for the Masai ... want no part of civilization.'[22] Charles Lindbergh, the famous aviator turned environmentalist, asked: 'Is Civilization Progress?' and answered: not necessarily. A safari in Kenya prompted him to understand 'that if I had to choose, I would rather have birds than airplanes.' Meeting the Masai, he realized that their spears were 'more impressive' than 'intercontinental missiles'; they 'do not think our civilization marks real progress.'[23] The Reader's Digest published a piece by Lindbergh's spouse, Anne Morrow Lindbergh, a well-known author in her own right, excerpted from Life. The best-selling inspirational writer recalled the month-long family safari in East Africa, a retreat that brought her, in the words of the article's title, 'Discovery and Renewal.' 'I am haunted by time in Africa,' she wrote, 'time as history and time as rhythm.'[24] Likewise, 'A Day in the Life of a Bushman' revealed that these South African indigenes 'live in a harmony,' with each other as well as nature, 'not found elsewhere.' The end of the day is marked by dancing and, at the end, 'the final wail of a lonely flute.' 'Thus it was 20,000 years ago for all men. Thus it is today for the dwindling bushmen of Africa.'[25]

One of Life's grandest treatments of Africa, Eliot Elisofon's 1961 photo-essay, hit the same note over and over again. Elisofon, who traveled 20,000 miles for the story, used his camera and (white) literature to evoke old, not modern, Africa. The texts were almost wholly from white adventurers, from Livingston to Hemingway. There were several photographs of wild and scenic Africa. Timeless Africans were at the heart of the essay. Indeed, the cover featured a 'Wild

Warega Warrior Poised for Attack,' a grimacing, gape-eyed man covered with white spots and bedecked with feathers, preparing to thrust his spear right through the cover into the reader's living room. The man reappeared on the piece's final page, with dilated pupils and bared teeth: 'intimating,' as Swedish academic Raoul Granqvist puts it, 'staggering fury at the other/the viewer.'[26] The accompanying poem, 'The Congo,' from Vachel Lindsay certainly suggested as much: '"BLOOD" screamed the skull-faced, lean witch doctors.'[27]

National Geographic's 1960 cover story on the new Africa contained little that was new. The cover photograph was a cut-out image of Africa filled with an anonymous horde of villagers gaping at an automobile. The lead article, written by senior staff member Nathaniel Kenney after five months of travel, opened with these words: 'At a time in the long ago, while Europe plodded forward, Mother Africa lay down to sleep in her incomparable sunshine.' Guns and the wheel were invented. Slavers came and went. Only after the arrival of western 'missionaries, traders, engineers, doctors, and teachers' and '[d]evoted scientists' did Africa at last awaken. Thanks to David Livingston, they learned of freedom, and they began to pursue it. Now, in 1960, the moment of African freedom had arrived. The issue presented photographs of modern buildings, dams, and economic activities such as mining, farming, and rubber making. But these represen-tations were dwarfed by photographic and verbal images of old Africa, such as a three-page spread of Victoria Falls. A collection of seven portraits of the continent's 'diverse' people included: a Nbele woman with massive neck rings; a

Congolese woman with a 'disfiguring' lip plug; a Congolese woman with a safety-pin necklace and sharpened teeth; a Masai man with red, plaited hair that 'draws flies'; Angola girls' breasts bordered by beads and 'tribal scars'; a Zulu rickshaw driver outfitted in a towering headdress featuring feathers and horns; and a Congolese woman with a child in a blanket. Nor did Kenney pay much attention to politics. He met President Nkrumah of Ghana but did not recount the independence struggles of the 1950s or Ghana's current political divide. He described a pleasant meeting with Ethiopia's Haile Selassie without addressing the nation's turbulent politics. The section on the Congo focused on mining, elided the long history of European savagery, then closed with a brief account of contemporary violence: 'Congolese troops turning on the terrified European community, murdering and pillaging in excesses that threatened the precious new democracy.' As for South Africa, he 'tried to stay apart from' its 'human strife.' Most of the people quoted on African politics were part of the continent's tiny white minority. Kenney's leading example of 'what human wisdom and understanding can do in Africa' was Schweitzer's project.[28] The issue's final piece was by L.S.B. Leakey, the British archeologist described by the *National Geographic* as perhaps 'the greatest figure in East Africa today.'[29]

Like other popular magazines, *National Geographic*'s coverage of Africa declined after the early 1960s and often focused on white protagonists and primitive Africans. The first photograph of 'Mozambique: Land of the Good People,' featured a bare-breasted 'chief's daughter, in beads and raffie skirt,' dancing 'between lines of warriors in battle dress.' The text dwelled on the lives and perspectives of the colony's small minority of Portuguese residents. The writer was relieved to find that on 'a continent seething with strife and ambitious hopes,' Mozambique appeared to be 'an island of tranquility,' where 'the people … will remain the same.'[30] Senior Assistant Editor Allan Fisher's Kenya piece reported no racial strife but dwelled not on that remarkable achievement of independence but rather on 'another Kenya, timeless and unchanging, the vast Kenya of the lion and the elephant and the antelope, of magnificent distances where one's spirit roams with the wind in a land so beautiful that it seems to cleanse the soul of the beholder.' His 'aha' moment occurred when he was aloft, in an airplane searching for Arab ruins and saw instead 'an old bull elephant, massive of tusk, ambling in solitary contentment.' He realized: 'Whatever changes white men had brought to Kenya, they had not affected this lordly bull, symbol of that amazingly fecund animal life, born free and living free.'[31] Anthropologist Catherine A. Lutz and sociologist Jane L. Collins in fact find that the number of white people depicted in *National Geographic* articles treating colonies and former colonies fell dramatically in the 1960s, part of a strategy of 'studiously' eliding the contested politics of these places so that their cultures could be presented 'as hermetically sealed worlds.'[32]

America's most popular magazines reflected a marked decline in both interest in and optimism for black Africa in the 1960s. Liberal journalist-intellectual Murray Kempton, reacting to Africa's outrage in the United Nations over the

West's treatment of the Congo in 1961, concluded: 'Africa hollers rape against us and does not even know that we no longer even care, let alone lust.'[33]

Popular films also betrayed America's declining interest in black Africans, though filmmakers tried much harder than Kempton to express respect for them. *The Drums of Africa*, 1963, features a significant African character, Kassango, who is an effective member of an otherwise white group that is fighting to free black captives. But he is something of a throw-away, stock character. The four white figures are allowed to develop: two fall in love and learn to trust each other; the hard-headed defender of undeveloped Africa learns that progress is not all bad; a boy becomes a man. Kassango just keeps on being Kassango.

The Last Safari of 1967 also tries to be sensitive to black Africans without surrendering its focus on white protagonists. Gilchrest is an aging safari leader disgusted with civilization, Ward is a callow and wealthy American who embodies everything that Gilchrest dislikes about his job and the modern world. The third character is Grant, a 'working girl' who is Ward's temporary consort. Grant is supposed to be local and half black, the product of an interracial relationship, though she is played by Gabriella Licudi, the light-skinned daughter of a Greek father and a Moroccan mother. Grant and Gilchrest critique Ward's reflexive racism. When Ward refers to 'half-witted savages,' Gilchrest retorts that their culture is older than 'your Christianity.' Grant tells Ward that he's 'offensive' to black servants because of how he smells. But the film does not take Jama, the leading black African, seriously. His independence and attraction to western technology gets him killed, for he disobeys Gilchrest by approaching some elephants that trample him when the alarm clock he is carrying goes off. In any event, the movie is not about Jama or even Grant, let alone racism. Like the classic African films of the early 1950s, it is about Africa providing a tableau in which white people can find their true natures.

Khartoum, from 1966, well illustrates how white protagonists inevitably shoulder aside gestures of racial inclusiveness or sensitivity. This account of the battle over the Sudan between Charles George Gordon (Charlton Heston) and the Mahdi (played by a darkened Laurence Olivier) has the former admitting that he and the Mahdi are cut from the same cloth, a pair of zealots bound to clashing and equivalent visions. But the film's sympathies clearly lie with Gordon, who lectures the Mahdi on slavery and claims that since the Sudan was 'the only thing that I have ever loved,' he 'cannot leave it to the sickness and the misery in which I once found it.' The Mahdi is simply a crazy man who displays severed heads and insists that all Muslims must 'tremble before me.' The viewer is not informed of rational reasons why the Mahdi and other Sudanese might want to resist British colonialism. As Pulitzer Prize-winning historian David Levering Lewis points out, the film cannot join British Prime Minister Gladstone in describing the Sudanese as 'a people struggling to be free, and rightly struggling to be free,' for to do so would overcomplicate the movie's simplistic message of white heroism, to wit: 'A world without Gordons would return to the sands.'[34] A world without the Mahdi would presumably be much safer and more civilized for all. *Khartoum*, then, engages in something of a bait and switch by simultaneously presenting its two main characters as equivalent even as it dehumanizes and depoliticizes the African leader and his anti-colonial movement.[35]

Dark of the Sun, 1968, tries harder to be about Africans. Curry and Ruffo are a pair of unlikely friends charged with extracting diamonds from Congo territory claimed by the Simbas, a group of fanatical anti-western and anti-government warriors. Curry is a jaded white mercenary, Ruffo a black Congolese patriot. When a white reporter refers to Ruffo (played by former football star Jim Brown) as a 'big ape,' Curry retorts that the sergeant knows four languages and studied at the University of Southern California. The most brutal figure in the film is a swastika-wearing soldier with a German accent who eventually kills Ruffo in the hope of taking the diamonds for himself. Ruffo is the most likable character and is given opportunities to explain the nature of his patriotism. He believes that the Congo is moving away from 'primitive, savage beliefs,' that the battle for a stable nation 'is our Bunker Hill, our storming of the Winter Palace.' The battle against the Simbas is also personal: 'I came down out of the trees by invitation, and I'll kill anyone who tries to send me up again.'

Ruffo the black patriot keeps mouthing western platitudes. The Simbas are caricatures, exotic, bloodthirsty, and irrational brutes. Once the film pays its respects to black liberation and racial reconciliation, it is free to indulge in hoary images of black rapaciousness. Moreover, at its center is a white man in black Africa. Ruffo may be Curry's moral superior, and they have their arguments. But Ruffo is ultimately loyal and devoted to his friend, a man whose physical and moral struggles are the story's driving narrative.

As in *Drums of Africa*, *The Last Safari*, and *Khartoum*, *Dark of the Sun* has a significant black character, and it sort of attempts an African point of view. But these black characters do not get to develop, are not the film's central concern, and Black Nationalism is treated crudely. '*Dark of the Sun*,' Cameron concludes, 'is constructed around a central conviction (white superiority) that it then cannot face,' an observation that neatly describes the modern white liberal dilemma.[36] Even these half-hearted gestures of racial inclusiveness evidently hurt the films at the box office.

Hatari was burdened by no such sensibilities. The 1962 action movie featured John Wayne and thrilling shots of a multi-cultural band of brothers risking life and limb to capture Africa's most dangerous animals. These men included an American-Indian and a Mexican, but no black Africans; they are exotic, servile backdrops, as if the last ten years had not occurred. Life imitated art when the film company hosted Julius Nyerere, soon to be the high-profile, radical leader of Tanzania. Director Howard Hawks' son marred the occasion by remarking: 'Dad, we never eat with black people at home. Why are we doing it now?'[37] The famously conservative Wayne had no use for Nyerere's socialism: 'The whole damn place won't be worth a shit in ten years.' After Tanzania gained its independence he lamented that 'the do-gooders had to give it back to the Indians!'[38] *Hatari* well expressed Wayne's belief that Africa was a wonderful, adventuresome place—if Africans remained in the background. The American public evidently agreed; at a time when more sensitive films about Africa foundered, *Hatari* was one of the ten top grossing films of the year.

Other successful films and television shows of the 1960s set in Africa ignored the politics of black independence or white racism in favor of noble animals and the white people who love and are inspired by them. The protagonists of *Clarence the Cross-Eyed Lion* of 1965 are animals or white people. Dark-skinned Africans are not so much stereotyped, though there is certainly some of that, as they are rendered invisible or inconsequential. *Born Free*, a British film released a year later and based on Joy Adamson's book, is more earnest, and associates the lioness Elsa with freedom. The Oscar-winning song of the same name was covered by American singer Roger Williams and sold very well in the US, and it well expressed the sense of freedom that Americans invested in Elsa: 'Born free to follow your heart' and 'Live free and beauty surrounds you.' Elsa proved to be a much more popular receptacle for American dreams for freedom than did African freedom fighters. *Clarence the Cross-Eyed Lion* and *Born Free* meshed with and encouraged a series of television programs that showcased African animals and neglected its humans. *Mutual of Omaha's Wild Kingdom* ran on NBC from 1963 to 1971 and often featured Africa's wild land and animals, places of 'untroubled, untouched, unaltered nature.'[39] *Daktari*, which aired on CBS from 1966 to 1969, features a white American wildlife biologist and his daughter in East Africa, but the true stars of the show are Clarence the Cross-Eyed Lion (the show took its premise from the earlier film) and Judi, a mischievous chimp. The most widely watched representations of Africa in the 1960s dwelled on white Americans making connections with wild, innocent Africa.

A few Hollywood films of the 1960s tried to take African characters and movements seriously without improving on the efforts of the late 1950s. *Hatari* (1962) and *Clarence the Cross-Eyed Lion* (1965) simply ignored black Africans. But perhaps the most notable trend about Hollywood's treatment of Africa during the 1960s was its lack of interest. Cameron's meticulous count shows a precipitous decline from fifty-seven US films in the 1950s to twenty-six in the 1960s to merely five in the 1970s. Tarzan and similar 'jungle fantasy films' produced by Americans fell from thirty-nine in the 1950s to seven in the 1960s to none whatsoever in the 1970s.[40]

The handful of Tarzan films that appeared suggest how difficult it was to make movies about Africa that were both racially sensitive and popular. *Tarzan and the Jungle Boy* of 1968 certainly hit some of the old notes. Tarzan informs a visiting photographer eager to find a white boy who had disappeared six years ago into the 'Segunda Country,' that she'll 'find life there—and death.' There are plenty of jungle scenes and exotically dressed natives and charismatic megafauna. And of course Tarzan eventually tracks down the wild boy. But the film is much more racially sensitive than its counterparts from even the late 1950s, let alone earlier.

Early in the film Tarzan makes an appeal for racial unity: 'Men are not different, ... only the sound of their words, and the color of their hearts.' Nor does this version of Tarzan, his bulging muscles notwithstanding, get to toss around hapless black Africans. Many of the film's action sequences are given over to a pair of black African brothers played by brothers Rafer and Ed Johnson, the former an African-American Olympic decathlon champion and both the possessors of highly chiseled, muscular physiques. In fact the two square off, appropriately enough, in a sort of African decathlon. Tarzan gets to intervene only when the evil brother cheats. He is otherwise a spectator. Likewise, in the final showdown Tarzan begins the hand-to-hand combat with the evil brother but then steps aside when the black hero turns up. It is the black protagonist, not the white one, who kills the evil man.

This racially sensitive Tarzan did not resonate with white audiences. After half a century and dozens of films that had taught two generations of Americans most of what they thought they knew about Africa, the franchise had at last, it seemed, expired.

Yet the earlier Tarzan, the white savage who dismissed and easily dominated black Africans, retained his popularity. The original Tarzan books underwent a renaissance in the 1960s even as the more enlightened Tarzan films disappointed. Liberal Hollywood may have lacked the stomach for such nakedly racist fare, but the general public, like John Wayne, was less squeamish.

TWO WHITE MEN AND A WOMAN IN THE NEW AFRICA

Robert Ruark was right; African independence made it much more difficult for white American seekers of adventure and restoration to make themselves at home in Sub-Saharan Africa. Three well-known Americans tried. Peter Beard, who became a celebrated photographer and artist/diarist, and novelist/travel writer Paul Theroux built the foundations of masculine identities and impressive careers on what they repeatedly characterized as unpromising African rubble. Journalist Martha Gellhorn came to Africa much later in life, seeking a refuge which proved ephemeral.

A child of wealth who had been entranced by Akeley's African Hall and then Dinesen's *Out of Africa*, Peter Beard first visited Kenya at age seventeen and found it 'perfect.'[41] From the start he approached Africa as an adventuresome male teenager. He recalled in *Zara's Tales*:

I had to find out what it was like to *escape* the drudgery of Mondays-back-to-school, delinquency, demerits, detention, dehumanization; to step into another time, to experience the open spaces, the 'endangered spaces,' the Big FIVE: lion, leopard, buffalo, rhino, and elephant. The enormous isolation, the impersonal solitude, the joy of escape, the need to set sail … RELIEF in a world without socks or underwear!

In Kenya he 'promptly lost myself in a child's paradise.' He spent a lot of time hunting and adventuring in the East African bush, but even as a college student at Yale Beard was working on *The End of the Game*, a pastiche of photographs, drawings, and rambling essays and travelogues which appeared in 1965 and betrayed his keen nostalgia for a disappeared and disappearing Africa. *The End of the Game* was suffused with a male adolescent celebration of wild Africa, interspersed with lament that 'ancient Africa' was slipping away.

Beard's touchstone for Africa from a young age was a colonial: Karen Blixen (Dinesen was her pen name). After his first visit to Africa in 1955 he made his way to Denmark to become friends with the famous author, who was near death. His portraits of Blixen's skeletal face (her 'death mask') became a favorite trope, and he purchased land adjacent to her beloved farm. *End of the Game*'s first section was devoted to her. The text closed with this admonition: 'This [Africa] is her world and we are different for having known it through her.'

But Beard's interpretation of Africa differed significantly from Blixen's more social and ambiguous one. She lived in Kenya for nearly two decades before finances forced a return to Denmark where she wrote *Out of Africa*, which became a beloved staple of Africana soon after its publication in 1937. Blixen commonly described 'her people' as a sort of extension of the landscape; black Africans were noble precisely because they were uncivilized. But Blixen differed from Conrad, Hemingway, and other popular male writers of Africa in taking relationships with black Africans seriously. Paternalism had weight, and the accumulated tragedies she bore witness to among 'my people' taught her about the unity of suffering and joy. *Out of Africa* can be read as an extended object lesson in coming to terms with the competing claims of personal fulfill-ment and loss, freedom and obligation, 'necessity and desire,' and 'infinite possibilities and absolute limits.'[42]

Beard, by way of contrast, approached Africa as a place to slough off rather than to acquire social responsibilities; it was a playground, a 'game.' Hunting was at the heart of the game, an antidote to modern mass industrial society, 'a private, personal experience for the few who find it meaningful,' he asserted in 1965. Beard, like Ruark, simply wanted to inhabit and lengthen the era of the British colonial system.

Though less blatantly than Ruark, Beard associated civi-lization, the end of the game, with 'Uhuru and the confusion it promised.' Black Africans were supposed to remain bit players. 'The Central symbol of African life,' after all, was 'the animal.' Humans of consequence did not exist until white explorers and colonists, 'equipped with a child's dreams and a man's courage,' brought light to 'and opened up' the country. But in the early 1960s, a new order was pushing out the colonial one. When he met two Belgian refugees from the Congo and learned what they endured: 'The business of Uhuru finally struck home to me.' Beard evidently had no equivalent conversations with black Africans. Many of them populate his book, but usually as '[s]kinners and gunbearers' or Dinesen's devoted servants, as helpers rather than actors.

Uhuru has hardly endangered Beard's status as a chic interpreter of Africa and its purported decline. One of his Yale mentors could not have been more prescient when he predicted: 'you could do the "end of the game" for the rest of your life.'[43] Beard was such a high-profile artist in part because he cultivated a mystique and friendships that made him famous for being famous: Andy Warhol, Jackie Onassis, Mick and Bianca Jagger, and his marriage to Cheryl Tiegs. His close identity with Kenya has been a central part of his persona and cachet, his fulsome authenticity.

Beard continued to associate old Africa with perfect freedom. A long-time colleague remarked that '[w]hat he likes most about Africa is to do your own thing there, ... He can't—won't—accept the normal responsibilities of society.' His fashion photography for *Vogue*, *Harper's Bazaar* and other magazines was highly nostalgic and associated feminine beauty with wildness. The tableaus often resembled *National Geographic* spreads, with occasional white models sprinkled among the bare-breasted, garishly clad natives. Naked women reclined with big cats. Dark-skinned models bared their teeth. 'Beautiful women,' he remarked, 'will be the last thing left in nature that's worthy of worship.'[44] He claimed to have discovered the Somali model Iman, the educated daughter of a diplomat, working as a goatherd in the desert.

Since he first set foot there in 1955, Africa's central purpose has always been to provide the playground on which Beard's authentic self could be created and burnished. 'Africans,' Iman observes, 'get in the way of his myth.'[45] He lamented the urban sprawl swallowing his ranch, the disappearance of his Eden. In a 1996 film, *A Study of Peter Beard*, he referenced modern black Africa when talking about the decline of modern civilization: 'A lot of pangas, a lot of robbery, cheating, stealing, murdering, torturing to death, a lot of imprisonment, army take overs, fascism, black, dark, horrifying, black totalitari-anism.' Nearly four decades after *The End of the Game*, Beard proclaimed from his sprawling home near the resort town of Montauk, New York: 'I have no need to go back to Africa.' 'Barking dogs in parking lots. It's really revolting. Africa has lost its authenticity, so what's the point of being there?'[46]

When the fiftieth anniversary edition of *End of the Game* appeared in 2015, Paul Theroux wrote the Foreword. Unlike Beard, who was drawn to Africa's animals and colonial residues, Theroux took a keen interest in black Africans. Yet, as for Beard, these people ultimately spoiled his Africa.

Like Beard, Theroux went to Africa in search of freedom and novelty. He begins his semi-autobiographical *My Secret History* of 1996 by noting that his protagonist's charac-teristics included 'a knack for knowing when I was happy.' Growing up poor in a conservative Catholic family and parish provided few opportunities to exercise this gift. He recalls seeing a missionary dressed as an Arab and thinking: 'That's for me—but it wasn't the preaching part, it was the travel. I'll get out that way, even if it means being a missionary, was my idea.' He would be doing not 'God's work' but 'my work.' In the Peace Corps he finds a 'special interval' of psychic and sexual freedom, the ability to at last 'pursue my secret life.' Indeed, Theroux was pleased to find that the Malawi Peace Corps was 'very vague and unorganized.' The volunteers were 'left alone,' and he could 'call my soul my own,' was 'completely at home in this distant place.'[47]

For the next half-century, through several novels and travel accounts, Theroux would argue with himself over whether or not Africa could be home. His first African novel, *Fong and the Indians* of 1968, suggests that outsiders could belong. The protagonist, Sam Fong, is an impoverished Chinese shop-keeper living with his family in East Africa. One of Fong's favorite aphorisms is: 'A man who is free to feed himself might choose poison.' Fong and his fellow Asian-Americans must negotiate between ruthless blacks and naïve whites, a position well illustrated when a man in a paramilitary orga-nization demands 50 shillings from Fong, then rides away in a new minibus with these words on the side: 'This Is a Gift of the People of West Germany.'

The tone of *Fong and the Indians* is farcical and absurdist. The protagonist is caught up in a struggle between witless Communist and CIA agents who are tone deaf to the nuances of native life. Fong, probably the most admirable person in the book, is an irritable racist who beats his wife. Black Africa is a place where nothing goes as intended. But despite or perhaps because of this Fong, and presumably Theroux, finds himself at home there. East Africa is a suitable refuge precisely because nothing really works—and nothing truly disastrous can happen. Fong reflects on his predicament and his pros-pects as he drifts off to sleep at the book's close: 'He was an immigrant, a stranger, and yet had been treated no differently from anyone else.' Africa is often cruel and absurd, but it was also interesting and, in its way, fair.[48]

Theroux's second novel, *Girls at Play*, appeared just a year after *Fong and the Indians*, in 1969, but it is much more pessi-mistic. Africa is still farcical, and the white misfits who live there constantly misinterpret it. But it is much more malevolent. Heather, the protagonist, 'began to imagine Africa a huge black carcass, inert in the ocean, with evil at its centre, and all Africa's vastness radiating mishap off its shores in dark smelly eddies.' Theroux provides no black characters of depth. Remarks one of his more sympathetic white characters of her African friend: 'Wangi was not dangerous. He was Africa, with all of Africa's dullness, simplicity and emptiness.' But she is wrong; Wangi, a former Mau Mau, evidently rapes her, and she commits suicide. Another of the 'white girls' is killed by a dim-witted African servant. Black Africa is malignant as well as farcical.[49]

Theroux's personal history mirrored his fiction. *My Secret History* pivots when promiscuous African girls start asking for money. In a later reminiscence Theroux recounted a similar turning point. A man in a bar invited him home for a night with his sister who 'liked you very much.' When Theroux prepared to leave in the morning, after a 'pleasant' night of love making, Nina and her brother insisted that he stay. They took Theroux to a local bar where he paid for everyone's drinks. The next day was more of the same, a day of drinking and growing tensions, and the next day, too; Theroux became their source 'for beer, for snacks, for presents.' It took him four days to escape and impressed on him the fact that he was just 'a presumptuous American ... little more than a tourist.'[50] In *Sunrise with Seamonsters*, 1985, Theroux recalled a third clarifying moment, after he had left the Peace Corps and was teaching in Uganda in 1968. He and his pregnant wife were attacked in a violent demonstration in the capital. The next morning Theroux learned that some of his students had been among the assailants. 'They were not apologetic. They simply said that Africans were being persecuted in Rhodesia.' Theroux was a white man to them, not a person: 'I had lost my confidence in these students. I needed different students and a new country. I remember, thinking: *I have no business to be here.*' Theroux would repeat that mantra again and again in the next half-century, as he kept revisiting the continent where he had first tasted freedom.

Several decades later, as recounted in *Dark Star Safari,* 2004, Theroux had become a highly successful, middle-aged author, and Africa now held out the prospect that he might become 'unobtainable,' like Kurtz, 'crawling on all fours like an animal, trying to flee into the jungle.' He was not disappointed. As he took his leave from Harar, Ethiopia, 'with children and adults howling at him,' he observed a screeching woman being beaten by an older man, an act that everyone else seemed to view as routine. Theroux realized that this is what drew him: 'the lepers, hyenas, ivory tusks, and garbage; the complaining donkeys, the open drains in the cobbled alleys, and the tang of spices; the butcher covered with blood … Being in Africa was like being on a dark star.' Beard was troubled by Nairobi's sprawl; Theroux celebrated the 'motley liveliness' that western cities had surrendered. Travel was an existential act, a commitment 'to see things as they are, not nostalgically, not as you wish they were.'[51] Living in bland America required rejuvenation on this 'black star.'

In 2013 he related a similar African pilgrimage in *The Last Train to Zona Verde.* He traveled up Africa's West Coast from

South Africa once again 'to get away from people wasting my time with trivia … to frustrate the stalkers and pesterers.' Africa was perfect for this 'because it is still so empty, so apparently unfinished and full of possibilities.' His journey promised 'a land unknown and undiscovered.'

But he ended the trip in Angola rather than Timbuktu; the misery he sought had become too miserable. Mali was rent by a coup, and radical Islam was loose in West Africa's interior. To continue would mean: 'decaying cities, hungry crowds, predatory youths, and people abandoned by their governments.' *The Lower River* of 2012, Theroux's fictional companion to *The Last Train to Zona Verde*, has a similar tone to the travel book. Protagonist Ellis Hock returns to the Malawi village where, forty years before, as a Peace Corps Volunteer, he had led 'his real life.' But the village is much changed, and Hock is lucky to escape with his life. Art here imitated life, for the last chapter of *The Last Train* bears perhaps Theroux's favorite refrain about Africa, one learned half a century before: 'What Am I Doing Here?' And this time he 'at last' had an answer: 'I am preparing to leave.'

So after a half-century of intense if sporadic engagement, Theroux shook the dust off his sandals in a promised final farewell, having discovered that there was poverty and desperation closer to home, 'on the red roads of the Deep South.' But, like Beard's, it had been a very long goodbye to the place that had first opened up his life. Malawi and Africa were ultimately unable to accommodate Theroux's paradoxical requirements, his desire for an Africa exotic and dangerous enough to provide a foil to the domesticated West, but not so much as to overwhelm. Perhaps the tirade Chief Manyenga addressed to Hock was intended for Theroux: 'You *mzungu* can go anywhere! You people can do what you like. ... This is a little holiday for you, but this is our whole life.' At the end of it all, this proponent of ordeal travel seems to sense that he has become that most despised of all Americans: a tourist.

A third prominent American writer also tried to make herself at home in Africa in the 1960s, and she failed much more quickly than did her male counterparts. Martha Gellhorn first came to Africa in 1962 when she was well into her fifties; it disappointed her at first and in the end. A distinguished journalist who was resentful that most knew her as one of Hemingway's wives, Gellhorn was before her time not only as one of the first women war correspondents, but also in her attitude. Brilliant and often acerbic, she did not at all fit the image people even of the 1960s had of how a woman should act. Always restless, she came to Africa for the same reason that most men did: in search of adventure. But upon her descent into Douala, Cameroon, as she wrote in her travel account, *Travels with Myself*, 'Africa presented itself as grey-green jungle swamp. ... Uninhabited and uninhabitable, except no doubt for reptiles.' 'I do feel that I am in Africa now,' she wrote a few days later, 'and it is oppressive.' She detested the African climate, accommodation, restaurants, social customs, officials, and often its people. The keepers of a Cameroon hotel 'are like something out of a bad play about Africa; a poor obese young man with open sores on his face and arms, and dirty clothes, a sluttish dark woman. It is appalling.'

Then she flew to Nairobi, and Africa, as it had for so many Americans, opened up. Soon she 'had fallen in love with the land and the sky, the fauna and flora, the weather of East Africa.'[52]

Gellhorn missed East Africa terribly after her trip ended and soon returned to make a semi-permanent home. For thirteen years she spent much of her life there, soaking up the 'moments of union, when walking on the long empty beach at sunrise or sunset, when watching the night sky,' she recalled in her travel memoir, or at her home in the Rift Valley, where she 'could look at four horizons, drunk on space and drunk on silence. Or always, driving alone on the backroads, when Africa offered me as a gift its surprises, the beautiful straying animals, the shape of the mountains, wild flowers.' 'I know Africa is my place,' she wrote a friend, 'there is everything to learn, everything: as long as my head and my legs hold out, I'll never come to the end of it.'[53] She loved Kenya's aesthetic, its nonhuman landscape.

In fact it was a tragic encounter with a fellow human being that drove Gellhorn out of Africa. During one of the drives she so enjoyed she struck not one of 'the beautiful straying animals' she so admired, but a child, and the child died. Gellhorn was disconsolate. 'What I cannot get out of my mind is this: the child is dead. How does one live with that.'[54] Africa had lost its luster; it was not home. She left and did not return.

She struggled to come to terms with what Africa had meant to her in three novellas eventually published in 1978 as *The Weather in Africa*. Some of her white protagonists reach a rapprochement with black Africans. Ian Paynter, a survivor of a prisoner-of-war camp, finds solace in his farm and in a half-white, half-black child that he adopts. In 'On the Mountain' the two daughters of a white couple who run a hotel are a study in contrasts. The racist, spoiled daughter falls apart as she becomes sexually obsessed with a ruthless black politician who humiliates her. The more practical daughter is comfortable with black Africans but falls in love with an English botanist who shares her passion for the African landscape. The most autobiographical piece, 'By the Sea,' features a white protagonist recovering from the loss of a beloved child. American Diana Jamieson comes to East Africa for two weeks and is rejuvenated by the air and the vistas. The climate energized her, the colors were vivid. 'I forgot time, I was free of it.' 'I could make a life like this,' she realizes. But just as this sliver of hope appears, she strikes and kills a boy. This parallel with her own loss unhinges her; she soon kills herself. 'Poor woman. She should never have come to Africa,' reads the ending.[55]

The white women who made themselves at home in Africa in the 1950s focused on relationships. Gellhorn did not. Like Beard, Theroux, and her protagonist in 'By the Sea,' she loved Africa as a place apart, a place where she could 'stop being me, lose my life, live by looking. It could be a way out, or part of a way out.' Her quest was more aesthetic than social. But she also noted in her travel account: 'not understanding Africans bothered me.' Beard and Theroux persisted in Africa well into the twenty-first century, their chronic grumbling over modern Africans notwithstanding, but Gellhorn's estrangement from Africa's people seemed to disqualify her for living there.

NOT QUITE HOME: BLACK AMERICANS AND AFRICA

Black Americans remained enthusiastic about black Africa in the 1960s, though by the decade's close that enthusiasm had become more abstract.

Ebony, aspiring to represent the swelling black middle class, remained both upbeat about Africa and resolute in drawing a distinction between it and black America. It routinely celebrated the independence and accomplishments of new, black-run nations and gave them the benefit of the doubt long after other popular magazines had written them off. The magazine's coverage of African history culminated when it published a five-part series entitled 'Africa's Golden Past.'[56] These articles focused on great leaders, empires and architecture. Africa had a history as rich or richer than Europe. But Africa was not home. An editorial, 'Brothers of the Skin' pronounced that: 'The American Negro, like Americans of Jewish Irish and Italian extraction, says his country is here.'[57] Perhaps the most telling examples of *Ebony*'s distancing from Africans were its safari articles. One featured Era Bell Thompson striking the sort of poses long reserved for white hunters: with her foot on a zebra she had killed and kneeling next to a gazelle she had dispatched, flanked by her white guide and two of his black assistants.[58]

If the moderate black middle class grew more comfortable with Africa, the growing number of young radicals fell in love with it. Black America's and black Africa's struggle for freedom and dignity continued to inform each other. Large numbers of black Americans protested at the complicity of the West in the coup that deposed and killed Congo President Patrice Lumumba in 1961. Demonstrators in Harlem alternated these chants: 'Lumumba!'; 'The word Negro has got to go!'; 'We're Afro-Americans!'[59]

Several hundred radical African-Americans sought a home in black Africa, particularly Ghana, by the early 1960s. W.E.B. and Shirley Du Bois, deeply disappointed by the US, moved there in 1961, where the ninety-three-year-old dean of Pan-Africanism was warmly welcomed by President Nkrumah, who asked him to direct the massive *Encyclopedia Africana* project.[60]

Younger radical black Americans also liked Ghana. William Gardner Smith, a distinguished journalist and novelist, lived in France (where he mingled with Wright and other African-American expatriates) for much of the 1950s and 1960s and in Ghana for some of the Nkrumah years. Ghana in many ways gave Smith what he was looking for. He lay in bed during his first nights in Accra listening to drums. Like Wright before him, he set out to find their source. Unlike Wright, he was gladdened by what he found. 'An enormous jolly woman in flowing robes' invited him and his companion to join the party, fed them, and invited them to dance. 'We were guests ... brothers,' he recalled in 1970. DuBois' widow, Shirley Graham DuBois, asked Smith to help organize Ghana Television's news department, and Smith 'was swiftly struck by the visible signs of black sovereignty,' the innumerable black ministers, directors, and other professionals running the country. On the streets he delighted in the clothing, laughter, and other mannerisms that made him feel 'as though I were walking down a street in South Philadelphia, Harlem, or Chicago.'

Leslie Alexander Lacy left the US in 1963 with high hopes, saying in his 1970 memoir: 'We had come from America because we hated it too much,' and Ghana 'was our promised land.' Upon arriving he was delighted to witness security officers and policemen who left white men feeling 'uncomfortable, not knowing what to expect from Blacks who did not move when they spoke.' The new, black Africa offered black Americans both familiar cultural features and the welcome spectacle of black political authority.

But African culture and politics could discomfit, too. E. Smith went to Ghana in search of 'that great mother country—Black Africa!' He was disappointed to find that Ghanaians seemed deferential to whites and uninterested in 'a unity of black men throughout the world,' and were still mired in a 'colonial mentality,' as he put it in his 1967 account. Lacy found that black Ghanaians often rejected his assumptions of racial solidarity. One accused him and most other black Americans of arrogance and 'taking jobs that are not rightly yours.' When Lacy protested that '[m]ost of us came out here to get away from America, to get the white man off our backs,' the Ghanaian countered that the US was a better place to live than Ghana. In retrospect, at least, Lacy found such stark difference in perceptions ironic and funny. Upon landing in Dakar, he recalled making this speech:

> Brothers, I'm so glad to be home. This is the greatest moment of my life. It was worth spending every hour

in America just to be able to live this moment. You have made me very happy. They tell black people in America that the Africans don't want them. I know now that they were lying to keep us apart. Black people in America belong on this continent, and I bring you greetings from all those who cannot be here. I am truly happy.

One of his new friends responded, with enthusiasm: 'Give us dollar.' Lacy was confused. The man expounded: 'You got plenty dollar. You be Big Man. American. Rich country. This be poor country. We need dollar. You give dollar.' Black Americans in search of a black haven and solidarity were shocked to find that poverty and ethnicity trumped race for most Africans and that black Africa had problems of its own.

Black Americans who adjusted their expectations found at least part of what they were looking for in Ghana. Bill Sutherland began working for the Ghanaian government in 1958 and later advised newcomers to be prepared for a certain amount of 'suspicion and hostility.' To seek out in Africa a sort of personal salvation, was 'putting too much of a burden on the country.' Robert E. Lee, who came to Ghana even earlier and stayed until his death half a century later, in the 1960s urged newcomers to learn local languages and customs. He 'didn't come here expecting to find all the Africans perfect.'[61] Pauli Murray, a civil rights veteran who would later become a pioneering feminist and Episcopalian leader, started teaching at the University of Ghana Law School early in 1960. Like her younger counterparts, she found Ghana alien. The languages confused her, life moved at an 'infinitely slow tempo,' driving unnerved her, the climate was 'intolerable.' Malaria 'plagued me throughout my stay,' she recalled in 1987. She became critical of Nkrumah's increasingly authoritarian government. But Murray also enjoyed many aspects of Ghana. Though at first reluctant to follow local custom by 'hiring a young male African as cook-steward,' she became close to him, and he eventually brought his family to live in her home. She was impressed by the 'innate dignity' and 'self-assurance' that even poor Ghanaians possessed, attributes that she felt had been bled out of black Americans by generations of slavery and racism.[62]

Maya Angelou, the famous memoirist and poet, turned avidly to Africa and Africans as an alternative to the US for several years. Vusumzi Make, a Xhosa civil rights activist in New York City to lobby the United Nations, told her soon after they met: 'I am going to take you to Africa,' she recalled in 1981. Angelou soon broke her engagement to a decent but prosaic man for the prospect of being at the side of this 'South African freedom fighter.'

This Pan-African romance was at first deeply satisfying, in part because it exposed Angelou much more fully to the black diaspora. In London she met women from South Africa, Uganda, Somalia, Sierra Leone, and the Caribbean. To the Africans' accounts of anti-colonialist struggles she added stories of legendary black Americans such as Harriet Tubman and Sojourner Truth. When she finished, 'the African women stood applauding, stamping their feet and crying. Proud of their sister, whom they had not known a hundred years before.' Though Angelou would not set foot in Africa for another year, 'that afternoon … I was in Africa surrounded by her gods and in league with her daughters.' She enjoyed a similar community in Egypt.

But other aspects of African collectivism alienated Angelou. This 'clash of cultures' most often arose when Vus asserted the prerogatives of being an African man. Angelou's American individualism manifested itself most badly when she was summoned before a court or 'palaver' in which Africans from across the continent attempted to heal this breach with her husband. Angelou indulged in a sassy tone and salty language not considered appropriate for an African woman. In fact she was offended by the idea that one's personal affairs should be mediated by the larger community: 'I never thought I needed anyone's approval but my own.' On this crucial matter, the right of the individual to control her or his own destiny, Angelou's feet remained firmly planted in American soil, in particular a tradition of black women's forthrightness.

Angelou left Vus and Egypt for Ghana. As her plane crossed the continent's interior she realized: 'It all began here,' the entire history of black America. All of her sufferings 'had begun just below our plane. I wept.' In Ghana she and the other 'Revolutionary Returnees,' as she termed, them, competed 'to best each other in lambasting America and extolling Africa,' she reported in her 1986 memoir. 'We would work and produce, then snuggle down into Africa as a baby nuzzles in a mother's arms.' But Mother Africa seemed indifferent to their presence: 'Our arrival had little impact on anyone but us.' They grew weary and then irritated by Ghanaians who wondered why they had left the comforts of America, then alarmed when the Ghanaian government began to accuse members of their community of sabotaging its revolution.

Angelou finally found what she was looking for in a personal encounter. Right before leaving she met some rural Ewe women who exclaimed and wept over her, for they 'saw their history in my face and heard their ancestors speak through my voice.' She could now leave the continent knowing 'my people had never completely left Africa.' English professor John Cullen Gruesser finds 'this ending … too easily manufactured at the last minute to resolve the problem of the book,' namely Angelou's struggle to form in Africa 'viable and ongoing connections.'[63] She and the other radical expats had come to Ghana in search of black solidarity but were a community apart.

Yet Angelou integrated Africa into her pre-existing identity. For some years after leaving Ghana she described Ghana as home: 'I never felt I belonged anywhere until I went to Ghana. … My soul relaxed.'[64] But she became more circumspect. In 2002 she recounted her consternation when after returning to the US in the 1960s the Ghanaian man who 'had taken the heart out of my body and worn it boldly on his shoulder like an epaulette' reappeared 'to collect you,' as he put it. The relationship had not lasted because 'I had no precedent for being who he wanted me to be. … He needed to be worshiped. Being an American, a black American woman, being Vivian Baxter's daughter, Bailey Johnson's sister and Guy Johnson's mother, I was totally unprepared to worship any mortal.' He returned to Ghana without her.

Angelou justified her unwillingness to surrender her identity to African men by citing her African-American heritage and kin. It was as if this American self that she refused to relinquish was not hers alone to give; it had been shaped by and was attached to other people.

Consummate individualist Frank Yerby and his widely read African novel of 1971, *The Dohomean*, could hardly have been more different from Angelou and her memoirs. Although by 1970 his novels had sold more than 20 million copies, with eight becoming best-sellers, Yerby was seldom recognized as a black writer. This was partly by design. After determining that he was unlikely to make a living as the next Richard Wright, he had settled for becoming wealthy by churning out 'costume novels' replete with sex, romance, conflict, and white protagonists. Black critics and radicals generally snubbed his work, and Yerby returned their favor, proclaiming that he left the US for Europe in the 1950s precisely because 'I wanted to be able to write without thinking about race or politics or religion.'[65]

The Dahomean features a black protagonist and aspires to be a serious if iconoclastic novel about race. Nyasanu is a man of great physical and moral strength and sexual magnetism trapped in the irrationalities and cruelties of his West African society, a way of life that he comes to despise. 'I'm out of step with life, as life has always been lived here in Dahomey,' he remarks near the novel's end, 'ever since our first King Tacodona ripped the guts out of Da, ruler of this City, then built a palace over his disemboweled victim's grave.' 'Even our origins,' he concludes, 'are drenched in blood.' Yerby finds much to admire in Dahomey society, and he finds it ironic that Nyasunu's owners in the US, where the nobleman eventually ends up, are ignorant of their slave's 'highly developed agricultural and mechanical skills.' But Nyasanu is great in spite of rather than because of Dahomey.

As a 'debunker' or 'rejecter,' black Africa provided Yerby not with an Edenic homeland but rather a backdrop for his solitary protagonist. Yerby believed, as Turner observes, that: 'Life has meaning only when man—frail and insignificant—sparkles as brightly as possible in his instant of eternity.'[66] Yerby posits a black superhero in steamy Africa as an archetypal American male individualist, a sort of black Tarzan.

Meanwhile, the Black Power movement that Yerby so detested expressed much less ambivalence over Africa. Malcolm X anticipated both Black Power and an orientation toward Africa in 1964. The Nation of Islam had possessed, at best, an ambivalent relationship with non-Muslim Africa, which it regarded as uncivilized. But when Malcolm broke from Elijah Muhammad and traveled to Africa, he liked what he found. 'Here in Africa,' he wrote from Lagos, Nigeria, 'the 22 million American blacks are looked upon as the long-lost brothers of Africa.' Weeks later, at the Organization of African Unity conference in Cairo, he presented a memorandum reminding the continent's leaders that we 'are your long-lost brothers and sisters, ... turning to our elder brothers for help.'[67] 'I'm from America, but I'm not an American,' he assured students at the University of Ghana. 'I didn't go there of my own free choice,' and 'I don't feel that I am a visitor in Ghana or in any part of Africa.'[68] Malcolm's efforts were more than rhetorical. He helped to found the Organization of Afro-American Unity, assisted by Maya Angelou among others. Though disappointed that Africa's young black nations were unwilling to jeopardize their standing with the US, Malcolm was clearly optimistic about the prospect of collaboration by black Africans and Americans at the time of his assassination early in 1965, not long after his second trip to Africa.

Stokely Carmichael, the Student Nonviolent Coordinating Committee (SNCC) leader credited with popularizing the term 'Black Power' in 1966, soon became a key link between black America and Africa. A SNCC delegation had gone to Africa in 1964 as part of 'broadening our struggle,' James Forman later recalled in 1972. 'We were going to become revolutionaries of the world.' Carmichael followed early in 1967, the year he left SNCC, as part of an international tour. 'The minute I got to Conakry, I said, "Oh, man, I'm home,"' he wrote in his 2003 autobiography. Carmichael was as good as his word. He soon married Miriam Makeba, the well-known South African singer, and moved to Guinea, where he would spend most of the rest of his long life, becoming close to both President Nyerere and the exiled Nkrumah, from whom he took his African name, Kwame Ture. Ture did not call for an immediate return to Africa. But it was essential for black people across the world to realize their unity: 'We are Africans, there can be no question about that. We came from Africa, our race is African,' he asserted in his 1971 collection. They were, as Africans, the world's 'most just' people, and they should work for justice wherever they lived—and for justice in Africa, because the struggle against colonialism in Africa was fundamentally the same as in America.

Maulana Karenga was another key Pan-Africanist of the 1960s. Much influenced by the writings of Nkrumah, Nyerere, and other African nationalists, he joined the Afro-American Association formed in 1962 which started Garveyesque schools, business, and cultural centers and had chapters in West Africa as well as the US. Karenga formed US (the name 'US' was a sort of ironic commentary on black Americans' exclusion from the US) in 1966, a highly structured, authoritarian organization patterned on what he took to be African lines. Members took African names, spoke Swahili, wore Afros and African dress, and performed African dances. Some even experimented with polygamy. Indeed, the Black Power and Pan-African movements of the 1960s often had masculinist undertones.[69] US declined beginning in 1969, but some of its outlook was assumed by LeRoi Jones, aka Amiri Baraka, who started the Modern Black Convention Movement in 1966 and then led the Newark Congress of African People. As these names implied, Baraka looked to Africa for models for black culture and politics. Like Karenga, to whom he had been devoted, Baraka believed that (African-inspired) cultural transformation must precede political independence. 'Faith in blackness' must come first, a belief in the essential distinctiveness and goodness of the African diaspora. But black political freedom and unity was the ultimate goal: 'American power over Africans around the world must be broken.'[70]

171

These pleas for Pan-African political solidarity failed for several reasons. Leaders sympathetic to the movement such as Lumumba and Nkrumah were overthrown with the active involvement of the CIA and replaced by black leaders more amenable to US influence. Some Africans found black American claims to brotherhood nonsensical. The Ugandan writer Taban Lo Liyong asserted that he had 'never come across a' black American 'who looks, talks, behaves, thinks like a full African.'[71] Kenya's radical activist Ken Mboya took a much more publicized and criticized swipe at black America's 'back-to-Africa movement' in a 1964 Harlem speech which elicited some eggs from an angered listener. He followed up with a much fuller treatment of the question in the *New York Times*. 'I have not found a single African who believes in a black demand for a separate state or for equality through isolation,' he remarked. Black separatism also implied a unity which Mboya found problematic, for black Americans came from a very different culture from their African cousins and too quickly mistook symbols ('a shaggy beard or a piece of cloth on one's head') for substance.[72] Ture (Carmichael), at home in Guinea, might pronounce himself still 'ready for revolution,' as the title of his 2003 autobiography put it, but his visions of global black unity seemed farther and farther away with each passing year.

Harry Belafonte, the singer who had promoted the interests of both Black Africa and the radical wing of the American Civil Rights Movement, in his 2001 autobiography identified Ture and Nyerere as two of the people who best personified his disillusionment at the decade's close. Nyerere 'set aside his youthful dreams of creating a utopian socialist state and became a vengeful tyrant,' Ture became more and more ideologically rigid. Indeed, Barack Obama in his classic *Dreams From My Father*, 2004, recalled listening to Ture speak at Columbia University in the late 1980s on how to 'circumvent white capitalist imperialism' by cultivating 'economic ties between Africa and Harlem.' When an audience member 'asked if such a program was practical given the state of African economics,' Ture cut her off, commenting that she had been brainwashed with 'bourgeois attitudes.' Ture lived, observed one of his biographers, 'inside a cocoon of political certainty.'[73]

Positing Pan-African political unity seemed to require a leap of faith at the close of the 1960s. Nkrumah was deposed, the radical black Americans he had drawn to Ghana long dispersed, and the growing number of freshly independent black states much more interested in placating the US state than in promoting Pan-Africanism.

Pan-Africanism's de-politicized cousin, Afrocentrism, had a much broader impact. Young African-Americans (the term itself was inspired by the Black Power Movement) learned Swahili, assumed African names, clothing, and hairstyles, and displayed African art. Critics such as Mboya pointed out that such symbols were often incongruent with any actual African ethnic group. But in asserting that blackness was a virtue to be celebrated rather than a stain to be lightened, Afrocentrism challenged long-held assumptions of white and European superiority. It asserted 'a greater pride in blackness.'[74]

Yet this was precisely the sort of ethnic identity that could be accommodated within, and often expressed, a broader commitment to American individualism and pluralism. Like the black bourgeois of *Ebony* they often criticized, Afrocentrists folded pride in Africa into African-American and American life. Pan-Africanism required organization, collaboration, and compromise with black people across the diaspora. Afro-Centrism could be pursued more symbolically and autonomously.

THE RISE AND FALL OF THE PEACE CORPS

Many white Americans were also heading to Africa early in the1960s, looking not for black solidarity but to help make their world and themselves better. For the first time in its history, a generation was coming of age whose majority knew little of toil or hardship, and many of them were extremely idealistic. When John F. Kennedy asked at an October 1960 campaign stop at the University of Michigan: 'How many of you are willing to spend ten years in Africa or Latin America or Asia working for the United States and working for freedom?' students seized upon the idea.[75] When Kennedy reappeared three weeks later, a graduate student asked if he was 'really serious about the Peace Corps?' Hundreds of students were already writing letters of interest.[76]

The Peace Corps became an integral part of Kennedy's New Frontier, his attempt to both reassert American power abroad and revive the nation's character at home. Sargent Shriver, the organization's charismatic founder, told early volunteers: 'The President is counting on you. It's up to you to prove that the concepts and ideals of the American Revolution are still alive.'[77]

Many early volunteers were enthralled by Kennedy's vision. John Coyne heard the University of Michigan speech and 'wanted to do something for my country.'[78] Jeanne D'Haem was just fourteen when she turned out in the hopes of catching a glimpse of Kennedy that night. When he spoke, she recalled in 1997, 'it seemed that he looked at me for a moment, and he began to talk about service in the cause of world peace.' Eight years later she was in Somalia. Roger Landrum recalled 'a sense of exhilaration about maybe carrying forth democracy.' 'When Kennedy said that Americans should do something for their country, I was captivated,' echoed Michael Moore.[79]

The Peace Corps aspired to create a new, more reciprocal model of development across the globe. Shriver termed it 'a genuine experiment in international partnership.'[80] Legendary anthropologist Margaret Mead in 1965 characterized the Peace Corps as 'an ethical enterprise, a way for an excessively fortunate country to share its optimism and generosity.'[81] Many volunteers agreed. George Johnson, recently returned from Tanjanyika, remarked that his decision to volunteer had expressed 'a personal affirmation of faith in the democratic ideal,' for volunteers were there to help people to help themselves, as many put it.[82] George Dewan wrote from Sierra Leone in 1962 that the Peace Corps provided 'visible and tangible evidence of Americans living and working here for someone else's interest.'[83] Such volunteers liked to contrast their willingness to live alongside Africans, as friends, with the colonial and racist Europeans. A volunteer in the Ivory Coast was delighted to quote a young boy: 'You know I don't like white people but I like Americans.'[84]

Many early volunteers shared a deep sense of idealism and optimism. D. Michael Warren wrote in his application essay that he believed he could 'help other people, who presently may be too hindered by disease and famine, [to] experience [a] love for life,' that serving would discharge 'a duty and responsibility to myself, to my country, and to the entire world.'[85] Other early applicants struck the same note: 'We have so much and others so little. May I help someone less fortunate than myself, giving them my time, my effort, my knowledge and my enthusiasm?' 'I wish to make the Peace Corps part of my conscientious effort in behalf of the peace race.'[86] Will Siegel left for Ethiopia in 1962 determined '"to save the world." I thought (hell, we all thought!) that by sharing my knowledge and myself, I could bring a small part of the world to new understanding and new motivation and improve their lives.'[87] Volunteers asked in 1962 why they had joined most commonly replied 'to help people and humanity in general.'[88] In their plane to Cameroon, a group of volunteers in 1962 chanted these words, to the tune of 'The Battle Hymn of the Republic':

> We got to teach believing education will create
> A world without the fear of war and people without hate.
> When we begin to think and learn, then freedom cannot
>   wait.
> Here we come, West Cameroon![89]

FROM POLITICAL TO PERSONAL

Such buoyant expectations were bound to founder on the shoals of reality.

Volunteers in Nigeria and Somalia found themselves in the middle of virulent conflicts. What Robert A. Randall 'really noticed, and have remembered' about Nigeria 'was the incredible frequency of illness and death.'[90] These tragedies accelerated with a 1966 coup and ensuing civil war. Tony Zurlo tried in vain to protect an Igbo man from being killed by a mob and then spent the next hours locating and driving three Igbo friends to the airport so that they could escape to Kano. The next day he learned that troops at that city's airport had 'killed all Igbo passengers.'[91] Jeanne D'Haem, the young woman who had been inspired by Kennedy as a teenager, had to leave Somalia abruptly when the government ordered them out of the country. When she resisted the attempts of four young men to commandeer her vehicle, one 'jammed the barrel of his gun into my mouth.' She left 'overwhelmed by the depth of the friendship and love I felt from my friends and by the depth of the hatred I felt from strangers who judged me by the color of my skin, my religion, my country.'

The degree of violence and hatred D'Haem confronted was atypical; her struggles to come to terms with a culture that struck her as alien were not. Her first morning in the Northern Somali town she had been assigned to brought a woman who told a screaming child that D'Haem was a devil. Children gleefully watched D'Haem weep in shame and frustration. 'I had had enough of being a goodwill ambassador for America,' she concluded. D'Haem eventually made friends and gained acceptance. But relations could easily become strained. When she showed a film of a moonwalk, for example, villagers pelted the screen and then D'Haem's group with rocks. 'Why do Americans think they can just go and take over the moon?' asked one. Other volunteers in Somalia grappled with more tedious challenges. Teachers in the mid-1960s felt 'useless and pointless, that they were accomplishing little or nothing of any value' as they struggled without paper and pencils and with students who struck them as unresponsive or rebellious.[92] Volunteers across Africa found that their hosts did not share their assumptions about work in general and education in particular. 'In West Africa the tortoise prevails not through perseverance but through trickery,' noted an anthropologist who evaluated the Peace Corps program in Sierra Leone.[93] Volunteers confounded African expectations and sensibilities by possessing a high degree of education and light skin but little visible wealth, such as fine clothes, an automobile, or a big house. An elderly Ghanaian called them 'the poorest white men I know.'[94] They espoused an educational philosophy that seemed to invite anarchy and criticized Africans' insistence on rote learning and authoritarian classroom management. 'When we tried to get them to think instead of memorize, they got very angry,' recalled Coyne. 'They didn't think we were real teachers. Some of them hated us, and we were devastated.'[95] 'The culture shock of Ethiopia,' summed up one, 'ripped apart my world.'[96]

The key to success seemed to be to lower one's expectations. John Demos, later to become a distinguished historian of colonial America, reported that he and his peers in Ghana reacted strongly to public perceptions of their 'youthful, naive idealism.' 'We were "hard-headed." We were "realistic." We were definitely *not* "salesmen for the American way."'[97] Their schools might be missing critical supplies, their pupils and supervisors resistant to modern modes of learning. But they were doing their best to make some small differences. A correspondent for the British magazine *The Economist* found that early volunteers commonly concluded that it took 'about two months to realize that "what we are doing has little to do with democracy or teaching the American way of life"; and then another two months to realize that "what we are doing isn't going to change the shape or destiny of the country."'[98]

African-American volunteers found that Africans commonly regarded them as white or European ('white Blacks') and that Africans could harbor prejudices toward each other that rivaled 'racism and segregation in Alabama.' 'You don't force your cultural things on people,' noted David Closson, 'but I thought some of my ideas were universal.' But most black Peace Corps workers in Africa in the 1960s, in the words of their historian, felt 'a growing sense of kinship' after their initial disillusionment.[99]

Volunteers were less likely to change Africa than to be changed by it. 'The intransigence of our preconceptions of ourselves and others gradually dissolved into a kind of affectionate confusion,' concluded David Schickele who served in Nigeria from 1961 to 1963.[100] Phillip Stevens, Jr. found that '"WAWA!" (West Africa Wins Again!)' could be 'spoken lightly and cheerfully with a shrug,' that 'efficiency-minded Americans' could develop 'patience, forbearance, and objectivity' by adjusting 'to "African time."'[101] Warren the young man who had joined the Peace Corps to 'help other people,' realized that Americans in 'the so-called "land of the free"' seemed much less happy than the Ghanaians he had lived among, people who made 'the harmony of and the dignity of the individual and the family ... the ultimate goal.'[102] Kathleen Moore realized that even taking a sip of water required great attention to detail in Ethiopia to avoid getting sick or wasting a precious resource. Returning home invited the danger of 'a life that would require less of me.'[103] Modernity fostered carelessness and thoughtlessness. Living in the Ivory Coast prompted Peyton to reflect 'that we have paid dearly for all our knowledge and high civilization: we have paid with fear and bitterness and anxiety.'[104]

This was a profound shift from early volunteers, who had come to Africa looking to share the 'American Way.' A decade later volunteers were wondering aloud whether or not America had much to offer. Tom Heidlebaugh, in Kenya from 1965 to 1968, recalled that he joined the Peace Corps because 'I wanted a culture.'[105] Earlier volunteers had been more likely to join because they believed that they had a culture to offer.

As the 1960s progressed, the Peace Corps' rapidly dwindling volunteers increasingly approached their service in individualistic terms. Darrell Dearborn in 1968 defended his peers from criticism that they were 'less thoughtful and committed than those of 1962–63.' 'We are no less committed to ourselves,' he argued. 'The basic force' motivating involvement in the Peace Corps was 'an individual's search of his own definitions and personal values.'[106] 'It is for each Volunteer to work out his or her "own bag,"' asserted Vernon L.

Washington.[107] Dan Douglas remarked that he 'came to Botswana, not because I cared a damn for the Peace Corps— it's truly not worth worrying about—but because Botswana is a good place to live and work for two years and the Peace Corps is paying me to do it.' The Peace Corps was good only inasmuch as it 'is still willing to subsidize individualism.'[108] James Skelton in 1991 recalled that he joined in 1970 hoping 'that the organization would serve him well in his quest for direction, purpose and, of course, his elusive self.' During the previous two years he had graduated from college, broken an engagement, twice 'dropped out of law school,' failed his army physical, quit his job, 'and given up on an attempt to qualify for the pro golf tour.'

The Peace Corps tried to shape the organization to the new times. A 1967 article in *The Volunteer* touted it 'as flower power without acid' and proclaimed that the United States remained 'a nation full of latent idealists.'[109] But the number of volunteers precipitously declined even as the organization became a destination for draft dodgers. Young idealists had become both more scarce and more critical of their government. By 1972 the number of worldwide volunteers had shrunk to under 7,000, a decline of more than 50% in just seven years. The Nixon administration guided the Peace Corps in more pragmatic directions. The 'B.A. generalist' who had done so much teaching and community organizing increasingly gave way to volunteers with more particular and practical skills, in agriculture, fish culture, or business, for example. Volunteers who specialized in the liberal arts fell from a peak of nearly 9,000 in 1967 to just 699 in 1982.[110]

But the long-term impact of the Peace Corps on American views of Africa was profound. By the close of the 1960s thousands of returned volunteers had lived for years among Africans and associated Africa with compelling and complicated people, not sublime tableaus or charismatic megafauna. Some, such as Theroux, were on their way to becoming writers and teachers who would spread their knowledge exponentially over the coming decades. As was so often the case with American overseas ventures in the 1960s, the Peace Corps did not go as planned. But the agency created something very new in the history of US interactions with Sub-Saharan Africa: a space in which young Americans had sustained interactions with Africans not as they imagined or wished them to be, but more or less as they were. Certainly it was no coincidence that such a large proportion of the Americans who would contest hoary tropes of Africa in the coming decades would be Peace Corps veterans.

Returned Peace Corps Volunteers often felt out of place in a fragmenting America. Mainstream America took the organization as proof that 'wholesome American youth, motivated by visions of self-sacrifice and adventure,' were fixing the world's problems.[111] Nor was the counter-culture much interested in digesting the moral complications that returned volunteers presented. When Siegel left Ethiopia for the drug-saturated, 'anti-war, free love' world of mid-1960s California, he learned to keep quiet about his time in Africa. Recounting the sufferings he had witnessed 'scared people off.'[112]

Leading American magazines and filmmakers lost interest in Africa and Africans even as America became more liberal and sensitive to racism. To be sure, part of this lack of interest could be attributed to the disappointing performances of some of the new African states. Ghana, Nigeria, the Congo, and others became autocratic, divided by bloody ethnic struggles, or simply acted against American wishes. Political scientist Martin Stanisland finds that American policy makers and other educated observers in the late 1950s expected the continent to become a sort of a laboratory for American-led modernization.[113] By the mid-1960s they had become pessimistic and uninterested in Africa, a place they now described as mired in tribalism and superstition, a trend, as we have seen, mirrored by mainstream American magazines and films. Peter Beard wrote off the continent even as it continued to provide him with materials with which to construct his own highly idiosyncratic identity. Black Americans remained much more positive about the new Africa than their white counterparts, though this enthusiasm became increasingly rhetorical as the decade progressed, more a matter of style than substance. Angelou and most of the other idealistic politicos came home.

The US had turned inward by the decade's close. The communitarian ideals of the Civil Rights Movement and the diverse socio-political movements it inspired had crumbled, leaving Americans disillusioned with causes beyond pursuing their own bliss. A wide spectrum of Americans had become less interested in as well as more tolerant of people other than themselves.

American interest in Africa would remain low in the coming years. But its very reputation as a failed continent would make it attractive to more extreme or unconventional types of American quests.

CHAPTER FOUR

GENDERED AMERICAN QUESTS IN 'TIMELESS AFRICA'

If idealism did not survive the 1960s, individualism continued to go from strength to strength. Obeisance to the Imperial Self became a sort of sacred obligation. '"Pleasure,"' remarked the French intellectual Pierre Bourdieu, 'is not only permitted but demanded, on ethical as much as on scientific grounds.'[1] Hedonism cut across class and ideological lines. Jefferson Cowie describes the economic elites of the 1980s as celebrating 'privilege without responsibility; wealth without obligation; noblesse without oblige.'[2] The fastest growing churches blended conservative politics with a therapeutic, non-creedal, and non-demanding form of Christianity.[3]

To be sure, Americans became less tolerant of intolerance. Blatant, public forms of racism receded, and liberation movements for women, Chicanos, homosexuals, and other oppressed groups flowered. But tolerance did not require engagement or accountability.

White America's post-Civil Rights approach to racism illustrates the new paradigm's limits. The great majority of white Americans expressed a belief in racial equality, and coverage of African-Americans in popular magazines increased several-fold from the 1950s to the 1970s.[4] 'Sanford & Son,' 'The Jeffersons,' and 'Fat Albert' arrived in the 1970s, Oprah Winfrey and Michael Jordan became cultural icons in the 1980s. 'Gangsta Rap' became the sound track of white suburbia. Black men became the poster boys of hip transgression, what cultural critic Stanley Crouch terms 'willful adolescence.'[5] Most white Americans also believed that racial equality had been achieved, and therefore any difficulties that African-Americans continued to face were of their own making. Scholars coined the term 'aversive racism' to describe practicing racial bias while denying its existence: 'racism without racists.'[6]

The nature of black society and culture also changed profoundly during these years. The expansion of the black middle class and the intransigence of black poverty widened economic and social divides even as the popularity of musicians and professional athletes obscured more traditional and conservative versions of black male success. As young black men were increasingly drawn to this individualistic 'Dionysian trap'—if not simply incarcerated—black women surged ahead of their male counterparts in college and graduate school.[7]

Gender remained a very significant social and cultural marker for both white and black Americans. Feminism splintered almost as soon as it emerged in the late 1960s. A movement whose slogan became 'the personal is political' was not likely to achieve consensus, could easily devolve into women simply doing what they wanted to do, which, some women argued, was the whole point. Growing numbers of men embraced androgyny or even worked at dismantling male privilege. But they were greatly outnumbered by men who sought to recapture rather than to retire traditional masculinity, from Robert Bly's 'wild men' to the ubiquitous 'male rampage films' such as *Lethal Weapon* and *Die Hard* featuring hyper-violent, anti-establishment heroes. Men remained much more committed to individualism than women by all sorts of measures, from who was more likely to desert their children to uses of leisure time, though black couples seemed to have a less gendered division of labor inside and outside the home than white ones. As political scientist Andrew Hacker put it early in the twenty-first century in *Mismatch: The Growing Gulf between Women and Men*, 'we are witnessing a *women's liberation* which grows from taking on obligations, while its male counterpart is based on abandoning them.'[8]

This splintered, masculinist, and hyper-individualistic America confronted an Africa that appeared hopeless and abject. By the 1980s, the promise of independence had faded. Western agencies and economists insisted that African governments cut their expenditures and encouraged foreign investment and the export of staples. But the subsequent suffering, like its beautiful vistas and charismatic megafauna, made Africa the perfect anti-modern foil on which to stage harrowing male quests. Those who actually visited, however, often found their quests thwarted or redefined.

EXTREME AFRICA

The news from Africa that the great majority of Americans received was almost always very bad during the last three decades of the twentieth century. As the high hopes associated with independence faded, black Africa seemed mired in a cycle of corruption, coups, and poverty punctuated by episodic famine and slaughter: starving Ethiopians and Somalis in the mid-1980s and early 1990s, respectively, followed by the Rwandan genocide. *Time* in 1992 termed Africa 'the basket case of the planet, the "Third World of the Third World."'[9] One particularly vivid photograph showed a tiny child, eyes lined with luminescent flies, sucking at a mother's withered breast. It was a pornography of suffering.[10]

Africa remained a place apart. The media coverage of the Bosnian and Rwandan conflicts illustrated Africa's singularity. Articles about the former were much more likely to describe individual leaders who pursued particular strategies. The Rwanda conflict was simply presented as an 'orgy.' Bosnia's bloodshed was the great European exception; Rwanda's represented all of Africa. A cartoon in the *Christian Science Monitor* showed a desperate woman thrusting her child not out of a Rwandan village but rather from the entire continent.[11]

Even American journalists who seemed determined to report good news out of Africa inevitably focused on atrocities. David Lamb ended the introduction to his 1983 book drawing from his years as Africa's bureau chief for the *Los Angeles Times* with the reassurance that 'troubled as these early years of nationhood have been, Africa needs not dwell forever in the uncertain twilight zone.' He closed the book's last major chapter by quoting 'a reasonable request' from an African: 'Give us time. We are young.' In between the bookends, however, was precious little hope: a dump truck full of corpses in Uganda; a note, almost in passing, that residents of Sudanese insane asylums 'are beaten twice a day'; his conclusion, drawn from reporting on Liberia's Samuel K. Doe, that 'below the paper-thin veneer of civilization in Africa lurks a savagery that waits like a caged lion for an opportunity to spring.' African-American Howard K. French seemed better prepared to write about a wider swath of Africa; he first visited the continent in 1976 while his parents were living in Ivory Coast, taught at one of its universities, married an African woman, and lived there much of the time from the 1970s to the 1990s, writing for *The Washington Post* and *New York Times*, among other western publications. French, too, ended his introduction referencing 'the continent's many cultural strengths.' But *A Continent for the Taking: The Tragedy and Hope of Africa*, 2005, put much more emphasis on tragedy than hope. Two pages into his introduction he listed his examples of '[t]he thrill of travel and discovery,' namely: 'a civil war in Chad, a coup in Guinea, a stolen election in Liberia.' French 'began to conclude that Africa was starting to kill me,' and resolved to leave. Getting from the Congo to '[g]entle Japan' became a sort of harrowing metaphor: the string of officials demanding bribes at Brazzaville airport;

the bloodied, bullet-pocketed walls that no longer supported a ceiling in the waiting area; an interminable delay in Douala, Cameroon, 'yet one more Central African exercise in decay.' He tried to use a telephone to reach his family to be told: 'Somebody ripped out all the cables. People are poor here. This is what we do to survive.'[12]

Robert D. Kaplan made no pretense of looking for good news in Africa. The opening photo spread in 'The Coming Anarchy,' a widely read 1994 article in *The Atlantic Monthly*, featured armed soldiers walking amidst the bones of Liberian civilians. Kaplan recounted the words of a disillusioned minister, 'the voice of hope about to expire,' telling of child soldiers willfully wrecking government cars, a leader 'who shot the people who had paid for his schooling, "in order to erase the humiliation and mitigate the power his middle-class sponsors held over him."' A generation later, after substantial economic and political progress, these events and anecdotes can be interpreted as exceptional episodes from a minority of West African nations. But for Kaplan in the mid-1990s they were proof positive that West Africa was suffused with 'criminal anarchy.' Kaplan's language seemed better suited to pesticide advertisements than to political science. 'A shack' was 'teeming with children.' Young men gathered in 'hordes.' Shanty-towns had 'scabrous walls' with children 'as numerous as ants.'[13] Kaplan reprised these themes in 1997 in *The Ends of the Earth*. He was appalled by everything African from its odors ('urine drying on sun-warmed stone') to land-scapes ('perhaps, the forest had made the war in Liberia'). As social scientist Kevin C. Dunn points out in 'Fear of a Black

Planet, Anarchy Anxieties and Postcolonial Travel to Africa,' Kaplan indulged in a Victorian environmental determinism in which Africa's fecundity is conflated with a primitivism so virulent that it might well pull down western civilization.[14]

The silver lining to Africa's sorry state for American journalists was that its misery often underscored the heroism of white protagonists. The coverage of African famines rose with the 'We Are the World' concerts and album of 1985. The conservative *Reader's Digest* was particularly apt to feature white American heroes in abject Africa: Ambassador Smith Hempstone's stand against Kenya's administration; a US official's extraction of Americans from Rwanda in 1994; biologists thwarting African poachers.[15] 'A Continent's Slow Suicide,' whose title aptly summed up its content, presented excerpts from twelve authors on the sorry state of black Africa. Not one of them was a black African.[16]

The venerable *National Geographic* continued to appeal to a more sophisticated audience than the *Reader's Digest* even as it largely ignored modern Africans. During the 1970s it focused on: animals, western adventurers, 'the emergence of modern man' (a sort of *Roots* for white people), and the survival of exotic peoples, all of which elided Africa's problematic present.[17] 'Drought Threatens the Tuareg World,' seemed more concerned with threats to the nomadic group's traditional culture than to their survival.[18]

The *National Geographic* became more sensitive to the new Africa in the late 1970s and 1980s. A landmark occurred in 1980 with the publication of a piece written by a Ugandan woman and her white Canadian husband, Sarah and Jerry

Kambites. The couple described a nation determined to recover from the ravages of Idi Amin's rule, and they presented their family as a truly intercultural endeavor. By the mid-1980s a sort of new synthesis had emerged in which the magazine could dwell on traditional cultures without indulging in baldly racialist and racist clichés. Photographer Angela Fisher embodied this approach; the people she presented seemed arresting but relaxed and happy, collaborative subjects rather than specimens. The text and captions put more emphasis on the beauty and ingenuity of their adornments than on their peculiarity, 'an Africa that is exotic, romantic, and ritualistic,' as one scholar puts it.[19] By the late 1980s, the magazine was also blurring the line between white and black in Africa. A piece on the tsetse fly featured several photographs of black helpers: a 'field researcher' using a microscope in Kenya; 'a World Health Organization team' in Ivory Coast' testing blood samples; ground crews spraying DDT.[20]

But this trend was fleeting. Coverage of African politics dwindled after 'The Twilight of Apartheid' and 'Tragedy Stalks the Horn of Africa' appeared in 1993.[21] Right after Rwanda's genocide, *National Geographic* featured several major articles well removed from modern problems and prospects. An article on Rwanda dwelled on how the war affected mountain gorillas. The year closed with a tribute to Jane Goodall.[22]

Indeed, much American interest in Africa hinged on relationships that Goodall and her American counterpart Dian Fossey formed with African primates, not people. Fossey found amongst the mountain gorillas a sense of love and acceptance that had otherwise eluded her. She wrote of one early encounter: 'I was overwhelmed by the extraordinary depth of our rapport. The poignancy of her gift will never diminish,' she recalled in 1983. Of course a woman who couldn't bear to see a rabbit or chicken mistreated often found herself at odds with black Africans, few of whom viewed animals sentimentally. Fossey professed to understand that an African country such as Rwanda 'has problems far more urgent than the protection of wild animals.' However, in fact she practiced and justified extreme tactics to defend her animal friends. She recounted the capture of a poacher: 'We stripped him and spread eagled him outside my cabin and lashed the holy blue sweat out of him with nettle stalks and leaves, concentrating on the places where it might hurt a mite.'[23] Fossey complained loud and often to and about local authorities, pretended to be a witch, and hired her own cadre of armed game wardens. Her controversial methods resulted in her being asked to leave Africa for several years and may have contributed to her grisly death in 1985 after she returned.

Americans empathized much more with Fossey and 'her' gorillas than with the black Africans they lived among. When her beloved 'Digit' died in 1978, Walter Cronkite announced his death on the CBS Evening News. *Gorillas in the Mist* was widely read, and it became the basis of a (generally sympathetic) movie. 'Dian Fossey,' conclude conservationists Jonathan S. Adams and Thomas O. McShane, 'personifies the ideal conservationist: a dedicated white scientist forced to take a stand against vicious poachers, with only a few loyal Africans at her side.'[24]

Adams and McShane make a similar point about Mark and Delia Owens, a pair of American scientists who lived in Botswana for most of the 1970s, then moved to Zambia in 1986. Houghton Mifflin published three of their books. Like Fossey, the Owenses liked their Africa wild and argued for a rigid separation of wild animals and black Africans. Wrote Mark of their arrival: 'we feel special, as if we are the only two people in the universe.' 'The whole attitude,' remarked one observer, 'was "Nice continent. Pity about the Africans."' Chief Chifunda, whose people lost their land when the British created a nature park, observed of Mark: 'The man has an illness. He loves animals more than he loves people.'[25]

By the 1980s a growing number of tourists were seeking out the wild places and animals that Fossey and others had written about, like the hunters who followed in the wake of Teddy Roosevelt at the century's outset. Now the peak experience was not to demonstrate one's courage by facing down a charging lion in a deadly duel but rather to touch, to connect with not-so-distant cousins. When writer Jane McIlvaine McClary drew within six feet of a massive silverback gorilla, it was 'a glimpse of Eden, of the world as it once was.'[26] Journalist Aaron Latham wrote a highly self-conscious account of his saga in Africa; the title alone, *The Frozen Leopard: Hunting My Dark Heart in Africa*, 1991, referenced Hemingway and Conrad. The book's second line evoked St. John of the Cross: 'It was the rainy season in my soul.' Readers were well advised that Latham set out for Africa in desperate need of vivification. The animals delivered. After one day 'I feel very much at home here.' As an attendee of Fossey's lectures and reader of her books, he sought an intimate encounter with one of the magical silverbacks and was not disappointed. He: 'escaped from my ragged self and felt glorious,' had 'broken free of the bars of my own personality,' had moved 'outside the cage of self.' Later, among elephants, he 'escaped from myself again. … I was the elephants. The elephants were me.' Witnessing the death of a wildebeest released his suppressed grief for his deceased sister and left him sobbing. This, too, was Africa's gift: 'I had found her once again, found her in Africa where she had never been, but where all memory started, a place that lives on in all our memories.' Unlike the great white hunters from earlier in the century, Latham's spiritual awakening did not require killing. But it was still Africa's charismatic mega-fauna, not its people, that brought transcendence and healing.

Wild Africa also lay at the heart of Hollywood's redis-covery of the continent. *Out of Africa* of 1985 is one of modern Hollywood's most ambitious and pretentious treatments. Produced by Sydney Pollack and featuring two Hollywood icons, Meryl Streep and Robert Redford, it reprised Dineson's trek from Denmark to Kenya in 1913 and her coming of age in Kenya. Indeed, Africa is arguably the film's main character. Unlike Dineson's memoir, the film gives much more weight to her white lover than to black Africans. Disney's *A Far Off Place*, 1993, offered a story of white self-actualization in the Kalahari Desert. Young Harry, visiting with his American father, is bored until he and an independent-minded white girl (Norrie) join a young black native (Xhabo) in a long trek to bring some evil poachers to justice. Xhabo of course has a mystical relationship to nature and gradually initiates the jaded Harry into the Kalahari's mysteries. Harry learns to hunt and to care, and the three survive and thwart the poachers. Xhabo is one-dimensional if noble. His role, like the Kalahari Desert, is to lead the white American to maturity. In *Cheetah* (1989), too, a pair of white children visiting from California find adventure in East Africa when they join forces with a native boy to save a beloved animal from evil men.

Popular films on Africa in the 1990s reprised familiar themes. *Africa: The Serengeti* of 1994 focused on animals and illustrated the theme of Edenic Africa. Here is its opening line: 'There is a place on earth where it is still the morning of life, and the great herds run free. Life streams across a land suspended in time.' The only black Africans to appear are the ubiquitous Masai, who are presented sans modernity, a simple, happy, exotic people. 'They, too,' like the animals, 'follow a nomadic existence.' Disney decided that its 1999 rendition of *Tarzan* would 'sidestep the racial issue by not including blacks at all.'[27] Then there was *Lion King*, Disney's much loved animated blockbuster of 1994 which dispenses with people altogether in evoking a timeless Africa of sublime beauty—save for a sordid den of hyenas whose voices and mannerisms seem calculated to suggest American inner cities. The film's 'circle of life,' Columbia University philosopher Robert Gooding-Williams observes, contrasted with this 'underclass of black and Latino scavengers.'[28] The other side of the African coin was vividly portrayed in *Outbreak*, 1995. Most of the film takes place in California, where a band of heroes must rescue a town from a horrible virus. But early in the film we are taken to the virus' origin, deep in Zaire's sticky jungle, the heart of darkness where the landscape and its people are bizarre and threatening, a fitting birthplace for a ruthless and deadly virus.

Michael Crichton's 1980 bestseller *Congo* mined similar African tropes. On page one of the Prologue we learn that it is 'an alien place, inhospitable to man.' Out of this steaming morass has arisen an undiscovered sort of ape man, more fearsome than any other mammal. The American research team dropped into this 'indifferent immensity' (Crichton is quoting the nineteenth-century explorer Stanley here) must somehow survive these beasts and their grotesque home. Civilization eventually triumphs, even in the Congo. But it is a close call. Writer Richard Preston's *The Hot Zone*, 1994, covers much the same ground. A horrible disease, ebola, which dissolves people from the inside out, relentlessly oozes out of Africa. The novel, which sold over a million copies, closes: 'it will be back.'

Another best-seller from 1980 presented a very different sort of story. James A. Michener added to his long list of interminable and widely read area novels with *The Covenant*, an epic story tracing the history of three South African families—Zulu, Boer, and English—over several genera-tions. Michener, a liberal married to a Japanese-American woman, strongly criticized South Africa's racist heritage. Alan Paton, long the nation's leading white reformer, praised the book, and South Africa at first banned it.[29] *The Covenant* begins with a lengthy account of a bushman clan, and Michener makes clear that their rudimentary life should not be conflated with primitiveness. A frail arrow, for example, was a remarkable feat of engineering that could kill an elephant. 'Any being who had the intellect to devise this arrow could in time contrive ways to build a skyscraper or an airplane,' Michener informs us.

But there is no doubt where Michener's deepest interests and allegiances lie. The book's title betrays the Boer perspective, and as the story proceeds, Michener's lens becomes whiter, his condemnations of racism notwithstanding. By Chapter Two he is writing about Prince Henry the Navigator's interest in 'this dark and brooding continent.' European explorers and settlers and their descendants are, to be sure, racist and cruel. But they are also the center of the story. In fact when Michener spent some forty days in South Africa in 1978 interviewing a great number of subjects he did not meet with a single black leader.[30]

In mainstream American culture, then, Africa remained a dream-like place on which any number of fantasies or nightmares could be projected without interference from black Africans. Toto's 1982 hit song *Africa* aptly represented the fluid associations that the continent conjured up in white American minds. Keyboardist-vocalist David Paich was inspired to write the song while watching a documentary about suffering in Africa, images which prompted him 'to imagine how I'd feel about if I was there and what I'd do.' But the song suggests safaris, not starvation and disease: 'drums echoing'; 'the rains down in Africa'; 'Kilimanjaro rises … above the Serengeti.'[31] The soft-rock rhythm connotes nostalgia for a lost world, not abject children. Somehow the latter easily morphed into the former. Starvation and safari had become, in American pop culture, intertwined, with white Americans at the center of each.

SELF-ACTUALIZED WHITE MEN IN BLOODY AFRICA

Producers of white masculine fiction liked Africa precisely because its people and landscape struck them as savage. These writers posited a harrowing Africa ideally suited for bloody, often sexualized masculine quests, an Africa reminiscent of the original Tarzan—without Lord Greystoke's civilized side.

Red Scorpion, from 1988, produced by controversial lobbyist Jack Abramoff, features the spiritual transformation and bloody exploits of a muscular Communist fighting machine, Nikolai Rachenko. In fitting with Abramoff's patriotic credentials, the government or system rebelled against here is Soviet, not western. When Rachenko fails to take out a virtuous black African freedom fighter, he is tortured by the Soviets, escapes, and wanders in the desert. He is found by an old native man reminiscent of the protagonist from the South African film *The Gods Must Be Crazy* (1980) who restores him to physical and spiritual health, a process which culminates with Rachenko receiving a scorpion tattoo and flinging away his Soviet dog tags. Since he 'now knows who' the villains are, he returns to the rebels, grabs a gun, and yells, 'let's kick some ass.' With the camera focused on him, he leads the rebels into the Communist camp and destroys it.

Lawrence Sanders' *The Tangent Objective* and *The Tangent Factor*, published in 1976 and 1978, respectively, present Africa as a bloody rite of passage. Sanders' genre was popular crime and detective books, not nuanced explorations of African or, for that matter, American culture. His protagonist, Tangent, goes to Africa in the employ of a western oil company and, like Rachenko, goes native. His initiation begins with a six-hour game called 'the Hunt' in which he joins a group of soldiers who track a fleeing fellow soldier. Tangent finds himself entranced by the chase, learning how to walk softly and read and smell signs. As they close in on their prey, Tangent's clothes are drenched in sweat, 'his face ... rasped with vines, and his bare forearms and hands oozed blood from a dozen small cuts and insect bites. He didn't care.' When they at last espy their man, Tangent runs 'dementedly' and gets to see 'the hunted' struck down. The men form a gauntlet for the 'captive' to pass through. He makes his way between their blows slowly, to show his courage, his back 'suddenly riven with red.' Upon completion he is met with 'a great roar of approval,' then 'carried aloft in triumph.' Tangent's word for the exhibition: 'Thrilling.'

Tangent is particularly drawn to Captain Anokye, a quiet, ruthless soldier who will lead a coup to unseat the nation's corrupt ruler. Sanders lays considerable emphasis on Anokye's sexual prowess. His white lover is 'a continent conquered by his hard blows,' calls him 'her "king," and her "master."' In fact it is this lover, Yvonne Mayer, who tells Anokye that Tangent is backing him not just to gain a more favorable deal for his oil company, but because: '*You* excite him.' Tangent, like Mayer, is drawn to Anokye's 'sureness, your resolve, your ambition, your singlemindedness, your power. He senses all this, and he responds to it. ... There has been nothing of significance in his life until this.'

Professor Duclos is Anokye's opposite, an effete black intellectual and nationalist planning Anokye's new country, perhaps even a new black civilization. Duclos is ambivalent about blackness, is himself 'no darker than a suntanned white' and has a narrow nose and thin lips. Duclos is repulsed by his doting lover's 'coal-blackness,' 'corn-rowed' hair, 'wide-spread nose, protruding lips. Put bones through her ears, he thought, and brass rings about her neck, and she might paint her breasts and dance naked under the moon.' For Sanders, African inauthenticity is signified by lightening of skin and intellectualism. The book culminates with Anokye's storming of the palace, the adoring Tangent in his wake.

The sequel, *The Tangent Factor*, finds Tangent still employed by Starret Petroleum Corporation but now part of Anokye's inner circle. Tangent explains that he was at first attracted to the physical aspects of the continent, then the people, and now the African way of life ... The Soul of Africa,' such a contrast 'to my dull, unfeeling, mechanical world.' He takes, or is taken by, a beautiful Hausa woman. But Anokye remains his pivot. Watching him plan for battle, Tangent 'wondered if he would ever get to the end of this man.' Again, Tangent inserts himself into the final battle and is transformed. He wields his warrior's blade with the rest of the troops, 'until the enemy was not only dead but minced, shredded, hacked, kicked, stomped and made to vanish utterly from the earth.' Togo and Benin were defeated, Anokye's power expanded. Tangent returns to his wise lover

who 'with closed eyes, swollen lips, whispered obscenities into his ear.' Africa is freedom through transgression:
violence, sex, vulgarity.

The Tangent books are remarkable in their white protagonist's quasi-homoerotic worship of a powerful black man,
a desire reminiscent of white suburban teen males' fascination with black rappers and athletes. Black Africa is here the
fount of true manliness, of courage, of military and sexual
command, all rooted in primal, violent desires the West
has suppressed.

William Harrison was a much more serious novelist than
Sanders. He founded the Masters of Fine Arts program at the
University of Arkansas and was a highly regarded short-story
writer. But in three novels published from the late 1970s and
early 1980s his white protagonists revel in bloody Africa.
Africana, published in 1977, features three people who find
themselves, literally and figuratively, in Africa: Leo, from
Wales; Val, a writer from London; and Harry, a roughneck
from Texas. Leo is the most extreme of the three, a visionary
warrior given to long speeches about the evils of civilization
and the necessity of redemptive violence. He is more brutal
than the wild Africans he leads. 'Welcome to real savagery:
play this on your drums village to village, he was saying to the
continent. Beat out the news of my arrival and get my name
right.' The purpose of life was 'to stare over the edge into the
fucking abyss.' Val is a good match for Leo. She insists on her
lover taking her to Africa, and in the Congo yearns 'to copulate
out in the open where nature would offer the python, the
mosquito, or some great jungle beast as interference.' When

a leopard threatens to break into their hut, her lover freezes in terror as she dances, 'thrusting her hairy mound toward the leopard, holding her breasts in her hands.' Val soon discards this urbane partner for Leo, who assures her 'I'm the first real man you've ever met in your life.' Val agrees. Val eventually takes up with the massive Harry, and she leaves Africa upon becoming pregnant. But she will regret leaving Leo, 'my lost love, my intellect, my father, my commander, my husband, my leopard of the hills.' Leo, having reached the end of the line, walks on to a Kenya beach weighted down with weapons and ammunition and blasts away at the bathers, having decided to go out in a homicidal-suicidal blaze of glory. As he dies, 'the thorns and leaves and weedy undergrowths of the continent shuddered and replied; pathways and streams, ... moaned softly in response; the savannahs answered with their doleful notes; the rivers whispered in their courses.' Africa loves Leo.

Africana has little to do with Africans. The major players are all outsiders who are more savage and effectual in Africa than the Africans are. Historical events such as Lumumba's assassination and the Biafra War are merely props for Leo's blood-soaked self-actualization. Speaking to a group of Biafran university students during one of the greatest tragedies of the twentieth century, Leo urges them on to battle: 'Civilization—a weakened, failed, hopeless civilization—has tried to embarrass you and reason you away from the mystic fire and the primitive blood! But I say walk on fire! Spill blood again! Enter the darkness!' Staving off modernity, keeping Africa from numbing prosperity and looking 'like California,' was not a job for the faint of heart.

Savannah Blue, which appeared in 1981, also features a violent anti-modernist. Quintin Clare, a Kenyan of American, British, and Asian ancestry, is poisoning businessmen visiting the continent because he is 'at war with all the businessmen and traders who had invaded his domain and, as much as possible, with the century itself.' In his young adulthood he had assumed the political views of his father, a refugee from American academia: 'The western world meant to take away culture, adventure, personal freedom, the arts, true science, nature and any wild spirit; it meant to instill efficiency, production, conformity, comfort, and the consumer mentality.' Charles Hazo is a middle-aged professor who shares some of Clare's sensibilities, a CIA agent eager to get to Africa whenever he can because machines are making the work of spies obsolete: 'there were few dark continents remaining, few adventurers needed, and fewer mysteries requiring personal attention.' Black Africans, by way of contrast, were too 'easily bought off by any coin. ... few had any of the old, dark warrior blood.' Clare fought on behalf of 'raw, wild nature itself,' and for 'profound freedom,' to be loosed 'from the restraints of all convention, from love, perhaps from life itself ... a soul adventure' culminating 'in a spiritual ecstasy.' Hazo shares with the man he is hunting a compulsion to embark 'on those darker journeys which are forms of suicide in thin disguise.' Clare, like Leo at the close of *Africana*, is blessed with a warrior's death, and as he bleeds out he imagines that he is following the old rogue elephant, part of a 'ragged file' of 'creatures and men ... going to its distant oblivion.'

Harrison's third African novel, published in 1982, is a historical one that explores the friendship between two famous African explorers, Burton and Speke, and it also closely associates the continent with masculine nihilism: 'I want to go to Africa,' Speke tells Burton, 'to die.' But it is Burton who is the more accomplished man, inside and outside of Africa. His young fiancé after they make love for the first time 'wanted to pray to him like an idol.' Aboard ship for a second attempt at penetrating Africa's interior, he 'felt truly free for the first time in his life,' anticipating:

> primitive kingdoms, swarming armies, naked women, ivory, unknown beasts, gold mines, human sacrifices, primeval jungles, languages that were the original tongue of men, dreams from which civilization was born, ages from which the present age was only a mere shadow and dim reminder. ... A whole continent awaited.

When Burton is finished with Africa he is finished with life. Separated from Speke and the other men he had gone adventuring with, he is stuck in England with his suffocating white wife: 'led by a woman ... fixed at a desk like a burned-out star in a dead orbit. My life is over.' Africa is manly life for Harrison's protagonists.

Philip Caputo also wrote highly masculinist fiction set in Africa. After a decade writing for the *Chicago Tribune*, Caputo vaulted to prominence in 1977 with his widely read and respected memoir of his military service in Vietnam, *A Rumor of War*. Three years later his *Horn of Africa* featured a journalist, Charlie Gage, drawn into a covert US operation to arm African forces. Gage is disillusioned, passive, at sea. His opposite number in the operation, Jeremy Nordstrand, is a heavily muscled American disciple of Nietzsche, a restless anarchist in love with danger and violence, with raw power. The third major figure or archetype, Moody, is a sensitive British man out to redeem a mistake he made in his previous military service when he shot three prisoners of war. Gage is in Africa to find his nerve, Nordstrand to kill and to conquer, Moody to absolve himself from a bloody act of passion.

Nordstrand seems the most likely to find what he is looking for in this desolate corner of Ethiopia and the Sudan. 'This is where I've always wanted to be,' he enthuses. 'This is the place I've been looking for. I can feel it.' Toiling through the landscape is like 'a journey back to the age of man's beginnings.' The same 'blind ferocity that had created those awful mountains burned inside' Nordstrand, 'drove him on.' Here he will find 'the fiery climax he sought,' the chance to kill without reason and thereby become a sort of god. Nordstrand does just that. He cuts apart and beheads five captives, is creating 'a new realm of existence for myself out here' so that 'the whole goddamned world' will 'know there's at least one man on this fucking planet with the guts and the nerve to do anything he decides.' He is soon initiated into the Beni-Hamid by having his cheeks slashed open. He has become a white savage.

Gage's route to self-actualization is more complicated and problematic. As Nordstrand becomes more and more vicious, he realizes that the right thing to do would be to murder him. But he, like others, is drawn by Nordstrand's strength. When the long-awaited battle comes, though, Gage finds within himself a primitive warrior, recalling 'the time when our naked progenitors went at each other with clubs and rocks.' He became, at last, 'myself, totally myself, a man released from all doubts, anxieties, and inhibitions.' He runs down an Ethiopian soldier and breaks his neck with his own hands. This plucking of 'a deep and primal chord' bequeaths to Gage the capacity to see Nordstrand for what he is: 'neither madman nor monster, but the embodiment of all that was wrong with me, all that is wrong with our crippled natures.' And Gage eventually does what must be done: kills a fevered and wounded Nordstrand at the moment that these weaknesses had at last 'put him in contact with the current of human suffering that flows through the world,' a moment when Nordstrand at last felt the weight of his sins. The killing was, then, a double gift: Gage at last acts decisively, and Nordstrand is released from life while in a rare state of 'guilt and repentance.'

But remorseless Africa refuses to give Moody what he wants. He again shoots two men in a moment of rage, then, realizing that he 'had failed again the standard he tried to live by,' turns his gun on himself. 'His flaw wasn't the streak of irrational violence' that kept surprising him, but rather 'his inability to accept that part of himself.' Win, lose, or draw, Africa forced your deepest self to the fore.[32] Like the great white hunters from the early decades of the century, or Hollywood's post-war protagonists, these men could slide along in life for decades in the flaccid West without revealing who they were until implacable, relentless Africa unmasked their cowardice or courage, exposed their essential natures that soft modernity had obscured and domesticated.

As literature professor Brenda Cooper argues in her aptly entitled *Weary Sons of Conrad: White Fiction against the Grain of Africa's Dark Heart*, even highly educated and ostensibly sensitive white male authors struggled, though not as hard as they might have, to escape the hoary tradition of white male quests in darkest Africa. T.C. Boyle is one of her leading exhibits.[33]

On the face of things, Boyle's *Water Music*, first published in 1981, seems a far cry from the blood and sperm-soaked Africa of Sanders and Harrison. True, it purports to be a historical novel of a heroic and tragic explorer of Africa, Mungo Park. But Boyle's Park is often shown to be an egomaniacal bumbler whose chestnuts are pulled out of the fire by his well-read Mandingo friend, Johnson. Park, moreover, shares top billing with a cockroach of a man, London low-life Ned Rise, who ends up as part of Park's last expedition as a convict and shows himself to be the better explorer of the two. As for sexual prowess, Park's great African conquest is a mountainous North African woman. True, black Africans are often depicted as savages, but then so are Londoners. *Water Music*, in sum, is a spoof.

But, as in *Henderson the Rain King*, 1959, spoofs often have a point, and there is a good case to be made that *Water Music* is more of an exercise in adolescent male fantasy than is Bellow's book from some two decades before. As Cooper points out, Boyle presents himself inside and outside of his fiction as a bad-boy searcher whose personality and outlook was forged in the rebellious 1960s. His depiction of Park is of an adventurer who, true to the genre, associates women with dull domesticity. This takes us to the heart of the matter. Park may be fool and Rise a knave, but these white males, as in the clueless protagonists of so many popular sitcoms and movies, are still at the center of the story. Boyle's use of irony should not distract the reader from recognizing that, at heart, this is the same old story: bold and solitary white men self-actualizing in savage Africa.[34]

Sanders, Harrison, Caputo, and Boyle were four very different writers who appealed to different classes or types of readers. But their work shared much in common. None of them evidently spent much time in Africa, and their African novels are little concerned with black Africans. Though abjuring the explicitly racist representations of their earlier counterparts, black Africans are backdrops in these white masculine quests of orgiastic violence requiring a setting so savage that only Africa will suffice.

WHITE SELVES DECONSTRUCTED

As before, writers who had sustained contact and friendships with African people often created relational and nuanced accounts. These memoirists and novelists, many of them former Peace Corps Volunteers, created a rich body of work in the 1980s and early 1990s that described Africans deconstructing, rather than confirming, their preconceptions of personal identity.

The feminine exception that proves the rule is Barbara Kingsolver's polemical and highly acclaimed *The Poisonwood Bible*, published in 1998 and shortlisted for the Pulitzer Prize. The novel follows the lives of an evangelical Baptist missionary family that moves to the Congo in 1959 and is written from the point of view of four diverse daughters and their long-suffering mother, Orleanna Price. The rigid patriarch, Nathan, is the odd man out here, literally and figuratively. The five females adjust, more or less, to life in the jungle. Daughter Leah progressively becomes the novel's moral authority; she is wise enough to learn from Africans. 'I wish the people back home reading magazine stories about dancing cannibals could see something as ordinary as Anatole's clean white shirt and kind eyes, or Mama Mwanza with her children,' she remarks. Leah eventually becomes Anatole's wife, which she describes as 'a very long convalescence' after the traumas of her childhood. Through her we learn of the western world's continued exploitation of the Congolese, particularly its support of the dictatorial Mobutu who supplanted the saintly Lumumba, assassinated with the active assistance of the US.

The novel is ethnocentric. Lumumba's government and Congolese characters must be without flaw because they represent, as literature professor Kimberly Koza observes, a 'backdrop for working out essentially American concerns.'[35] Historian Diane Kunz characterizes *The Poisonwood Bible* as 'a simple morality play: Africa was a premodern Garden of Eden' that fell 'not from corruption within but because of European sin without.'[36] All the sinners—and interesting people—in this book are white, and the best of them, Leah, aspires to become black, '[t]o scrub the hundred years' war off this white skin till there's nothing left and I can walk out among my neighbors wearing raw sinew and bone, like they do.' She will 'leave my house one day unmarked by whiteness and walk on a compassionate earth,' for 'time erases whiteness altogether.' Kingsolver's Congo is the anti-America, an Eden where even the unbearable burden of whiteness dissolves.[37]

Lesser known women authors who spent substantial time in Africa wrote more truthful and morally complex fiction. Roberta Warrick, whose pen name was Maria Thomas, joined the Peace Corps in the early 1970s with her husband 'because of not being able to find anything else to do.'[38] She lived in Ethiopia, Nigeria, Tanzania, Kenya, and Liberia, and her fiction features highly diverse and realistically rendered African and western characters.

Thomas' Africa seldom provides what its western protagonists seek. The American couple in 'Come to Africa and Save Your Marriage,' published in a 1987 collection of short stories, drift apart. The Texas veterinarian who left for Kenya feeling 'like a combination Connecticut Yankee in King Arthur's court and Albert Schweitzer' kills a man while playing at bumping Africans on bicycles. The white physician protagonist of *Antonia Saw the Oryx First*, also published in 1987, was born in Tanganyika, feels at home in East Africa, but knows that the hospital's 'filth and disarray' were unredeemable: 'she had to accept it or get out.'

Knowing black Africans is the compensation for Africa's privations and absurdities. They are no longer 'the shadows behind you cleaning up, washing thousands of sheets and

dishes, hands bringing you things, carrying your stuff.'
Antonia forms an improbable friendship with a young black
African who assists her in her work, and the story becomes
Esther's, too. Antonia, despite herself, becomes entranced
by the little healer whose powers defy science and logic. The
metaphor of 'touch' figures strongly in the novel. Esther's
touch entails, in the African tradition, '[q]uite literally, challenging the universe, changing the way things were. A disease
materialized, falling away to the floor.' She prompts Antonia
to realize that she 'had lost touch,' merely 'looked at patients.'
The Africa of Esther and Antonia is not the sharply defined
images of heavily beaded nomads and stark vistas but the more
complicated terrain of interracial friendships and understandings, 'an Africa seen from within rather than from without.'[39]

Thomas' Africa is relational and feminine, allusive and
elusive. Her characters are interior, feminine doubles of the
solitary males that populate Caputo's *Horn of Africa* and Harrison's bloody fiction. The male existentialists face their demons
through violent confrontation—risking their lives, killing,
being killed. Thomas' protagonists, black as well as white, risk
their equilibrium for a chance to touch life more deeply and
vulnerably. 'Abdullah and Mariam' reveals an elderly Islamic
couple who have cared for each other despite their inability
to have children, a deep shame for them both. Mariam ran
away from her parents in Dar es Salaam as a young girl to care
for her beloved while Abdullah languished in a prison in the
Congo: 'they had precious debts to each other.'

Warrick herself was deeply committed to an Africa she
often found problematic. In an autobiographical short story

published in 1991, she wrote that to go to Ethiopia in the early 1970s 'was to drop suddenly, not back in time to when men lived as primitives, romantic, close to Eden, but to an area that reflected, like a mirror, the real condition of our species.' One was surrounded by beautiful 'women in white veils' and 'a child rushing toward you who has nothing left of his face,' all of it 'governed by some holy mathematic that I never figured out.' In *Antonia*, the protagonist reflects that she stays in Tanzania because of 'a world opening out behind her in the textures of silence. … This was her depth.' In a 1987 interview the author remarked that '[o]ne of the problems' of living in Africa 'is the realization that you're never going to understand the people you're living among.' Yet her 'greatest fear is eventually having to leave for good.'[40]

The short story 'Second Rains,' 1987, is a particularly compelling story of Africa's 'holy mathematics.' Charlotte is an attractive foreign-service worker not many years from retirement when assigned to Ethiopia in 1972. 'She had a stock portfolio. She wasn't worried about anything,' Thomas assures us. There, for the first time, she dates a local man, Kassahun, a widowed father of two young children. She finds herself attracted to his dignity and honesty. He eventually proposes, but explains that he is 'doing this to protect my children. I want them to have an American mother.' She feels used. He explains that he is not asking her for himself. The emperor will soon die, and he is likely to be killed by the new regime. He wants a way out for his children. '"You want me as an insurance policy against famines and coups, is that it?" She laughed.' '"Yes," he admitted. "But it isn't for *me*." He thought that made a difference. He amazed her, awakened her, when she thought she knew it all.' She decides that night to marry him. Her American neighbor's objection ends with this warning: 'How can you do it, marry the fate of this horrible country.' Charlotte moves to Kassahun's compound and blooms. She learns Amaharic ('each new phrase was a gift'), worries about her children, makes plans with Kassahun for retirement. Then Selassie is deposed. Executions ensue. Kassahun is arrested and thrown in prison, just as he had predicted. But his wife refuses to leave with his children, as he had planned. 'This is my home now,' she pleads, 'I want to be an Ethiopian.' 'She was,' Thomas explains, 'a romantic.' Her husband is not: 'You don't understand Ethiopians. Don't even try. We're not worth it. I warn you, get my sons out of here.' She decides to leave only when she sees the corpse of a twelve-year-old on their street. She visits the proper authorities, makes the necessary bribes, and maneuvers her children through the airport and onto the plane. She leaves Ethiopia no longer thinking that 'she knew it all.'

Africa, despite or because of its tremendous challenges, is where Thomas' most endearing and enduring white protagonists are both at home and unable to live. Some of her characters are too racist or frightened to stand Africa, like the well-meaning white woman in *Antonia* who 'wanted the trip but it turned out that dark people bothered her. And that was hard to admit.' But even those who commit themselves fully to the place are exiled in the end. Africa brought 'an inevitable loss of idealism.'[41] It humbled. There is a whiff of declension in her writing—and life. 'After 20 years of trying,' she remarked from Liberia in 1987 of her aid work, 'it seems as though it has all been a failure. You have the sense of a flame dying out.'[42] That same year she wrote of Isak Dinesen's classic question: 'Will Africa remember me?' Thomas' answer: 'of course, … "No."'[43] Two years later she and her husband died in a plane crash, on their way to a refugee camp on the border of Ethiopia and Sudan. But if Africa never quite managed to be home for Thomas or her white protagonists, the relationships they found there deepened and humanized them in a way that life in the US had not.

Much of the fiction of Eileen Drew is devoted to puncturing the idea that white Americans can be at home in black Africa. A respected if less widely known author than Thomas, this daughter of a diplomat grew up in West and North Africa as well as Korea and the US and then returned to Africa as a Peace Corps Volunteer. The teenaged girl protagonist of the 1989 short story 'Blue Taxis' is living for the summer in Accra, Ghana, where her father is in the foreign service. She is bored, comfortable, flirting cautiously with her Ghanaian tennis instructor. Then one day she takes a taxi and finds that the other passenger is angry with her:

> Always without worries, without cares, so high in your skyscrapers and airplanes, your homes like botanical gardens. Your father keeps you comfortable, isn't it? He puts gold on your fingers, and your mother hangs traditional masks in your parlor. I've seen your houses, I've been inside them to see. You think nothing can happen here because you are white. White people can't

AFRICAN, AMERICAN

be poor in Africa. You never get our problems, there's
nothing can touch that watery skin.

She tries to flee, but he confronts her alongside the road,
orders her to beg on her knees and 'tell me that you are shit
and your father is shit and your mother is shit and England is
shit and your life is shit,' or he will beat her, rape her, maybe
attack her father. She stammers out the words, then runs to
a different taxi. Crying, she tells the new taxi driver what
had happened. And he sympathizes, shakes his head, says
'[t]hose men are bad.' 'He was the kind of African I loved.'
The next day she watches Kwame, her athletic instructor,
interact carefully with the ambassador, and then deftly fend
off her flirtations; becoming romantically involved with a
young white woman of privilege could not end well for him.
Now, many years later, 'I have to respect that man in the taxi.
Everything about him was honest, from his wire rim glasses
to his aching hate.' Drew's 1996 novel *The Ivory Crocodile*
features a protagonist named Nicole Spark who, like the
author, had returned to Africa as an adult after spending
much of her childhood wishing that she could get beyond
the chain-link fence of her privileges 'to live among Africans
in the endless bush.' That quest proves to be, at best, futile.
The book closes with the death from a botched abortion of
a student she had befriended and whose independence she
had encouraged. Sparks had been determined to escape her
'American impulse to exploit, to exoticize what lurks beyond
the fence.' She failed. But ten years after again leaving Africa,
her African friends 'refuse to fade; they temper who I am.'

Drew's female protagonists want to connect with Africa and Africans on their own terms, endeavors complicated both by privileges they cannot shed and by the often unpredictable agency of black Africans.

Wendy Belcher, who spent much of her childhood in Ghana and Ethiopia, also wrote a novel, *Honey from the Lion*, published in 1988, in which the protagonist grows up feeling 'caught between' America and Africa and 'hoped by my return to this African country to free myself.' Before she can even get out of the airport, however, Ghana exposes her ignorance and privileges, the first of many such episodes in her missionary experience. But these painful experiences bequeath to her a sense of humility and generosity, the germs of a more fruitful life.

Some male novelists also explored the painful dissolution of white selves and sensibilities in Africa. Norman Rush drew on his five years in southern Africa in writing short stories, including three published in *The New Yorker*, and a novel that won the National Book Award. All are rife with irony and moral complexity. 'Bruns', published in his 1992 collection, *Whites*, features a sensitive Dutch volunteer who confounds South Africans by his generous treatment of black people. He evidently chooses to martyr himself rather than fight back when a powerful Boer man beats him, but his death causes no end of problems for the very people he professed to love. An aging diplomat in 'Official Americans' cannot find a way to shut up his powerful black neighbor's dogs, which come to symbolize his dis-ease in Africa. They are keeping him awake, driving him mad. Desperate for relief, he submits himself to an indigenous ritual that nearly kills him. But the feel of a knife cutting his skin also gives him, at last, 'the sensation of conviction.' He survives, and finds out that the dogs no longer bother him. Perhaps the healing worked. In 'Alone in Africa' another diplomat, his wife away, finds himself confronted by an attractive young Botswana woman who comes to his house to seduce him. He tries to control and contain this opportunity. 'If this was going to happen, sobeit, but it was going to be with reasonable amenity and taking an amount of time worth the risk he was running.' But a succession of disasters ensues, not the least of which is the young woman's assertive nature. Then her younger siblings turn up. A sanctimonious white neighbor investigates, and the protagonist fears a scandal. But the young woman disarms all of these land mines while the object of her affections founders. At last he has them all out of the house, has somehow survived the prospect of being caught, of losing his job, and endangering his marriage. He lays down on his bed, is near sleep, when there's a scraping at the window. 'She was back.' Rush's black Africans rearrange relationships in unpredictable ways.

Mating, Rush's 1992 novel, features an archetypal white protagonist whose African quest ends badly. A brilliant but obsessive graduate student discards eighteen months of dissertation research on nutritional anthropology for Africa's promise. Here are the book's first two sentences: 'In Africa, you want more, I think. People get avid.' Once in South Africa she is soon obsessed with Denoon, a famous American academic who has been pursuing his own African dream: a secretive utopian community in the desert called Tsau.

Though, as its title implies, *Mating* is first of all a study of romantic relationships, Africa is integral to its plot and content. As in his short stories, it destabilizes white identities and expectations. During a sudden sand rain, the protagonist remarks: 'all I could think was Africa! What next!' Hence Denoon's utopia is fated to fail. To avoid being just another western imperialist or manipulator he must step back and let Africans lead. This works well enough until more men filter into Tsau, opposition to him builds, and he is blamed for the disappearance of his principal adversary. Tsau and Denoon unravel. The protagonist now feels trapped by Africa. She wants to shout at the villagers: 'You are consigning me to a boring position.' A near-death experience takes away Denoon's critical edge, the intellect that had made him attractive to her. He has discovered that 'Consciousness is bliss,' reads nothing but the *Tao Te Ching*, dresses in dazzling white, avoids eating meat, has become 'like the Basarwa are, apologizing to the animals they kill and praising the totem of the genus.' Her plan to 'restore him' and thereby 'restore me' is lost. She finds him a new lover, one younger, more beautiful, and less intellectual than herself. Denoon returns to Tsau. She returns to Stanford. Africa has sorted the parts of this couple to where they belong, though Denoon had to lose his mind to be at home.

As with Thomas' protagonists, Africa has both expelled her and made her unfit for life in the West. She appropriates her experience and Denoon's ideas to achieve academic success and respect. But: 'Being in America is like being stabbed to death with a butter knife by a weakling.' She is a poser among fools eager to believe reassuring stories of Africa she knows to be false.

These subtle, often disturbing fictional works by white Americans who had lived in Africa for years were joined in the late twentieth century by dozens of memoirs from returned Peace Corps Volunteers. The best of them rode the razor's edge of ambivalence, of belonging and not belonging, revelation and desperation, suggesting how deeply it cut. These young Americans struggled both to belong and to confront their privileges, contradictory impulses that often left them transformed if seldom transcendent.

Sarah Erdman joined the Peace Corps late in the 1990s hoping to start 'my life there from scratch' only to find that she had brought with her incredible privileges, as she wrote in her 2003 memoir. An African friend soon confronted her with their radically different fates: 'We die all the time here. Africans just keep dying.' She then asked, with a 'frantic note in her voice': 'Why am I black and you white?' Erdman's mumbled response 'about both being the same in the end' rang false. Indeed, after many frustrating months of trying to fit in, she realized that her very reasons for coming to Côte d'Ivoire set her apart: 'I have the liberty to be an idealist, a romantic. ... I'm here to suck the marrow out of life, but I have the luxury to leave when I wish.' Her quest to begin 'my life ... from scratch' was ridiculous.

Monique Maria Schmidt's quest, 'a utopia' that would 'consume all my thoughts and energy,' was also incongruous in West Africa late in the 1990s.[44] Benin, she wrote in her 2005 memoir, confronted her with a 'barrage of sexual advances, the eternal heat, the never ending screams of beaten children, the polio beggars, the AIDS victims, the women with clits sewn shut, the husbandless woman with three children and no food' and 'the latrine battles and the discipline battles and the intestinal battles, … and the loneliness.' 'I had thought,' Schmidt recalls, 'I was invincible.' One of the girls she had poured herself into is found raped and bleeding shortly after Schmidt leaves. 'I have never "gotten over" my Peace Corps experience' she wrote years later. Africa brought not transcendence but submergence in sufferings easily elided in the US.

George Packer, the son of a distinguished academic and now a public intellectual, wrote one of the most incisive memoirs. In *The Village of Waiting*, 1988, he recounted that he joined the Peace Corps because 'I wanted to leave the path for a while.' Instead, his path led him into new dilemmas.

Packer wanted desperately to belong in Togo but remained an alien. He was not surprised to learn that 'yovo,' the word that children constantly flung at him, could be translated as '"cunning dog."' So '*yovo* got into my brain and became an evil word, the single most evil word I heard in Africa, with a dozen nuances: derision, hostility, inanity, a mocking reminder of wealth, an unwillingness to learn my name, to see past my skin color. It was an introduction to being a privileged minority.' His monthly salary, paltry by American standards, 'amounted to a peasant family's annual income,' but he had been told not to give away money and create dependency. He was outraged when some of his ample possessions were stolen, hurt when the village seemed uninterested in

221

finding the thief. The culprit turned out to be his hostess'
ne'er do well son: 'They had to protect a boy who, though
the family thought him a rotten papaya and cursed his birth,
could not be thrown out, for he was flesh and blood. And I?
A stranger, an ill-cut patch sewn temporarily onto the tight
fabric of relations in the village.' In fact this insight made
Togo all the more compelling to Packer. Unlike efficient but
impersonal America, Togo required dependable social relationships; 'things personal somehow survived and muddled
through, against the grimmest odds.' Yet Packer could never
really be part of this.

He came home 'prematurely aged'; having stepped 'off
the path,' he could not get back on track. 'The rational, moral
world into which I had been born, and in which my own place
was taken for granted, had crumbled,' he recalled in 2000.
He argued with his mother over the deeper meaning of *Heart
of Darkness*, which she interpreted as a study in 'the need
for self-restraint.' He countered that Kurtz 'became a killer'
precisely because he 'was a liberal,' and had buried rather than
confronted his 'irrational and destructive forces.' Son and
mother were really arguing about 'my parents' view,' which
'had failed me over there.' Nor could he forget the sadness and
futility of Togo, for he had 'left behind in Africa an obligation
I can neither fulfill nor escape.' Letters kept arriving, news 'so
invariably sad that they lie on my desk for days before I can
bring myself to open them,' he wrote in 1988. The tragedies
never stopped. Yet he was homesick for the village where he
had felt so out of place: 'I missed the intensity, the surprise,
the sense that life was real and hard and lovely.'

Mike Tidwell went to Africa, to Zaire, in 1985 expecting to be 'stripped nearly naked of my own culture' so that he would 'travel my inner continent,' he recalled in 1990. His first insights were not comforting. Despite his riches, he did not share as readily as the other villagers, a greedy impulse that he realized was connected to a deeper problem, his desire 'to take as much from this African world as I could, to learn and experience, without surrendering any large part of myself.' Then the rainy season came, and 'the number of people dying in the villages made me shake.' A man he was teaching to fish farm named his son after him, then insisted that he mark this honor by eating a whole chicken, though 'the rest of the family hadn't tasted fresh meat for weeks.' These paradoxes eventually drove Tidwell to alcoholism. 'You can't,' he explained, 'without injury, attend two hundred funerals in two years and watch stooped elderly people approach your house begging for gasoline to pour on aching teeth. You can't without inner lacerations, take a two-month-old diarrhetic baby in your arms and listen while the parents tell you his name is your name. Living amid such things is like drinking the local water. Sooner or later you pay.'

Josh Swiller came to a village in Zambia in 1994 hoping 'to find a place past deafness,' for 'I'd already looked everywhere else,' he wrote in 2007. It worked. The villagers found Swiller exotic primarily because of his color and nationality; his deafness, for the first time in his life, was beside the point. They were, moreover, warm and welcoming: 'never in my life had I felt so integrated into a place.' But 'then almost immediately I learned how … irrelevant my self-absorbed

searching was.'[45] In the rainy season 'children started dying
in droves.' Swiller felt out of his depth, helpless in the face of
the villagers' great faith in the white man from America. 'Our
first three sons died,' a friend told him over a meal, 'but we
know you will keep our last alive.' Swiller also experienced
the underside of social solidarity. A mob captured a killer and
delightedly tore him apart. A boy's leg was severed for stealing
a fish. Swiller's friend Jere convinced him to build a medical
clinic, but their hard work became worse than pointless when
a local politician appropriated the project, stole the building
materials, and coated the walls with lye, killing some patients
and permanently poisoning the building. Swiller's anger over
such problems got him and Jere thrown out of the village, and
enabled him to see, 'for the first time, how much they must
have hated me.' Three months and a bout of malaria later, he
was back in the US. His last conversation with Jere, his closest
Zambian friend, left much unsaid. 'Remember me,' Jere
asked. 'Remember? How could I ever forget? I will meet other
men, remarkable men in this life, but you, there will never be
anyone like you.' Losing touch with Jere after leaving Zambia
became 'the great frustration of my life,' a sort of microcosm
of Swiller's African transformation—and expulsion.[46]

The best of these memoirs, like Swiller's, are not just
interested in what Africa means to them. They also struggle
to fathom the lives of the Africans they lived among. They
form deeply meaningful, if often challenging, friendships.
But it is this empathy that often persuaded them that even
as Africa brought them closer to the core of life, to a much
greater degree of self-awareness, it would inevitably spit them

out. So Packer went home early, Swiller was expelled from the very village where he had at last felt as if he belonged, then lost his dear friend.

Tony D'Souza, who became a prominent novelist and journalist, also found much more than he wanted to in Africa upon arriving in 2000. The son of an East Indian father and a white American mother who had served in the Peace Corps had broadly counter-cultural goals: 'to travel,' protest capitalism, be close to nature, 'experience black Africa, for adventure, a challenge, to be able to brag about being in the Peace Corps for the rest of my life, to do something good in the world.' Instead, in Cote d'Ivoire he 'abused my position as a whiteman to get things or get away with things,' from making 'a kid get me a cigarette' to much worse. Like Conrad before him, 'I found my own heart of darkness in Cote d'Ivoire, found that the darkness was in me.' The war 'excited and attracted' him, a realization that left him profoundly dismayed. The Peace Corps taught him 'that I had fucked up, and that human life is fucked up.'[47]

D'Souza poured this pain into *Whiteman*, a highly auto-biographical novel published in 2006. As the title suggests, the protagonist, relief worker Jack Diaz, realizes early on that the central fact of his existence in the Ivory Coast is his color. No amount of language training, name changes, or even a willingness to take up arms and die with the villagers would change the fact that 'this was a place I did not belong and, more than that, a place where they would not let me belong.' Diaz's struggles with sexual desire illustrate his incongruity. Painfully aware that every mature male mammal in the village seems to be having regular sex but him, after much effort he is able to convince a young woman to kiss, but when he attempts intercourse she flees or fights him off, then leaves the village to marry. Finally, a year later, Jack thinks everything has changed. The language and customs are more familiar, and he successfully woos Djamilla, a beautiful young Peul woman. Then, on the brink of this improbable marriage, he abandons her. His next lover, a savvy prostitute, has already had her heart broken: her daughter, her 'best and only thing,' had died. She confronts Diaz with his privilege: 'Oh man, why is this the life? Why is it? Why is one rich and the other poor? Why is one black and the other white?' Diaz persists in trying to go native. He gives away his western possessions, toils in the fields, goes hunting, and learns witchcraft. But this takes him too far. He kills a woman and, when warfare breaks out, leaves to wander around other parts of war-torn Africa, perhaps remembering the words of his former Peace Corps supervisor shortly before she returned to the US: 'I've liked who I am here. I don't know who I'll be back there anymore. … I'm going to be lonely back there.' For Diaz, like D'Souza, Africa has revealed that he will never be at home.

Women volunteers, in the main, seemed more able to integrate African sociality into their post-Africa lives. Susan Lowerre in her 1991 memoir *Under the Neem Tree* describes how her early days in a Senegal village in the mid-1980s were spent enduring the taunts of children who threw stones at her house, chanted '*tubab*' (white man) at her, and overturned her trash for the pleasure of watching her pick it up. 'The whole land seemed to jeer at me, the white woman who knew nothing, who did not belong in this country—but the children did it deliberately and wickedly, and they were as inescapable as the flies.' Then she fell dangerously ill and had to come back to the US. After fighting for the right to return, the villagers disappointed her by 'saying with glee that I had forgotten their language.' She came down with an awful fever and had to leave again, this time for good. But this leave-taking was much more meaningful. The family she had been closest to sang her a song: 'Love, it hurts. It comes from God. ... If you leave I will cry, if you leave I will cry, if you leave I will cry, but when you return I will be happy.' Meg Sullivan, too, followed her account of enduring frustrations and humiliations in Kenya during the early 1990s by detailing the warmth of her students and neighbors. Leaving them required taking 'the gift of their pain, and yours, for that is love.'[48] Margaret Szumowski, who volunteered in Zaire and Ethiopia in the mid-1970s, most valued 'our friendships, the friendships with Africans,' a warmth that helped her to feel that: 'Living in Africa was having a look at the heart of things.'[49] Kris Holloway celebrated an especially close friendship with a midwife named Monique in Mali. She and her husband returned to Mali upon Monique's death to research her life story, published in 2007 as *Monique and the Mango Rains*, and arrange for her three children to go to school.[50] Allison Flynn Fitzpatrick left her high-pressured sales job in Los Angeles for two years in Botswana, where she enjoyed 'life with accepting, kindly people, with spontaneous singing and joyful dancing.' Upon returning, she 'longed for the easy, the communality of my life in Africa' and moved back home to Connecticut to work for a non-profit. 'Family and roots and comfortable connective tissue were what Africa taught me to value.'[51]

Perhaps the abundant memoirs produced by so many Peace Corps returnees is an artifact of being separated from that 'connective tissue.' Anthropologist Sharon Abramowitz, a Peace Corps volunteer in Cote D'Ivoire from 2000 to 2002, remarks that the modern US frustrates this basic need for sociality: 'Our fundamental desire, as human being, is to be close to others, and our society does not allow for that.' Hence Peace Corps Volunteers commonly become depressed upon leaving their materially poor but socially rich communities in developing countries for the wealthy, atomized US.[52]

Ethnomusicologist John Miller Chernoff is a leading example of a white American who invited Africans to recon-struct his view of the world. As the title of his classic *African Rhythm and African Sensibility* from 1979 implies, he found that learning how to perform and to understand West African drumming required, above all, listening and waiting. Like Theroux, Chernoff asked himself: 'What am I doing here?' Rather than respond with introspection and pessimism, he made himself at home by becoming more deeply involved with Africans. Since both learning and performing African music were highly social activities, personal commitment to African musicians and communities brought rapid progress. Children began calling him by his first name 'because you have made yourself low to us. That is respect.' 'Music-making in Africa,' he concludes, 'is above all an occasion for the demonstration of character.' Human beings, then, were not, as modern westerners believed, captains of their own ships, atomized individuals. Rather: 'a person is what others see him to be and ... he finds himself insofar as he is accessible to their influence.' The self was porous.

It is highly suggestive, then, that Chernoff's other two books are not reflections on his explorations of Africa, but rather episodes from the life of an intelligent, resourceful but obscure young West African woman—never named—who lived by her wits. In his lengthy introduction to *Hustling Is Not Stealing: Stories of an African Bar Girl*, 2003, Chernoff argues that positing modern Africa as a violent, chaotic jungle serves to problematize and keep it at arm's length. But 'the people I met in West Africa were the best reason for the years I spent there.' Africa was not so much a place to discover or to perfect one's self as a place to allow one's self, and one's entire conception of self, to be shaped by remarkable people.

Chernoff notes that western accounts of Africa seldom feature such Africans. Unlike most American journalists, observers paid to present the American public with the spectacles of suffering it demanded, writers such as Chernoff and Thomas were drawn into the rich and engaging lives of ordinary Africans, people who transformed their assumptions about identity and purpose, who challenged the American Dream of lives pursued within silos of untethered selves.

GENDERED AFROCENTRISMS

In the mid-1970s an extraordinarily popular and powerful book and mini-series boosted African-American interest in

Africa to an extent not seen since Garvey's United Negro Improvement Association half a century before. Alex Haley's 1976 novel *Roots* won millions of readers, and the TV mini-series had some 130 million viewers, more than half of the country. The compelling saga dovetailed with the inward turn of American popular culture, black as well as white. As literary scholar David Chioni Moore puts it: *Roots* asked Americans to ponder 'who you really are. Perhaps no image of identity is more compelling in the present age.'[53]

The book describes a rigorous but idealized African childhood. Kunta Kinte's village is a self-contained world of stiff challenges modulated by warm, all-encompassing relationships. There are seasons of famine, and the harmattan winds prompted even the Mandinkas to bickering. 'It seemed to Kunta,' by age seven, 'that his people were always enduring one hardship or another.' But this is a minor theme. Villagers treat each other with reverence and care. There are no armed rivalries between groups. The village and its environs are a womb. But as he walks away from his favorite place, on the limb of 'an ancient mangrove tree' where 'everything he could see and hear and smell from the top of this tree had been here for longer than men's memories, and would be here long after he and his sons and his son's sons had joined their ancestors,' he is torn away by a white slave catcher.

Roots the miniseries of 1977 made West Africa still more familiar and idyllic. The Mandinka village is full of familiar people such as Cicely Tyson and Maya Angelou. There is little dirt or dust or blood, let alone hardship. The villagers are gentle. The leader of the manhood training explains to the initiates that they must use violence very judiciously, even if attacked: 'we believe not in death but in life.' Again, the slavers even in West Africa's interior are white, not black, a historical anomaly congruent with Haley's Edenic depiction of black American origins.[54]

Haley's wildly popular saga was a signal event in the spread of Afrocentrism, of what Austin terms '*integrationist* black nationalism.' As opposed to Pan-Africanists who had argued and worked toward actual economic and political affiliations between black Africa and America, Afrocentrism asserted the sort of 'symbolic ethnicity' commonly articulated by ethnic groups upon achieving major aspects of the American Dream of prosperity and acceptance. Adherence to Afrocentrism correlated with high incomes and especially higher educa-tion. Its determination to locate the heart of African culture in Ancient Egypt suggested an internalization of European norms as to what constituted an ideal state. Austin cites the career trajectory of Maulena Karenga, the radical black nationalist who led US in the late 1960s and early 1970s, then emerged from prison more focused on culture. He became best known for inventing Kwanzaa, the black holiday.[55] As historian Elizabeth Pleck points out, Kwanzaa by the 1980s had morphed into a celebration of black middle-class identity and consumerism, the sort of 'symbolic ethnicity' that enabled celebrants 'to "feel black" while residing in a largely white suburb and/or attending a largely white university.'[56] Indeed, the locus of black radicalism and Pan-Africanism shifted in the 1970s and 1980s to university campuses, where scholars such as Molefi Kete Asante at Temple University oversaw extensive programs of Afrocentric research, publication, and teaching. In sum, educated African-Americans had become less likely to claim Africa as a place to live or to defend politically, more likely to stake a more symbolic affiliation to the continent, a gesture of 'therapeutic essentialism,' as English professor Ann Ducille puts it.[57]

By the 1970s the growing black middle class, its substantial political and economic gains notwithstanding, increasingly posited Africa as an alternative home in an America that continued to treat them as interlopers. But this affinity for Africa was frequently abstract, rhetorical, a matter of style.

Essence, the magazine for successful black American women founded in 1970, often featured commercialized Afrocentrism. "'I Thee Wed'" began by identifying 'African-inspired dresses' as one way of 'saying to the world, "This is the way we are."'" The piece both elided attachment to any particular African place, since 'we have a continent to pick from,' and provided the names of particular US merchants.[58] Somali supermodel Iman was on the cover of a 1980 issue largely devoted to Africa, which included a piece on African-themed home furnishings and the names and addresses of the US businesses selling them. *Essence* promoted a black, feminine version of 'the American dream of individualism' and fulfillment through consumption.[59]

A variety of black American artists expressed Afrocentrism in the late twentieth century. Wise Intelligent of the Poor Righteous Teachers rap group contrasted 'warm [black] people' with '[t]hese cold people, these cold hearted, cold blooded [white] people.' 'It's time to take off the red, white and blue,' he concluded. 'Time to put on the red, black, and green,' the colors of Black Liberation.[60] Likewise, hip-hop artist Sister Soujah contrasted 'one dimensional, flat, and pale' white women with 'multidimensional, round and creative' black women, 'the women through whom all life that exists on this earth, all human life came through our womb.'[61] Photographer Chester Higgins, Jr. set himself to the work described in the title of his massive 1994 book: *Feeling the Spirit: Searching the World for the People of Africa*, pairing photographs of black people in Africa and the US suggestive and illustrative of cultural parallels, such as a Muslim man tending his drums in Senegal on the same page as a New York City vendor barbequing chicken in Harlem.

Black American children's authors were particularly susceptible to representing Africa as timeless. For example, Eloise Greenfield's 1977 picture book, *African Dream*, featured an African-American child who falls asleep:

And landed in Africa
Long-ago Africa

She goes to a city that resembles North Africa to shop '[f]or pearls and perfume,' reads old books about Egypt and visits '[t]all stone buildings,' with pyramids in the distance. There are donkeys and camels. Growing tired, her 'long-ago grandma,' who closely resembles her mother, holds her and rocks her, and the book closes.[62]

Not all children's books by black Americans portrayed Africa in such an idealized, rustic fashion. Margy Burns

Knight and Mark Melnicove's *Africa Is Not a Country*, 2000, pointed out that only 10% of the continent was rainforest and depicted African children in cities and watching television. Rita Williams-Garcia's 2004 *No Laughter Here*, intended for older readers, tackled the cultural complexities of female genital mutilation through the friendship of a Nigerian and an African-American girl.

But most picture books intended for black American children evoke an ancient Africa that is a source of strength in the long and often painful history of black Americans, the touchstone of African-American culture and life.[63] In contrast, by the 1970s modern Africa presented black Americans with thorny complexities.

To be sure, the great majority of African-Americans could agree in condemning Africa's remaining white regimes. In 1972 the inaugural African Liberation Day in Washington DC drew up to 30,000 people. A few years later black American leaders founded TransAfrica, a powerful anti-apartheid group that enjoyed broad support in the black community. The movement for divesting in and imposing sanctions on South Africa became powerful on American campuses among black and white students alike, peaking in the mid-1980s with impressive legislative victories, before apartheid finally crumbled in the early 1990s. *Ebony* grew increasingly critical of American policy toward Africa in these years.[64]

But black Americans often disagreed over how to approach and characterize Africa's black-led nations. Travel writer Eddy L. Harris came to Africa with high hopes: 'Africa was suddenly like a magnet drawing me close, important in ways that I cannot explain, rising in my subconscious and inviting me,' he recalled in 1993. Like 'perhaps … every person with black skin,' he had deeply ingrained images: 'Africa as motherland. Africa as a source of black pride, a place of black dignity.' But his time there underscored an uncomfortable truth: 'I am not African.' Expelled from Mauritania for taking photographs, he soon tired of being immersed in poverty and fending off beggars. 'I felt a little as Jesus must have felt, surrounded by misery, approached at every turn by lepers wanting a miracle from me, beggars after a meal, jobless men wanting to go to America.' He was offended that so many black Africans wanted to lighten their skin and change their facial features and that they would neither accept him as one of their own nor grant him the same privileges afforded white westerners. Harris concluded that Africans were incredibly resilient and deserved assistance. 'But Africa is not home. I hardly know this place at all.' Keith Richburg, a reporter for the *Washington Post*, came to Africa in 1992 hoping to force American politicians to pay attention to the continent but soon soured on it. He was put off by its prejudices and corruptions, as well as the hypocrisy of black American radicals who pretended that these problems did not exist and fraternized with corrupt or brutal African leaders. Richburg did not hate 'Africa or the Africans' but rather 'the senseless brutality, the waste of human life … the way repressive systems strip decent people of their dignity,' he remarked in 1997. 'In America,' he concluded, 'I may feel like an alien, but in Africa I *am* an alien.' He cannot help, then, 'celebrating the passage of my ancestor who made it out.' Richburg's book received a great deal of criticism from black Americans. Tunde Adeleke, a Nigeri-an-born scholar based in the US and an outspoken critic of Afrocentrism, argued both that Richburg had 'made erroneous and silly statements that made him seem racist' and that he had hit a nerve; like DuBois early in the century, black American radicals were reluctant to confront abuses committed by black African heads of state.[65] One of Richburg's many examples is Jesse Jackson's praise of Nigerian President Ibrahim Babangida, a leader widely criticized for his abuse of political power and human rights.

Black American women seemed less apt to sanctify or demonize Africa than their male counterparts. *Essence*, founded in 1970 to appeal to the growing population of black American women of means, approached Africa more warmly. Unlike *Ebony*, its male-dominated and more conservative counterpart, it at first reflected 'a 1970s Black nationalist rhetoric and discourse.'[66] An early column by Karama Fufuka described how she and her husband chose African names to 'cast off much of the European mind-conditioning that has been forced on us.' 'We are,' she concluded, 'an *African* people and this concept has become the guiding principle of our life.'[67] *Essence* was much more likely than *Ebony* to publish the work of African writers. In 1976 it published 'The Mermaid,' a short story set in Nigeria by Ode Okore. Two years later a long article on South Africa featured extensive interviews in which black South African prostitutes described their struggles. Herb Boyd in 1977 took *Roots*, the mini-series, to task for using American actors and speech in its representation of Africa. Kofi Quaye tackled 'The African Stereotype.'[68]

Essence also confronted unflattering aspects of black Africa that *Ebony* elided, particularly male dominance. The 1980 issue on Africa featured pieces on both the brutalities of Idi Amin and the imperfections of Kwame Nkrumah. In 1985 it featured three excerpts from the book *Sisterhood Is Global*, treatments by women of South Africa, Nigeria, and Ghana that addressed aspects of women's subordination. Dr. Gwyned Simpson, a psychologist, kissed the ground when she at least reached 'the motherland' but was soon put off by what she found in Ghana, including male dominance and privilege.[69] Marriage to African men presented many challenges. A lengthy article by Marita Golden Kayode on such relationships described how one of her interviewees learned that in Senegal 'the person cannot exist as an individual.' Extensive social commitments both supported and intruded upon the lives of black American wives. 'I was losing myself by living here,' she concluded. Black American women married to African men and living in Africa often felt that they remained outsiders even as they struggled to adjust to more hierarchical and patriarchal social systems. Husbands seemed more attuned to the needs of their birth families than to the needs of their wives. But much of the adjustment, as with Golden's, had to do with negotiating a new definition of identity and self. One wife was taken aback that her Nigerian husband expected her to eat Nigerian food. Another reported that her husband was offended that she had not learned his language, but 'I feel I have to hold on to what I was and knew before. There's a lot to be said for keeping your own roots intact.' For this administrator at a Nigerian university, eleven years into marriage with a Nigerian man, roots meant maintaining her American culture, not a Haleyesque African homecoming. Golden concluded the article by recounting her own discovery that 'intense personal growth and change' was incompatible with her marriage. Her closing piece of advice underscored her fundamentally American point of view: women's adjustments to such marriages 'must be made alone.'[70]

Golden explored the tension between her American identity and intermarriage to an African man fully in her memoir, *Migrations of the Heart*. Coming of age as Black Power and Pan-Africanism crested, Golden upset her father by letting her hair grow naturally, then found herself swept up by a Nigerian man, Femi, whose 'presence was obtrusive and irresistible,' she recalled. 'I'd read about my past,' she noted in her 1983 memoir, 'and now it sat across from me.' For Golden, marrying an African and moving to Africa offered the prospect of healing. She, Femi, and his brother talked long into the night to unravel the stereotypes that had separated black Americans and Africans, '[s]parks of revelation and admission of sin bouncing among us as we moved toward understanding.' An ominous note sounded when she first told Femi that she loved him. 'It's not enough for you to love me,' he retorted. 'You can't love just me alone. You must love my mother, my father, my family.' Though this challenge made her feel 'fear ... like an electric bolt,' she imagined being 'pressed against their bosom,' leaving behind 'this cosmic loneliness, the disconnectedness' brought on by her parents' deaths on top of the struggle to be a black woman in white America.

But marriage to an African man in Africa stretched Golden too far. Her fundamental duty was 'to set the stage on which' his life would 'unfold.' But she had difficulty accepting that their marriage was secondary to larger kin obligations. Her pregnancy emboldened her to teach about feminism at the university and write for publication. Fearing that Femi's indifference would 'kill the new me bursting forth,' she took a lover, endured a beating, and escaped with their son back to the US, where she could focus more fully on self-actualizing. In the end, this woman who had been 'saved' from a chaotic childhood by reading 'all of Jane Austen and Charlotte Brontë,' made the quintessentially American turn inward, away from an African marriage in Africa.

Indeed, in Golden's 1986 novel *A Woman's Place*, the well-educated African-American woman radical who goes to Africa remains single, and her life in Africa remains very woman-focused, even as she is more 'permanent guest' than black sister. Research of black Americans living in Ghana in the late 1980s in fact found that most felt socially but not culturally integrated and more concerned than their African hosts with matters of personal identity.[71]

The black American protagonist in Florence Ladd's 1997 novel *Sarah's Psalm* continually wrestles with this tension between the personal and the collective. Sarah Stewart, child of the black bourgeois, a brilliant graduate student, has been drawn to Senegal from a young age and goes there not simply for her dissertation research on a brilliant author but to pursue 'my own liberation, the freedom to be my authentic self.' Ibrahim Mangane, the writer she had come to study, overwhelms her, and when his wife dies she turns her back on academic security and America to make a life with him in Senegal. Mangane expects a helpmate. As she is folded into the great man's life, she feels as if 'I was drowning.' Yet mothering proves to be deeply rewarding, and by the time her husband and step-son tragically die she has begun to find her own way, working with village women in Chad that her husband had viewed largely as backdrops for his films. She becomes at home in Senegal as a facilitator of Pan-Africanist womanism, even as her African-born son decides he is more at home in the US. Sarah's achievement is hard-won, the result of many years of sacrifices and disappointments, and it is more social than ideological. *Sarah's Psalm*, remarks literature professor Eileen Julien, illustrates that 'building political solidarity with women across class and national boundaries around women's felt needs ... is firmer ground than identity politics.'[72]

Julien describes the fraught romances of Ladd, Golden, and Angelou as progressions toward complexity and integration. Each woman, or her protagonist, is immediately swept off her feet by the power that male African leaders exude, a raw sexuality not available to black American men after centuries of enduring American racism. Living in Africa with these men inevitably entails disillusionment; the husbands and Africa expect sacrifices of their American selves that they are not prepared to offer up. Yet these selves emerge deeper and wiser. These are 'narratives of maturity, of success in coming to see individuals and societies in multiple dimensions.'[73]

The most widely read and celebrated black American writer of the 1970s and 1980s, Alice Walker, expressed much less complex views of Africa and Africans. 'The Diary of an African Nun,' an early short story published in the 1967 collection *In Love and Trouble*, features a suppressed black African protagonist. '"[C]ivilized" by American missionaries,' she always wears her habit, bathes 'in cold water,' and obeys her white superiors. But she has more sensuous, more African, desires. 'Must I still tremble at the thought of the passions stifled beneath this voluminous rustling snow!' As the bride of Christ, should she tell Christ of the delights of the African earth? She resolves to 'help muffle' the village drums, to teach 'my people ... how to die.' Unlike so many actual African Christians, Walker's nun brooks no syncretism, no hybridity of cultures. Africa is warmth and life. The West and Christianity are cold and dead.[74]

Walker's view of Africa became less rosy as she discovered that modern Africa often failed to meet her progressive western standards. The highly popular *The Color Purple* novel and movie appeared in 1982 and 1985, respectively, the former winning the Pulitzer Prize and National Book Award, the latter being nominated for eleven Oscars, though winning none. The protagonist's sister, Nettie, ends up being adopted by black missionaries who go to Liberia, and Nettie's letters to Celie provide a commentary on that place. She is disturbed by its stratification, the lack of educational opportunities for girls and respect for women, by Africans' unwillingness to take any responsibility for the enslavement of her African-American ancestors.

Later books more explicitly criticized Africa. *The Temple of My Familiar*, a 1989 novel, contrasts a woman-led, utopian

Africa with the violent patriarchies that supplanted them. *Possessing the Secret of Joy*, published in 1992, came to Walker during the filming of *The Color Purple*. A beautiful Kenyan actor had caused Walker to think about how 'little girls were being forced under the shards of unwashed glass, tin-can tops, rusty razors and dull knives of traditional circumciser.' So Walker wrote a book on women's sexuality to combat the practice of genital mutilation. It felt like her duty, for: 'I do not know from what part of Africa my African ancestors came, and so I claim the continent.' Walker was by this time perhaps the most influential black writer in the world, and her blunt criticism of black Africa constituted a major rupture in Pan-African solidarity.

Africans have found her claim to speak for and moralize toward Africa presumptuous. Kadiatu Kanneh, a literary scholar, is troubled that Walker draws so heavily from her own Eurocentric 'unconscious' in establishing 'a universal feminine Unconscious' that diverse African cultures are measured against and found wanting.[75] As for many of her male counterparts, Walker's idealized Africa is bound to disappoint, in part because its roots are more western than African.

Other leading black American women novelists incorporated African culture into their work through deep explorations of African-American culture. Paule Marshall, child of Barbadian immigrants, continually weaves connections between black people of the US, Caribbean, and West Africa. Caribbean academic Velma Pollard observes that the term 'submarine' unity coined by Caribbean scholar Edward Brathwaite aptly captures Marshall's subtle Afrocentricism.[76]

Both *The Chosen Place, The Timeless People* of 1969 and *Praise-song for the Widow* of 1983 are saturated with African culture. *The Chosen Place* is prefaced by an aphorism of the Tiv of West Africa. The very title of *Praisesong* references a common African ritual. A key scene reprises an oral tradition of enslaved Ibos who, upon arriving in coastal South Carolina, turned around and walked back to Africa, a story the protagonist remembers from her great-aunt. This memory moves this repressed, middle-class black American toward an appreciation of her African heritage and self as she begins crossing literal and metaphorical waters. Both novels are rife with rituals and with casual African references to Africa: 'a face that might have been sculpted by some bold and liberal Bantu hand'; palm trees with 'fronds tossing in the wind like headdress of a Tutsi warrior,' a face that resembled 'a Benin mask or a sculpted thirteenth-century Ifé head.' The history of slavery and a rebellion led by Cuffee Ned constantly inform the island's life in *The Chosen Place*, and the place is located as close to Africa as a Caribbean Island can be, awash in a 'perpetually aggrieved sea which, … continued to grieve and rage over the ancient wrong' of slavery that 'it could neither forget nor forgive.' At the novel's close Merle, a passionate and radical local woman, decides to go to Africa to attempt a relationship with her son and a rapprochement with her former husband, a Ugandan she had met in England. She will be flying there not through London, but backward in time: to Trinidad, then on to Recife in Brazil, and from Recife, that city where 'the great arm of the hemisphere reaches out toward the massive shoulder of Africa as though yearning to be joined to it as it had surely been in the beginning' to Dakar, and then to Kampala. Then she will return to the island to take up the ancient fight for her people against oppressive economic and political forces.[77]

Praisesong's transformations are also informed by deep, Pan-African histories. When Avey Johnson unaccountably steps off her cruise ship and onto a Caribbean Island, she has begun the process of retracing her steps, reversing the march away from her childhood and culture that her hard-working husband had undertaken as the price of entry into middle-class prosperity, the repression of emotion and pleasure and music. At the book's end she is resolved to take up the house the great-aunt had left her, a place to bring her grandchildren and other children to pass down the sacred story of the Ibos that had been told to her.

Remembering and cultivating an African past, then, is a social and political act. The journeys of Marshall's protagonists, notes professor of literature Missy Dehn Kubitschek, are 'no longer an isolated if perhaps lengthy incident in the quester's life but a lifelong commitment and, ... a continuous modification of identity.'[78] Their Pan-Africanism is grounded in the archaeology of kinship, of lineage.

Gloria Naylor emerged as a powerful and popular novelist in the 1980s, and *Mama Day*, 1989, features a matrifocal community redolent with West African antecedents. Kelley characterizes Naylor as an evoker of an 'Africana womanism' employed for human liberation.[79] Indeed, the mythical Island of Willow Springs is the closest locale in the US to Africa, a place where the usual American standards are inverted:

the key historical figure is a slave woman; women have more power than men; African-Americans covet darker skin. This is a highly woman-centered Afrocentrism.[80]

Mama Day's male protagonist, George, is a good man but represents the modern African-American's rootlessness and soullessness. When the woman he loves, Baby Girl, takes him home to Willow Springs, he cannot find his rhythm and pays with his life. 'Words spoken here,' he realizes too late, 'operated … through a whole morass of history and circumstances that I was not privy to.' As in Marshall's *Chosen Place*, storms and history roll into Willow Springs from 'the shores of Africa … Restless and disturbed, no land in front of it, no land in back, it draws up the ocean vapor and rains fall like tears.' It is Baby Girl's great-aunt, Mama Day, who shapes and adapts to these powers, who teaches a new generation the necessity of bending one's life to the requirements of community, love, and—inevitably—loss and pain.

A highly ethical and feminine Afrocentrism also lies at the heart of some of the most celebrated novels of Toni Morrison, winner of both the Nobel and Pulitzer Prizes. Morrison draws on a strong knowledge of African culture, religion, and folk tales. In *Song of Solomon*, 1977, black people can fly, as in Africa. In *Beloved*, published a decade later, in 1987, people are more powerful after death, as spirits, than they were while alive, as in Africa.[81]

As with Naylor and Marshall, Morrison's Afrocentrism is not academic or abstract, is not simply the assertion of an identity. It has a community-oriented, moral core. The wisest characters are deeply committed to caring for each other no matter how difficult the circumstances. Milkman, the protagonist of *Song of Solomon*, is pampered and heedless. The love of women and hard experience form him into a more compassionate and courageous man who is determined to find his kin and to be worthy of good people's love and trust. Life is to be survived with the help of others, not transcended on one's own. *Beloved*'s couple, Sethe and Paul D, are each engaged in the 'work of beating back the past,' as slavery exposed them to repeated and horrific cruelties and choices, including the one on which so much of the book turns: is it better to kill your daughter than for her to survive and be re-enslaved? The hard truth of life is: 'That anybody white could take your whole self for anything that came to mind. Not just work, kill, or maim you, but dirty you.' But Paul D comes to understand that this is not quite true. Those who survive can choose to forgive and care for each other. The answer comes from the old man, Stamp Paid, in response to Paul D's anguished question: 'Tell me this one thing. How much is a nigger supposed to take? Tell me. How much?' Stamp Paid replies: 'All he can.'[82] Culture and history embody pain, but also a tradition of coming to terms with and surviving it.

The Afrocentrism of Marshall, Naylor, and Morrison, then, is imbricated not only in their stories' material culture and rituals. It is also embedded in an ethical and spiritual sensibility that is relentlessly social and inclusive, not just a dash of Egyptology here and Swahili there but a deep anthropology of collective and hybridized memory, of shared suffering and survival. This feminine Afrocentrism is organic, not invented.[83]

Life imitated art when the efforts of academics on both sides of the Atlantic Ocean brought Mary Moran of coastal Georgia to Sierra Leone in 1997 to sing a mourning song with Bendu Jabati that the two women and their ancestors had kept alive, an event commemorated a year later in the film *The Language You Cry In*. Moran's ancestor had taken the song with her across the ocean upon being captured and enslaved some three centuries before. Back in Sierra Leone, where Moran's ancestors had once lived, the same song had been passed down to Jabati. Suffering and mourning and surviving against the odds were in their DNA. So Moran and Jabati sang and wept together. A Mende elder explained: 'To cry over your dead, you always go back to your mother tongue, the language you cry in.' One can imagine Moran as a character in the work of Marshall, Naylor, or Morrison, novelists who evoke an Afrocentrism of love and resilience in the face of fragmentation and suffering.

Gender strongly shaped American views of Africa in the twentieth century's last three decades. This was particularly true of Afrocentrists. Black American men posited a more abstract and theoretical version than women novelists, who fashioned deeper, more organic continuities with Africa. Popular white male novelists turned Africa's purported savagery and hopelessness to the advantage of male protagonists who required extreme, ungoverned physical and moral landscapes in which to self-actualize. White women novelists and men who were former Peace Corps Volunteers were much more likely to feature Americans whose sense of self dissolved in Africa, a necessary if shattering transformation.

There was, then, a very strong contrast between the Africa presented to Americans through popular media and the Africa experienced by people who went to and lingered in Africa. The Africa of most Americans was bifurcated between timeless and hopeless: *The Lion King* and *Roots* on the one hand, famine and genocide on the other. But those who spent years in African villages reported a very different and compelling Africa, one that often splintered their quests and the assumptions behind them, replacing them with more compelling if unsettling ways of approaching and pursuing one's life.

Africa and Africans would become more and more difficult to ignore on both sides of the Atlantic Ocean after the millennium's turn.

CHAPTER FIVE

AFRICA COSMOPOLITAN IN THE NEW MILLENNIUM

Three major, intertwined events have marked and reshaped America in the early twenty-first century. The 11 September 2001 attacks brought a surge of foreign wars whose consequences, at home and abroad, remain far from clear. The election of a black US President in 2008 gladdened and appalled major sections of the American electorate, exacerbating political divisions that led eight years later to the improbable ascendance of a narcissistic and coarse reality-TV star to the status of the US President elect. All three events suggest an America that has become increasingly polarized and agitated.

The 9/11 attacks infused Americans' long-standing sense of exceptionalism with anxiety and rage. Fear of and prejudice toward Muslims in particular and outsiders in general rose steadily in the US from 2002, particularly among

Republicans. Wariness of outsiders meshed with a renewed sense of America's distinctiveness and virtuousness. A 2010 Gallup poll recorded that four out of five agreed that the US has 'a unique character that makes it the greatest country in the world.'[1] Confronted with the fact that the US push for war with Iraq put it at odds with the rest of the world, Fox News' conservative pundit Bill O'Reilly had a ready explanation: 'Well, everywhere else in the world lies.'[2]

Political, social, and cultural divides widened in the new century. For less-educated white Americans, whose economic prospects have languished since the 1970s, the threat of terrorism seemed of a piece with other unwelcome developments: racial and ethnic diversity and a black President. For more educated and prosperous white Americans, cosmopolitanism has become a mark of distinction, even superiority. Black America also divided in the new millennium. As journalist Eugene Robinson points out in *Disintegration*, the infusion of large numbers of black immigrants from Africa and the Caribbean since the late twentieth century has contributed to other divisions among African-Americans, particularly around class. As before, Afrocentrism most often appeals to more educated black Americans who are less likely than their poorer counterparts to be immersed in black social environments, professionals who often feel alienated from the very American mainstream they seem to have joined. Poorer black Americans are both more likely to experience African immigrants as economic competitors and less likely to be interested in Africa. For them, Harlem is 'African-Americans' Africa.'[3]

In sum, educated Americans of means, black or white, were more disposed than their poorer counterparts to express interest in Africa. For black Americans it still held out the prospect of home, for whites a canvas on which to demonstrate and develop one's sensitivity, 'the benevolence and inevitability of American hegemony,' as historian Larry Grubbs puts it in *Secular Missionaries*.[4] After 9/11, observed prominent economist William Easterly: 'We had this sudden awareness that there were all these people out there who hated us, and we needed people who, as far as we know, don't hate us, and are in great need and we can help.' Africa's suffering, its supposedly patent neediness and helplessness, filled an 'existential vacuum,' for a public 'antsy to feel its goodness and influence.'[5] *New York Times* columnist Nicholas Kristof learned that the secret to drawing attention to suffering in the developing world was to link an attractive victim with a heroic 'bridge character,' an American protagonist 'who's off in the middle of nowhere' saving lives.[6]

But the Africa that twenty-first-century Americans encountered, abroad and at home, was changing quickly. The fifteen years following 1995 saw the most substantial median growth in per capita GDP since 1960, and in the early 2010s many of the world's fastest growing economies were in Africa. More and more countries achieved political stability. The number of highly educated Africans inside and outside the continent was skyrocketing, and many of them were making themselves heard.[7]

In the third millennium of the Common Era, America's growing number of Africa-bound questers have had to come to terms with both Africa's modernity and modern Africans.

THE PERSISTENCE OF WHITE QUESTS

The biggest news out of Africa in the twenty-first century was largely a non-event: an ebola outbreak that was confined to a handful of small African nations. Most Americans ignored the contagion until they feared that it would spread from Africa, whereupon they widely exaggerated its extent and threat. In the absence of epidemics or other atrocities, news of Africa dwindled. The amount of time devoted to Africa during network news shows, never high, plummeted by a factor of about three from the 1980s to the 2000s. A majority of these infrequent treatments featured Americans, and Africans seldom appeared in a flattering light. Hence when journalist Alan Huffman arrived in Liberia he was startled to find that 'most people are remarkably friendly and crime is typically the petty kind.'[8] The news from Africa he had absorbed in the US left him unprepared for a safe and pleasant visit.

Hollywood regained its interest in Africa in the twenty-first century, but the films almost invariably feature white protagonists, often aided by admiring black Africans. *Hotel Rwanda*, a 2004 film nominated for several Academy Awards, was in some ways a departure. The film's protagonist was the hotel's African manager, Paul Rusabegina, though played by the well-known American actor Don Cheadle. The film has been criticized for oversimplifying the complex historical, political, social, and cultural roots of the genocide and for trying to reduce the horrible tragedy to one person's story. *Sometimes in April*, Haitian-born filmmaker's Raoel Peck's 2005 offering, is much more nuanced and realistic. But *Hotel Rwanda* stood alone among major Hollywood movies until 2016 in its focus on black Africa and black Africans, including a noble black protagonist who is easy to empathize with. The film paid a price for its Afrocentrism at the box office, as acclaim from critics and Academy Award nominations were barely enough to lift it into the top 100 films of the year in the US for 2004.[9]

Other films about Africa were more likely to cast major black characters into the 'Magic Negro' role that became so common for black Americans in twenty-first-century American films, with black Africans providing guidance and encouragement for white vision quests.[10] In *The Ghost and the Darkness*, 1996, another rendition of the battle at Tsavo between British railroad builders and man-eating lions, Samuel comes to the aid of Colonel John Henry Patterson (Val Kilmer), protecting him from Africa's many dangers and then imparting to him the courage to stand up to them. Samuel is also the narrator who relates Patterson's African transformation. *The Four Feathers* of 2002, another American film about British colonialism, is set in the treacherous Sudan of the 1880s, where Harry Faversham (Heath Ledger) hopes to prove himself worthy of his fiancée's (Kate Hudson) respect. The massive Abou Fatma befriends and ministers to Faversham and helps him to escape the fiendish Mahdi. They part, but the African's gifts will stay with him. Back at his sweetheart's side, he quotes his devout Muslim friend on why he has never stopped loving her: 'God put you in my way.' The magic black African had done his work.

Africans hardly play even supporting roles in the Bruce Willis 2003 action movie *Tears of the Sun*. Willis plays A.K.

Waters, a jaded lieutenant who leads a SEAL team on a rescue of some western humanitarian workers during a Nigerian coup. He tells a pious priest: 'God already left Africa.' And in fact it would certainly seem so, given the way in which black Africans are hacking off each other's heads and other body parts. But then the white woman doctor whom he has saved against her will shames him into turning their helicopter around and going back to rescue the black Africans. 'I broke my own rule,' he later explains. 'I started to give a fuck.' One of the film's key moments is when Waters stands in the midst of a burning village, with sad music in the background, and soaks up all the suffering, all the death. This empathy brings him much adoration from: the beautiful young doctor; his men, black and white; and the black Africans he is trying to save. In fact when one of them, the son of the recently assassinated president, stops to grieve a dead companion, Waters tells him 'to become a fuckin' man. ... Now cowboy the fuck up.' With enough bullets, rockets, and explosions careening across the screen to annihilate a small army, Waters leads the key players to safety.

In one of the era's few films to feature a female protagonist, it is Africa itself that seems to exercise agency. In the aptly entitled *I Dreamed of Africa* (2000), jaded Italian socialite Kuki Gallman (Kim Bassinger) retreats to East Africa, works hard, and, accompanied by a soaring musical score, finds herself. Even the death of her beloved son, bitten by a poisonous snake, cannot shake her love for her home: 'We came to this extraordinary place, and Africa let us lead extraordinary lives, then Africa claimed an extraordinary price. That was Africa's privilege. And now it is my privilege to look after Africa herself.' Gallman does this by teaching the local black Africans not to poach and otherwise devoting herself to African conservation. Africa has given her a sense of purpose. Black Africans are mere backdrops.

It is the best-known movie about Africa of the new millennium, *Blood Diamond* of 2006, which most clearly spells out the incidental roles of black Africans. To be sure, one of the major characters is a very likeable Sierra Leoneian, Solomon Vandy, who joins Maddy Bowen, a western reporter, and Danny Archer, a white Zimbabwean arms smuggler, in an unlikely alliance that includes a search for Vandy's son, who has been forced to become a child soldier in West Africa. The film is also notable for implicating western actors (diamond traders) in West Africa's political miseries. But the film fails to rise above its many trite precursors in two respects. First, nearly every black African in the movie is either a pathetic victim or a psychotic killer. Second, the movie is not about Vandy or any other black character. It is about bad boy Archer (Leonardo DiCaprio). Archer dies nobly so that Vandy can reunite his family and Bowen can unmask the western world's complicity in the brutal war. The film's climax arrives with Archer bleeding out, gazing at the beautiful continent that he adores, intoning the film's mantra: 'This is Africa.' Vandy is noble and boring, too simple a man to notice, let alone expound upon, sublime Africa. When he finally is front and center, introduced to an admiring white audience, the film ends right before he is to begin his speech, a silence that speaks volumes about his role in the movie.

Lord of War, 2005, resembles *Blood Diamond* in many respects. Endorsed by Amnesty International, its ostensible message is to depict the horrible impact of arms trafficking and the West's complicity in it. The protagonist, Yuri Orlov (played by Nicholas Cage), is a Russian immigrant, a likable brother, husband, and father whose character is progressively corroded by his participation in the arms trade. By the film's end Orlov has got his brother killed and been disowned by his parents. His wife has taken their son and walked out. 'I would tell you to go to hell,' intones his nemesis, the international agent who finally catches him. 'But I think you're already there.' Orlov, unlike *Blood Diamond*'s bad boy, remains evil. But the movie is all about him, not Africa. The most finely drawn African character is the American-educated Andre Baptiste, a Liberal leader who literally shoots his own soldiers for practice, a man whose son eats still-beating hearts to absorb their deceased owners' strength. Here, again, is a landscape full of corpses and wild-eyed, crazy Africans butchering women and children.

Black Hawk Down of 2001 simply celebrates the bravery and character of US soldiers killed in Mogadishu in 1992. Somalians are irrational and bloodthirsty swarms. As one of the few allowed to speak puts it thus: 'In Somalia, killing is negotiation.' Conflict films depict black Africans as innocent doves or ravenous lions, guileless victims or sadistic killers. The only well-rounded characters, the only people who grow and develop, are white.

Transplanted Americans were the heroes of reality shows filmed in Africa, including *Survivor, The Amazing Race*, and

National Geographic's *Worlds Apart*. Such shows presented the continent as an undifferentiated whole. 'Africa' provided ample opportunities not only to compete for prizes, but to self-actualize through communing with nature, learning Maasai customs and to love 'mother Africa,' caring for village children, and savoring one's privileges. As cultural anthropologists Laura Hubbard and Kathryn Mathers remark: 'Africa again recedes to the backdrop as the contestants come face to face with themselves.'[11]

The Legend of Tarzan, a big-budget film released in 2016, managed to turn the legendary vine swinger into a (albeit heavily muscled) social worker. By the film's end he has not only defeated King Leopold's attempts to plunder the Congo and enslave its inhabitants but has healed ruptures between his beloved homeland's human and animal residents, an effort that keeps this white man, as before, squarely in the middle of this purportedly African story, loved and celebrated by man and beast.

At the millennium's turn the *National Geographic* presented extensive coverage of American Michael Fay's 'greatest adventure of all time,' as they claimed in their 2001 TV show of the expedition: *Africa Extreme*. Ostensibly a scientific expedition for the Wildlife Conservation Society to research Central Africa's 'still pristine forests,' the accounts read more like a sort of vision quest. The opening photograph of a shirtless Fay striding across a jungle stream with black porters in his wake meshed with Quammen's description of him as 'a postmodern redneck who chews Red Man tobacco, disdains political correctness,' and, most important of all,

'views the landscape of modern America with cold loathing.'
Fay explains: 'I plan on dying out here, … I'll never go back to
live in the US.' In the second installment, nine months into
the expedition, Fay's party is fighting exhaustion, disease,
and the prospect of ebola, all of which underscored Fay's
steely resolve: 'He had begun to remind me of a half-mad,
half-brilliant military commander gone awol into wars of his
own choosing,' remarks Quammen, in an excerpt placed in
bold type above a photograph of a nearly naked Fay looking
out over a bleak landscape of hills and trees. The caption
quotes him: 'I have been to the mountaintop.' Fay's journey,
like Dr. King's life, had assumed biblical proportions. Several
months later, the third and final installment brought Fay and
his party to the Gabon seashore. For Fay, this is bittersweet:
'Reluctant to leave the place he so loves, Fay lingered on the
beach for days. "I would gladly have turned back and done it
all again."'[12]

Celebrities, Americans' 'exalted versions of ourselves' or,
as Packer calls them, our 'household Gods,' have rushed to
Africa in the twenty-first century: Clay Aiken, Drew Barry-
more, Don Cheadle, George Clooney, Matt Damon, Mia
Farrow, Angelina Jolie, Quincy Jones, Ashley Judd, Alicia
Keys, Lucy Liu, Madonna, Brad Pitt, Jessica Simpson, and
Oprah Winfrey, among others.[13] Madonna's 2007 shows
paired her usual trope of crucifixion (she was affixed to a glit-
tering cross) with images of mournful African children. When
Winfrey took her annual Christmas Kindness show to South
Africa in 2005, her millions of viewers learned not about the
root causes of poverty and their unexamined complicity in it,

or about the lives and perspectives of poor South Africans, but rather how viewing all this suffering affected Winfrey. The show was not really about South Africa at all but rather 'Oprah's quest for a meaningful (read emotional) Christmas.'[14] Winfrey 'found her true north' in South Africa in 2003 and soon undertook the Oprah Winfrey Leadership Academy for Girls.[15] Her collaboration with the government of South Africa dissolved as criticism mounted that the $40 million should instead be spread out over several projects serving many more children from impoverished homes. Winfrey's response was highly autobiographical: 'I wanted this to be a place of honor for them because these girls have never been treated with kindness. They've never been told they are pretty or have wonderful dimples. I wanted to hear those things as a child.'[16] Winfrey was determined to offer the luxurious childhood that she wished had been provided to her and projected onto these children a sense of physical and emotional deprivation that they may not have felt. As writer Rebecca Traister points out, Winfrey's charity reflected her 'desire to set the world right not simply for other young women, but for her own prepubescent self.'[17]

The hard-partying heiress/celebrity Paris Hilton got much less done in Africa. In 2007 she emerged from prison determined to rehabilitate her character and image by spending five days in Rwanda doing charity work, along with a film crew that would document 'how hard I work.' But the trip was canceled. She did make it to South Africa for the 2010 World Cup, where she was arrested for marijuana possession.[18] Africa's healing and redeeming touch has its limits.

American celebrities, movies, TV shows, and news consistently presented Africa as an abject tableau for American journeys of generosity and other forms of self-actualization in the twenty-first century. More so than ever before, we seek the admiration and gratitude of Africans.

TRAVEL AND AFRICANS

But ordinary Americans who went to Africa found it more and more difficult to ignore Africans.

Many of the over 500,000 Americans a year visiting Africa by 2000 were looking for adventure. In the 1970s MacCannell observed that tourism often expressed travelers' reaction to the perceived 'shallowness of their lives and inauthenticity of their experiences.'[19] By the new century entrepreneurs in southern Africa were providing the sort of outdoor thrills that had become popular in the western world several decades before, such as river running, jet boating, bungee jumping, and mountain biking. Young vacationers spoke of 'doing Africa' through thrilling outdoor activities; Africa mediated an 'encounter with the self through adventure.'[20] *The Rough Guide to West Africa*'s 2009 edition urged readers to strike out on their own, into the countryside, away from the 'tawdry banality of the cities,' out to 'termite mounds, baobab trees and ... stands of rainforest resounding with birdsong and ... tantalizing side-roads of red earth disappearing into the bush.'[21] More visitors sought 'the Africa still rough around the edges,' as a writer in *Outside* magazine put it, not just the usual 'packaged tour' of 'game parks and ... fine hotels.'[22]

An industry grew up around what Theroux in 2004 termed 'safari-as-struggle.' 'Poverty tourism' emerged in South Africa in the mid-1990s. By 2010, perhaps fifty companies were taking 300,000 tourists a year through poor Cape Town's townships to visit historical or cultural sites, pre-schools, residences, *shebeens* (informal pubs), even healers. Some wished to donate their time or money to help poor Africans. A growing minority traveled as part of Global Exchange or Reality Tours, groups devoted to combating global inequality, others as students. By the century's turn, sixty-one study-abroad programs were sending nearly 4,000 American college students a year to Africa. Americans who return home after a Global Exchange Tour or study-abroad stint are often motivated 'to work toward helping Africans,' such as donating money or materials or pursuing a career in public service, aid work, or journalism.[23]

Entrepreneurs try to regulate or contain visitors' African experience so that it provides just the right mixture of danger and safety, exotica and familiarity. Hammett and Jayawardane discuss how tourists to South Africa commonly conflate 'authenticity' with 'primitive,' that tourism has increasingly fulfilled a sort of religious function in which 'alienated denizens of modernity tramp to former colonies in search for mystical possibilities,' not disturbing evidence of contemporary inequality and exploitation. For example, the *shebeens* tourists visits are 'sanitized' to ensure that too much authenticity (rowdy patrons, street children) does not intrude.[24]

Accounts of African adventures still sell. Jeffrey Tayler, a former Peace Corps Volunteer, traveled *Through Muslim*

Black Africa by Truck, Bus, Boat, and Camel, as the subtitle of his book published by Houghton Mifflin in 2005 put it. Five years later Harper Perennial offered Julian Smith's *Crossing the Heart of Africa: An Odyssey of Love and Adventure,* the author's retracing of a young British man who in 1899 walked from the Cape of Good Hope to Cairo in the hope that this would win him sufficient fame and fortune to impress his beloved's parents. Though Smith's fiancée, and presumably her parents, seemed to be perfectly happy with him as he was, he resolved that in the interests 'of true autonomy' and, especially, 'love,' he, too, must cross Africa. William F. Wheeler's *Alive in Africa: My Journeys on Foot in the Sahara, Rift Valley, and Rain Forest* of 2008 described a series of extreme adventures. Brandon Wilson's ambitious itinerary included: running the Zambezi River, trekking the Sahara Desert, and climbing Mount Kilimanjaro. They had, he reported in 2006: 'Vaulted up volcanoes and marveled at gorillas. We'd hunted with Pygmies, traded with Masai, celebrated with voodoo villagers, and out-scammed the scammers.'

An academic variant of adrenaline tourism emerged with the Rem Koolhaas Harvard Project on the City, which presented sprawling cities of the developing world not as abject failures but as fascinating and even functional harbingers. *Mutation* featured a section on Lagos larded with aerial photographs in which the city's innumerable shacks, vehicles, and people were represented from above and afar as geometric patterns. The authors found the city 'resilient, material-intensive, decentralized and congested,' perhaps 'the most radical urbanism extant today, but … one that works.'[25] The project contested the ready association of slums with chaos and futility, but with little examination of its subjects; its rosy conclusions were more rooted in a theoretical aesthetic than in the actual lives of the ant-like, anonymous people of its illustrations. Tim Hecker argues that the photographs in fact presented Lagos 'as the radical other ... a de facto celebration of poverty via a laissez-faire aesthetics of the status quo, ... a dystopic voyeurism.'[26]

But much travel writing culminated in transformative cross-cultural exchanges. Bradley Charbonneau described how after 'never-ending scams' he had at last found peace on a pleasant Malawi beach when a pair of boys approached him, no doubt to demand that he 'buy their woodcarvings' or contribute to their school's fund raiser. But instead one of them asked softly: 'Excuse me, sir, could you help me with my mathematics assignment?' And he meant it. For several hours they labored together over 'word problems and calculated angles.' Then the happy boy turned and left, and Charbonneau

> remembered why I wanted to do this trip in the first place: to see something of the world, to see things I'd never seen and would maybe never see again, to learn things I didn't know and teach things that I did, to do that with people I didn't understand and who didn't understand me. To share something of me with someone else.[27]

Deborah Fryer's 'Cause for Alarm' recounted a similar interchange on the other side of Africa, when Toka, a teenaged boy on crutches, negotiated her through the streets of Djenné,

Mali. The plucky young man fended off a variety of suppli-
cants: children demanding candy; women pleading for
aspirin; Koran scholars wanting her sunglasses. But when an
angry imam emerged from the mosque, Toka explained: 'You
can't ignore him. He wants you to come with him.' The Jewish
Fryer felt like 'a target.' The man took her into the compound
and slowly revealed to his fearful guest ... his prayer clock. He
asked her to set it for him. She did, and the old man 'cradles
it with the gentleness of a new mother' and 'thanks me with
his eyes.'[28] Travel writer Kevin Fedarko's African friends
were less benign. In *Esquire* he related his time with Djibou-
ti's khat addicts, men whose lives centered around enjoying
the widely used narcotic. The city was dirty and dangerous,
proof 'that some parts of the world are beyond redemption.'
But he came to respect the band of ragged khat chewers who
befriended him, people 'who sail the inside of the toilet bowl
in such marvelous style' with 'such unapologetically defiant,
fuck-you élan.' Their secret, he decided, was sociality. One
explained: 'What's important is being together. To talk. To
laugh. To help one another out. Without that, we have no
community. That's everything, is it not?'[29] In fact this was a
common theme among travelers across Africa, that it was in
some sense the converse of mainstream America: desperately
poor but filled with friendship and generosity.

Most tourists, to be sure, were more engaged in a search
for self than in connecting that self to others. Cultural
anthropologist Kathryn Mathers traces the manifold ways
that Americans continue to use Africa as a 'foundation for
finding their better selves.' Service is often construed in self-

serving ways, with Africa approached 'as a hapless place that Americans can save and where they can do good.'[30] Likewise, journalism professor Melissa Wall's analysis of YouTube videos created by Americans in Kenya suggested that such visitors generally 'saw Africa as the setting through which to discover themselves rather than the place itself.'[31]

Yet Africa and Africans often intrude, disrupting carefully constructed itineraries and narratives. A group of tourists on their way to nature reserves in Tanzania passed through several poor villages in which 'emaciated children dressed in rags ran after the cars with outstretched hands.'[32] For several days after they reflected on their responsibility, if any. Africa's people have become more and more difficult to segregate from its safaris. Smith, the young man who decided to follow Grogan's route across Africa, could not manage to capture his inspiration's 'blunt approach, … his confidence in his own cultural superiority.' The artificial and contrived nature of many of his interactions with Africans troubled him. A village of dismayed Pygmies at a national park quickly spread out their 'craft items,' and Smith realized that there is 'nothing cultural about' this visit: 'We're interested in their size; they're interested in our cash.' Likewise, Casey Scieszka recounts in *To Timbuktu*, 2011, how she went to Mali to learn the local culture and language but realized that the very presence of people like her was eroding the culture that she came to see, that children quickly dispensed with traditional greetings 'before demanding water bottles or candy' and that a colorful funeral dance had been staged for the benefit of 'a wealthy Frenchman' who 'paid for the village to reenact one for him.'

Peter Chilson, who had lived in West Africa as both a Peace Corps Volunteer and journalist, recounted in *Riding the Demon* of 1999 his return to travel its highly dangerous roads to better understand its people and to indulge his desire for thrilling danger. Driving in Africa was at once an act of desperation and a search for transcendent freedom, 'as if life must be chased mercilessly to its end and finished in a bright flash.' But Chilson became more and more aware that he was playing. At the book's end, his driver, Issoufou, is acerbic: 'You white people, ... you come, you stay a bit, you gather your information or whatever you came for, and then you leave.' Chilson's money and white skin were a passport to an adventure he could abandon at his pleasure. His driver has one word for him when he at last departed, the ultimate insult for American questers: 'Toureest.'

Kira Salak set out to paddle 600 miles of the Niger River, following Mungo Park's route, just hoping that 'by the end of the trip, I have learned something.' Villagers fed her a rotten fish head, made sexual advances, tried to steal her equipment. By the last day she was out of food and fleeing from a succession of 'screaming and scolding' people. Finally in Timbuktu, she decided to redeem her quest by purchasing the freedom of two women. But this act brought no closure. A baby was left behind. One of the women spoke of feeling 'ashamed that she was sold like some animal.' Both spoke of how their former master beat them. As she got up to leave, they told her that 'God will bless me, will take care of me for what I've done.' But 'I don't know what to say. ... I don't have words.'[33] Africans complicated American quests.

Marie Javins noticed early in 2001 that many of her friends had become locked into routines with their families and jobs. She decided to spend a year traveling the globe and loved Africa so much that she moved there for much of 2005. But she often admitted to feeling out of place. Ethiopia was particularly challenging. Its 'hunger-inspired … con artists' were relentless, and 'I'd been poked, touched, and yelled at on a regular basis,' she recalled in her 2016 travel memoir. Determined to see Lalibela's rock-hewn churches, she and a friend, as *faranjis*, or white foreigners, were allowed to get onto the bus park early, as they were 'considered incapable of fending for themselves against the wild-eyed locals' preparing 'for the mass sprint to the buses.' But their privileges did not go unnoticed: "'Run, *faranji!* Run, run!" An old man hooted at us gleefully.' Karen Blixen's refrain about Africa: 'This is where I ought to be…' didn't ring true for Javins.

Jeffrey Tayler wrote eloquently of the often awkward juxtaposition between his desire for adventure and the conditions of the Africans he met while pursuing his quests. Like many such trekkers, he was inspired by a Victorian traveler: Henry Morton Stanley had gone down the Congo River in the 1870s, 'fighting cannibal tribes all the way,' he recalled in *Facing the Congo* (2000). Re-creating part of Stanley's trip 'would be my defining achievement … would strip myself of encumbering personal concerns, remake myself.' The river became an obsession. But realizing his dream proved to be very difficult, and in unexpected ways. Tayler first had to deal with a succession of government officials determined to separate him from his money. But it was Zaire's poverty that most fully dismayed him, the skeletal people scavenging through garbage heaps or simply laying on them, 'too weak to move.' 'We are sick here,' explained a driver. We are a sick people. Sick with malaria and other diseases.' In Kinshasa Tayler found 'a posh, Japanese-owned restaurant,' with *Baywatch* on the television. But there were polio-stricken beggars at the door who made it 'tough to eat my food.' It occurred to Tayler that US support for the corrupt but staunchly anti-Communist Mobutu 'had helped to create this hell.' Who was he 'to risk my life amid people who had nothing.' But 'I had come too far to turn back.'

Tayler gathered his equipment and gained a berth on the ramshackle boat that would carry him up the Congo, to his destination. In spite of himself, he began to take an interest in the many struggling passengers that he met, people who 'could maintain their dignity, command respect, and suffer hunger at the same time.' They found his quest absurd. 'We Africans don't like adventure,' proclaimed one. 'We don't understand it. Part of your problem will be that no one will believe why you are on the river. They will be suspicious and afraid of you.' These challenges persisted into his expedition. Many villagers were distrustful, and Tayler found his guide, Desi, unfathomable. In fact Desi's failing health eventually convinced Tayler to end his expedition. But it would take some time before he could acknowledge the 'obvious: that I had exploited Zaire as a playground on which to solve my own rich-boy existential dilemmas.'

But Tayler, as he recounted in a 2005 travel memoir, was back in Africa a few years later, drawn to the Sahel by the growing conflict between the Islamic and western worlds. As before, Africans puzzled over his presence. In Chad, a commander explained: 'this is a war zone. We're fighting off rebel attacks every night. I don't understand what you're doing here.' Later his tour of a palace ended when an aide confronted him: 'You whites! You whites fear *nothing!* You just don't get it.' His guide reassured him of his entitled position: 'if anything happened to an American here, the whole town would flee back to their villages, fearing the bombing that would come from your government.'

Tayler's experiences and goals were idiosyncratic. But more and more American tourists have found Africa, or, to be more precise, Africans, more discomfiting than they had anticipated.

MISSIONARIES AND OTHER DO-GOODERS

The stream of missionaries going to Africa, secular and religious, has become a torrent in the twenty-first century. They, too, have often been discomfited by Africans.

The broad Christian consensus on the value of missionary work fragmented in the second half of the twentieth century as liberal Christians became increasingly uncomfortable with proselytizing. 'The New Missionary' of 1965 was 'liberal, practical, secular,' more interested in 'helping the African achieve full economic, social and political equality' than in evangelism, observed a writer in the liberal *Christian Century*.[34] Evangelicals more than took up the slack. One scholar in 2009 estimated that about one US congregation in three had taken a short-term mission trip of some sort.[35]

Many of these evangelicals were rediscovering the social gospel. Ron Sider's *Rich Christians in an Age of Hunger* from 1977 was seminal. In 1985 an article in *Christianity Today*, evangelicalism's flagship publication, expressed criticism of the well-known Jerry Falwell's support of South Africa.[36] Early in the twenty-first century Gary Haugen lamented, in *Just Courage*, that American Christians lived in a 'Disney-land island' of affluence, ignorant 'that there are millions of people crying out every day to be rescued from aching, urgent hunger; from degrading and hopeless poverty; from the ravages of painful disease; from torture, slavery, rape and abuse.' World Vision President Richard Stearns asserted: 'We are not commanded to be a docent in the art museum. We are commanded to love the poor. To bind up the brokenhearted, to care for the widow, the orphan, and the stranger.' To the concern that Christian activism should focus on abortion, he retorted: 'Five times as many children die around the world of preventable causes than die in abortions.'[37] Of course many conservative Protestants and Catholics have continued to focus on the keystone issues that brought conservative Christians into politics in the 1980s: abortion and gay rights. But younger evangelicals have been drawn to human trafficking, AIDS, and poverty.

Though this emphasis on helping the poor often leads to charity rather than to justice, paternalism rather than collaboration, the new missionaries are more likely than before to respect local cultures and work with local people. The Mennonite Central Committee strives for collaborative projects that become self-supporting. Its magazine, *A*

Common Place, is dominated by the stories of local people. Conservative evangelical publishers such as Intervarsity, Moody, and Baker have offered books such as *When Helping Hurts: How to Alleviate Poverty without Hurting the Poor ... and Yourself*, and *Serving with Eyes Wide Open: Doing Short-Term Missions with Cultural Intelligence*. A 2009 *Christianity Today* article even suggested that polygamy, long a bugbear of western missionaries in Africa, should be treated with care and compassion, even toleration.[38]

Evangelical Christians have begun to realize that Africa may be more Christian than the US. At the turn of the twentieth century, roughly one in ten of the world's Christians lived outside the West. A century later, seven in ten did. Africans were much more likely to attend church regularly than Americans. Wilbert R. Shenk, a professor at the conservative Fuller Theological Seminary's School of World Missions, suggested that 'churches in the West urgently need resources of responding to the challenge of evangelizing their own culture, which regards itself as postreligious, resources that may well be found outside the West.'[39] Africa has increasingly become the source rather than the target of religious renewal. Perhaps, one scholar noted in *Christianity Today*, 'African Christianity was not just an exotic, curious phenomenon ... but ... the shape of things to come.'[40]

In fact some evangelicals wondered if it was really necessary or even appropriate to send American missionaries to Africa, as indigenous Christians could do God's work much more effectively with less expense. A mega-church in suburban Chicago decided late in the 1990s to shift its financial support from large, western relief organizations to churches in Africa and Latin America that were already doing outstanding work in combating problems such as AIDS.[41] As American churches have been sending more money to Africa, Africans, particularly Nigerians, have been sending more missionaries to the US. In 2001, Anglican archbishops in Asia and Africa started ordaining American priests for American congregations that found the mainstream Anglican Church of the US and England too liberal.

African Christians have had a growing voice in the theory and practice of mission work. Nigerian Archbishop John Olorunfemi Onaiyekan in 2006 criticized the West, especially the US, for: its program of regime change in Africa and elsewhere; propping up corrupt leaders; accepting patently bogus election results; and overemphasizing African conflicts. But he also discomfited western liberals by criticizing western acceptance of same-sex relations, abortion, and declining fertility rates. Ugandan-born Emmanuel Katongole, of Duke Divinity School, challenged *Christianity Today* readers to understand mission as a true and radical partnership, a transformative journey less 'about fixing northern Uganda,' for example, than 'to *feel* the gifts and needs of the world.' This might mean learning that 'it is America' rather than Africa 'that needs saving'; certainly it would include 'a new sense of community with those different from us.'[42]

High-profile American Christian initiatives in Africa have met with various degrees of resistance from Africans. Rick Warren, dubbed 'America's Pastor' by *Time*, started paying attention to Africa after his wife, Kay, became deeply concerned over the spread of HIV/AIDS on the continent. She soon drew Rick in, and he at last 'found those 2,000 [bible] verses on the poor' that had hitherto escaped his notice.[43] So Warren brought his 'Purpose driven model' of godly problem solving to Africa, and by 2008 had sent nearly 8,000 of his Lake Forest, California church members on mission trips to foster stronger churches, leadership, education, and economic development to places like Rwanda. Some observers found Warren's faith in Rwanda's much criticized President Kagame naïve and his reliance on top-down development anachronistic. Critics charged Warren with playing a cynical game, capitalizing on his fame and concern for African poverty to whitewash Kagame and Ugandan President Museveni while colluding with them to push a conservative social agenda no longer achievable in the US. Such critiques prompted Warren in 2009 to oppose anti-gay legislation in Uganda, which in turn elicited a rebuke from the Uganda National Pastors Task Force against Homosexuality.[44] Warren's African enterprises have provoked criticism in Africa as well as the US.

The African ministries of Bruce Wilkinson, author of the best-selling *Prayer of Jabez*, collapsed under African criticism. Wilkinson moved from Atlanta to Johannesburg in 2002 because 'God ripped open our chest, took out our heart, dug a hole in Africa, put it in, covered it with soil and said, "Now, follow your heart and move to Africa."'[45] There Wilkinson worked to strengthen Africa's churches, ease the burdens of its many poor, turn back the spread of AIDS/HIV, and build an orphanage for 10,000 children. It would be, he asserted, 'the largest humanitarian religious movement in

the history of the world from the US to Africa.' His Dream
for Africa sent hundreds of Americans a month to the continent, and the Bush administration granted him $108,000
for abstinence education there. But Wilkinson became frustrated at local resistance to his request for a ninety-nine-year
lease on 32,500 acres. 'Why can't he simply tell us that he
wants to be given the whole country so that he can gloat to
his friends overseas that he owns a modern day colony in
Africa,' remarked an op-ed in the *Swazi News*. 'Are We Really
a Nation of Fools?' read another op-ed. In 2006 he went
home. Not all Swaziland residents were pleased to see him
go. 'How can he leave everything in the middle of the road,'
remarked a volunteer in one of the anti-AIDS programs.[46] An
editorial in *Christianity Today* asserted: 'Wilkinson mistook
his vision for God's plan' and demanded that Africans accept
it as 'God's divine will for Swaziland.'[47]

Sam Childers, aka the 'Machine Gun Preacher,' also
became certain that God had called him to Africa for great
things. His account, published in 2009, related how the
biker and drug dealer turned born-again Christian found
his life's work in South Sudan late in 1998, when he saw the
corpses of children killed by the Lord's Resistance Army
(LRA). Upon returning he realized that 'I left a piece of me
in Africa.' Childers adopted a novel two-pronged solution:
an orphanage/school and a heavily armed militia group, a
sort of blending of Mother Theresa and Rambo. He is often
photographed holding children or brandishing weapons. In
2011 a film detailing his life and work in Africa appeared.
But in 2012 Childers faced accusations from a variety of

Sudanese that the orphanage's children were neglected. Not everyone agreed with the charges, and Childers vigorously denied them. But his own book laid considerable emphasis on the military aspects of his Christian ministry, and Childers obviously saw the project as an extension of himself: 'I'm not going to let anyone just come in and take my orphanage over,' he told *Christianity Today* in 2011.[48]

Katie Davis' 2011 best-selling *Kisses from Katie: A Story of Relentless Love and Redemption* tells a much less violent but similar story. Davis first went to Uganda while in high school and soon felt that it was where she belonged. 'My heart had found its joy as I served the beautiful people the world calls "poor" but who seemed so rich in love to me.' By age twenty-two Davis had moved to Uganda, adopted fourteen children, and was running a large orphanage/school. The book focused on Davis' life rather than the Ugandans who transformed it. Like many evangelicals in Africa, she was particularly interested in assuming a parental role. When the birth mother of one her adopted daughters appeared, Davis fought to retain custody, and she interpreted her failure as 'horribly unfair and totally unjust.'

These celebrity Christians have shared the blind spots of their more secular counterparts, such as Oprah Winfrey, in weaving the continent's sufferings into their own highly public autobiographies, a curious blending of self-emptying and self-enhancing. These stories were too self-referential to be much distracted by the prosaic work of learning about and helping to improve Africa on its own terms, of working with Africans rather than simply ministering to them.

A much lesser-known Christian, Christine Jeske, recalled in 2010's *Into the Mud* a quest for a more modest and painful form of self-actualization. She and her husband came to South Africa in 2006 as managers of a micro-finance organization and attended a conference on youth entrepreneurship. She was out of her comfort zone, staying at a cheap hostel in a dangerous part of the city as one of only a few white attendees. A young black man confronted her: 'I don't understand why you Americans come here,' he remarked. 'What do you do? Just drive around in your four-wheel-drive vehicle and hand out things and feel good about yourself?' Jeske tried to explain and defend the choices that she and her husband made about where to live with their young children, all the while wondering 'if he believed me, or if I even believed myself.' The young man softened, showed her some photographs of his wife and child, and they parted 'on terms something like friendship.' Then on impulse she decided to walk to the Indian Ocean just ten blocks away, through a very dangerous neighborhood, praying that God will *'show me You love me. And I want to see how much You love all these people, too.'* Then, on the way back to her hostel, she panicked as she heard a pair of young men talking 'street Zulu and English.' They brushed against her, then one wheeled and said: 'Sister, I just want you to know we're human beings, too. God loves us, and God loves you, and we love you, too.' They 'were watching out for you' while she was on the beach. They talked on and on, then had a request as they parted: 'We want you to remember when you're waking up in your warm bed and going about your day doing whatever you feel like doing, remember we're here on the street. Just remember us.'

John Donnelly's *A Twist of Faith*, published in 2012, is a compelling study of how a devout North Carolina carpenter, David Dixon, struggled to square the strong calling he felt to help orphaned Malawi children with the complexities and challenges of actually doing so. He unwittingly ignited village rivalries and even violence in choosing to work with some locals and not others. Like so many American evangelicals, Dixon had a particularly soft spot for orphans and orphanages, this despite the fact that Africans excelled at taking care of children without biological parents. When a government official pointed this out and urged Dixon to instead focus on the provision of food and education, Dixon followed his advice. His African call required humility and flexibility as well as persistence.[49]

Of course Christians and other Americans wishing to do good have more commonly participated in one of the mass movements to aid Africa, movements not noted for their sensitivity to African agency. Following on the heels of *Hotel Rwanda*'s tale of American indifference to African suffering, the 'Save Darfur Movement' seized on the slogan 'not on our watch' in staging massive rallies and lobbying efforts in 2006. The endeavor foundered on the shoals of political and ethical complexities inside and outside of Central Africa, challenges exacerbated by what scholar-commentator Mahmood Mamdani terms the movement's tendency to privilege emotion over sound knowledge and judgment. Save Darfur appealed to a nation wishing 'to feel virtuous even when acting on the basis of total ignorance.'[50] Engendering a sense of crisis, the sort of moral indignation necessary to ignite popular opinion, proved to be incompatible with a nuanced and accurate assessment both of Darfur's problems and how to remedy them.

Journalist Nina Munk's harrowing *The Idealist: Jeffrey Sachs and the Quest to End Poverty* is a cautionary tale of how the hubris of even brilliant Americans often leads down disastrous paths in Africa. She details how the prominent economist's version of what he termed 'Extreme Village Makeover' ran roughshod over local contexts and sensibilities, often failing to improve villagers' standards of living while sowing division and other unforeseen problems, such as intra-community quarrels provoked by massive and sudden infusions of cash and deepened dependency on external aid that would, inevitably, dry up.[51]

One of Sachs' leading critics has been an economist who once studied under him: Dambisa Moyo of Zambia, author of *Dead Aid: Why Aid Is Not Working and How There Is a Better Way for Africa*. A growing number of economists, development specialists, and missiologists, African and otherwise, insist that Africans must lead African development. They point out that western aid has too often: ignored the western agricultural subsidies that have devastated so many African economies; fostered corruption and dependency; linked aid to western political and economic interests; and maintained relatively lavish standards of living for western aid workers, at a time when more and more qualified Africans are eager and able to do the work for more modest salaries. These scholars urge western donors to honor and assist the work of African-initiated programs, from distributing mosquito nets to preventing AIDS to rehabilitating child soldiers to running universities. It is more and more difficult to justify programs conceived of and executed by western outsiders when a growing number of African organizations are doing such work effectively and economically.[52]

In fact, first-hand accounts from American aid workers have become more self-critical. Emily Meehan's 'The Humanitarian's Dilemma' described her friendship with a boy named Aimé in the Democratic Republic of Congo. Meehan was far from naïve and set and maintained some boundaries with the charismatic Aimé. But many of them blurred or crumbled, and she found herself devoting more and more money to a boy who claimed, just as she was about to leave, that the $120 she had just given him for tuition had been stolen. 'I realized that I didn't know anything. I didn't know whether Aimé was tricking me. I didn't know why he would trick me. I didn't know if anything I have told you about his life was true, and I didn't know if foreign aid works.'[53] Lisa Shannon in *A Thousand Sisters* (2010) recounted how her life was changed by an episode on the *Oprah!* show when she learned of atrocities against women in the Congo. Raising money through Women to Women International became her 'solution' to her father's death; becoming less absorbed with her personal life and 'putting human beings before stuff' restored her. But traveling to the Congo exposed her to many dilemmas: showing preference to a particular woman might place that woman and her family under suspicion; there were too many needs for her to meet; the women's difficulties were rooted in political and social complexities not easily solved. In *Blue Clay People* (2006) William Powers of Catholic Relief Services related at length his struggle to come to terms with the possibilities and limitations of aid work and his own capacity to help others. He went to Liberia in 1999 armed with a graduate degree from Georgetown's School of Foreign Service and a strong dose of idealism. He promised himself to 'learn from the people who live there.' These pledges were soon tested by begging and desperate Liberians and western aid workers who were insulated, privileged, and often racist. 'Don't care so damn much,' a colleague told him; 'this is all beyond your control.' Powers progressed through a combination of determination and humility, of learning to listen to and connect with desperately poor people whom he would have rather kept at arm's length.

Invisible Children is a particularly vivid example of Africans' growing power to contest even wildly popular US movements. In 2009 its leaders wrangled several minutes on *Oprah!* and pulled off the largest lobbying day on an African issue in the nation's history. The cause especially drew young, earnest white Christians from privileged backgrounds who, as one of them put it, did not 'feel like I have a right to live a normal life if other people aren't.'[54] Then, in 2012, Invisible Children's thirty-minute video, 'KONY 2012,' catapulted it into the American mainstream by drawing more than 100 million viewers in just one week. 'KONY 2012' starred one of the organization's founders, Jason Russell, explaining to his young son why he wanted to bring warlord Joseph Kony to justice. He recounted how he and two college friends discovered the evil acts of Kony and his Lord's Resistance Army nine years ago in Uganda and promised Jacob, a young survivor, 'we are going to stop them.' Confronted by the US government's lack of interest, they created a movement (Invisible Children) strong enough to engage even President Obama; in 2011 he dispatched 100 US troops to help African soldiers combat Kony. If only enough of us made it clear that we cared, then, according to Russell, 2012 would be the year that Kony was brought to justice and Uganda was healed. Russell blended idealism and grandiosity. 'I am going to help end the longest running war in Africa, get Joseph Kony arrested and redefine international justice,' he pronounced. 'Then I am going to direct a Hollywood musical.'[55] At the heart of 'KONY 2012' and its stunning popularity was the story of a white American who traveled to Uganda, discovered a purpose for his life, and invited the rest of us to 'change the course of human history.'

But the African-led backlash to the video became as noteworthy as the video itself, especially when it contributed to Russell having a very public mental breakdown in which he stripped, pounded on the pavement, and yelled obscenities along a busy San Diego street. Several Ugandans found 'KONY 2012' highly misleading. 'Arresting Kony in 2012 will not rebuild the lives of the people in northern Uganda,' remarked Victor Ochen, director of the African Youth Initiative Network.[56] Kony had left Uganda years before, and money spent on capturing him would be better used to help those recovering from the war. Putting more military pressure on Kony might also have unintended and bloody consequences.

Anywar Ricky Richard, a child soldier for the LRA who went on to become the director of Friends of Orphans, noted that earlier US-backed military campaigns prompted Kony to retaliate against civilians and disperse his forces to make them more difficult to locate and eliminate. Since the African armies battling Kony had also been accused of abusing civilians, escalating the conflict might well cause more suffering than it stopped. 'What is certain,' Richard concluded, 'is that this is not a simple problem that can be solved with a simple solution.'[57] Capturing Kony would not address the factors that fostered his rise: poverty and inequality; conflicts over land and other resources; and authoritarian, corrupt governments. Critics also noted that a disproportionate amount of the considerable amount of the money Invisible Children raised went to staff costs in the US and that the organization had no Africans on its board.[58]

The video's style also offended Africans. As Ugandan journalist Rosebell Kagumire observed, 'this is another video where you see an outsider trying to be a hero trying to rescue African children.'[59] It did not address the remarkable work that Ugandans had done over the past several years to rebuild their society. It in fact did not require viewers 'to learn anything about the children, Uganda, or Africa,' lamented Ethiopian Solomone Lemma. 'You just have to make calls, put up flyers, sing songs, and you will liberate a poor, forgotten, and invisible people.'[60] Public intellectual Teju Cole offered an especially acerbic and widely shared set of tweets on the 'White-Savior Industrial Complex.' Cole later explained in *The Atlantic* that the video should be understood as the

latest installment of Africa 'as a backdrop for white fantasies of conquest and heroism. … Africa has provided a space
onto which white egos can conveniently be projected,' often
'under the banner of "making a difference."'[61] A showing
of the film in Northern Uganda was halted when audience
members pelted the screen with rocks. 'We wanted to see our
local people who were killed,' complained one; 'these are all
white men.'[62]

Russell has shown little evidence of taking these criti-
cisms to heart. In a May 2013 interview with the Canadian
Broadcasting System's Jian Ghomeshi he gave no ground,
and Invisible Children's board still had no people of African
descent.[63] Nor did it early in 2016. But certainly the chorus of
objections from Africans across the globe made an impression on a substantial proportion of the millions of Americans
who had been supporting or at least following the campaign.
The 'White-Savior Industrial Complex' remains a powerful
trope. But it is often contested by African-authored books,
articles, blogs, and tweets of Africans through such vehicles
as 'Africa Is a Country,' 'The Africa the Media Never Shows
You,' and 'This Is Africa.'[64]

Anthropologist Roderick L. Stirrat's study of development
personnel suggests that they share a common assumption
'about the nature of the person as a free agent,' 'free from
social or other forms of constraint.'[65] But by the twenty-first
century, missionaries and aid workers alike have increasingly
faced criticism from the black Africans they have purported
to help, Africans who are representing themselves as partners
rather than abject victims.

BLACK AMERICANS AND AFRICANS

Black Americans have embraced black Africa's recent rise more readily than have their white counterparts. But they, too, have faced increased criticism from black Africans.

Both *Ebony* and *Essence* articulated a much more permeable black diaspora in the twenty-first century than they had before. Michael Jackson's return to 'the motherland' in 2007 prompted an *Ebony* issue devoted to Africa and a shift to more Africa-centric coverage.[66] 'The Africa You Don't Know' presented some of Africa's many underpublicized success stories to counteract the pervasive 'disaster porn' of the mainstream white media: oil production in Nigeria; coffee pickers in Kenya; a nightclub in Senegal; a well-stocked grocery story in South Africa.[67] *Ebony* celebrated successful black women and men who moved between continents: musicians Akon and Angelique Kidgo; supermodel Alek Wek; architect David Adjaye; novelist Chimamanda Ngozi Adichie; scholar Manthia Diawara; and athlete Mikembe Mutombo, among others. *Essence* also elided the line between North America and Africa. Tributes of distinguished black women routinely included Africans: Ellen Johnson-Sirleaf, Iman, Liya Kebede, and Olufnmilayo Falusi Olopede—a politician, two supermodels, and an oncologist—in '40 Fierce & Fabulous,' for example.[68]

For black Americans who traveled to Africa, however, forging a common culture proved to be much more challenging. Columbia University professor of literature Saidiya Hartman's *Lose Your Mother: A Journey along the Atlantic Slave*

Route, published in 2007, was a particularly honest and painful account of such a quest. The chasm between what Hartman was hoping to find and what she experienced began with the name that Ghanaian children and others quickly attached to her: '*obruni*,' or 'stranger.' Her attempts to escape the legacy of slavery by taking an African name and crossing the Atlantic to trace the slave routes of 'the commoners, the unwilling and coerced migrants' seemed anachronistic in modern West Africa. Her light brown skin, her walk, her dress, her language all identified her as an alien. Hartman struggled with both the complexity of slavery's history and Africans' lack of interest in it. Most Ghanaians were nonplussed as to why an American, blessed by wealth and other privileges, would be so troubled by history. They 'had too many pressing concerns in everyday life to ruminate about the past.' Hartman noted the irony that the African-Americans who would have felt most at home in Ghana were the very 'prim, Bible thumping, flag-waving black Christian conservatives' who seemed least interested in Africa. Ordinary Ghanaians tended to be Christians who deferred to authority. But she also struggled with more educated Africans. Traveling north with a group of African academics, she felt as if '[m]y presence tainted the glory of precolonial Africa … the flesh-and-blood reminder of its shame and tragic mistakes.' By the time the bus neared Burkina Faso, she was accused of privileging the American point of view, of being 'just another Alex Haley.'

Other recent black American sojourners in Ghana have wrestled with similar paradoxes. The Ghanaian government began to cultivate heritage or Pan-African tourism early in the 1990s to attract black American visitors and, it hoped, investment. These events have usually elided or excised discomfiting subjects such as domestic slavery and African agency in the trans-Atlantic slave trade in a celebration of what anthropologist Jennifer Hasty terms 'Pan-Africanist essentialism.'[69] Even so, the idea of making money from the history of slavery has upset African-Americans, particularly when it has entailed prettifying the dungeons in which their ancestors suffered. 'Are flowers being planted in the ovens at Auschwitz,' asked one?[70] Diasporans were offended when required to pay much more for entry to slave castles than Ghanaians were. African-Americans 'talk too much and don't deliver!' countered the chair of Ghana's National Commission of Culture.[71] 'They come in here and they cry and throw themselves on the ground, but they don't want to contribute anything to what we're doing,' added the regional director of Ghana's Museum and Monuments Board.[72] Many Ghanaians wished that one of their ancestors had been forced across the Atlantic Ocean so that his or her descendants would have 'escaped the poverty and hopelessness that we are now living in Africa.'[73] Ghanaians also complained that to focus on the trans-Atlantic slave trade neglected other historical aspects of Ghana in general and the slave castles in particular, as if history stopped once the ancestors of returning black Americans had left the continent. Even the noted Pan-Africanist Dr. Ben Abdallah asserted that responsibility for maintaining the slave castles should fall to black people outside of Africa. 'We do not have the money' and, in any event: 'It is your history.'[74] Radical black Americans have been puzzled over Ghanaian's pride in their European buildings, as well as their attraction to western skin tones, grooming, and religious beliefs. Black Americans in search of durable African traditions may hear Ghanaians remark that Ghana has 'too much culture,' that it must look to the future, not the past.[75] 'Looking diasporic' refers to the hip, western clothes purchased on trips to the UK or US that signify socio-economic mobility, not a Pan-Africanism rooted in the past.[76] Successful black performers represent not some sort of traditional collectivism but 'individuated success and cosmopolitanism.' And although music historians might locate modern hip hop, like most other forms of contemporary western music, in West Africa's past, modern West African youth often dismiss traditional music, ironically, as 'colo,' shorthand for colonial and out of date.[77]

Sorting out what constitutes 'traditional' and how the history of black Americans and Africans intersect is a highly contested and complicated business. Writer Caryl Phillips reported an episode from Panafest, the festival for black people across the diaspora. At the '"Thru the Door of No Return" ceremony' run largely by a group of black expats from New York City in Ghana, a blonde woman and 'her confused Ghanaian husband and even more confused son' left upon being told that 'this is not a place for white people.'[78] American definitions of race often seem out of place in contemporary West Africa's very different ethnic and social milieu.

Henry Louis Gates' monumental six-part TV series *Wonders of the African World*, which first appeared on Public Broadcasting in 1999, and the reaction it generated is perhaps the most salient example of differing definitions of black identity. In the well-illustrated companion book Gates, one of the world's leading black scholars, described the series' aim as: 'to discover who, indeed, "the African people" were and what, in fact, they had contributed to civilization,' especially before the arrival of Europeans.

But as historian Joseph C. Miller points out, Gates' 'quest … revolves around the profound sense of loss that he takes as basic to the experience of African-American descendants of Africans seized as slaves and sent to America and thus deprived of their own heritages.'[79] When an Asante leader in Ghana remarks that now 'most people are very sorry' about slavery, Gates counters that he is 'trying to explain it away.' Much of the episode on the Swahili coast is taken up with his critiques of the residents' color consciousness and the closely related subject of slavery's legacy. Gates often expresses wonder and respect for what he finds in Africa and is more nuanced and culturally sensitive in the book than he is in the film. But several African scholars accused Gates of ethnocentrism. Ali Mazrui, a distinguished Kenyan scholar of African history, politics, and society, characterized the series as 'obsessed with race in American terms,' of being tone deaf to the cultural and historical contexts of slavery and other practices that most of the world now finds objectionable.[80] He and others found Gates to be flippant and disrespectful toward African dignitaries and religious sites and neglectful of contemporary African scholars, philosophical systems, and civilizations.[81] Gates often appeared in Harvard gear and assumed a jocular tone sharply at odds with his subjects' earnestness. Stopping at a village on his way to Great Zimbabwe he met a young man named Albert who spoke of his difficulty in pursuing an education. 'Good luck,' retorted, Gates, 'do well and come to Harvard.' 'The problem is money,' replied Albert. 'If you smart,' Gates assured him, 'they'll give you the money,' as if every bright student in Africa could claim a free Ivy League education. Gates and the Africans he met often talked past each other.

The black African quests for home and meaning in the slave castles and slave routes of Ghana and elsewhere in Sub-Saharan Africa have often been tragic. They have entailed not only touching the acute pains and sorrows of what one's ancestors endured but have also revealed that West Africa was not, as Haley had implied, where one's ancestors eagerly waited to clasp their lost grandchildren to Africa's warm breast. West Africa's history has continued and branched, creating its own varied blends of tradition and modernity, often in ways that black Americans have found bewildering, if not offensive. In *Lose Your Mother* Saidiya Hartman related the bitterness of an ex-pat couple who after nearly twenty years in Ghana felt snubbed or played by the locals. 'I won't die here, John,' asserted Mary Ellen Ray to her husband. 'Not in a place where people will spit on my grave.' West Africa can be many things to black Americans. But it is seldom 'home.' 'When you really *really* realize you are not African' a black ex-pat in Ghana told Hartman, 'it's the loneliest moment of your life.' But 'if you can withstand that, you can make it here.'

Making oneself at home in Africa required painful adjustments. Dr. Robert Lee, a dentist who came to Ghana in the 1950s and persisted through sundry political, economic, and personal upheavals, including the execution of his own son, cautioned black American seekers that Africa 'isn't ready' to 'solve their problems.'[82] But those who came willing to offer something beyond their wounds would be welcomed. And Lee much preferred Ghana to America. 'I just know that living in this society, where I am living now, I feel better. I feel like a person.'[83] When he passed away in Ghana in 2010, sixty-five years after arriving, he was laid in state, President Mills praising his 'selfless service.'[84] Likewise, Auntie Gladys first came to Liberia with the Peace Corps and moved to Ghana in 1996 to serve as a nurse. Nearly two decades later she remarked that although she did not consider Ghana home and still thought herself as a black American, she felt connections between 'her calling to treat sick children in Ghana to her own experience of growing up poor in North Carolina.'[85] Emily Raboteau, the light-skinned daughter of the distinguished black historian Albert Raboteau, became consumed by the concept of Zion that had long occupied so many black Americans. Her Jewish friend, Tamar, could go to Israel. 'So where was my home?' She went to Jamaica, Ethiopia, and Ghana, visiting many of the same places and people as Hartman before her. No Zion materialized. But in her 2013 memoir *Searching for Zion* she recounts the advice offered by expats in Ghana who had made a life there by accepting small gifts, such as seeing faces like theirs on the currency and by staying curious, 'by listening.' Raboteau carried this humility back to the US and learned to make a home there by visiting family in New Orleans, striving 'to find the right words to forgive my father for his failings, and to thank him for his many gifts,' loving her husband and bearing a child. Martin Luther King's Promised Land was 'about human relationships.' 'Zion is within.'

Former Black Panthers Pete and Charlotte O'Neal moved to Tanzania in 1972, two years after they fled the US, and provide somewhat contrasting studies in adjustment through a pair of documentary films made about them. Charlotte is the subject of *Mama C: Urban Warrior in the African Bush*, from 2013. On the one hand, she asserted that she has always felt 'right at home' in Tanzania. But she also recounted painful adjustments. A poem entitled 'I Almost Lost Myself' described how she tried to curb her African-American brashness to better fit into her new home. After forty years she was still asked 'where are you from, from, from.' Charlotte's eclectic ideals, from veganism to advocating for peace to creating a shrine for her ancestors, represented to her a synthesis of her two worlds. Her husband seemed less resolved about his cultural identity. In *A Panther in Africa*, made in 2004, Pete describes himself as 'a grumpy old man.' Unlike his wife, he felt as if they had 'gone too far' upon arriving in Tanzania, and he continued to struggle with how long it took to get things accomplished, how regular bouts of malaria were taking 'too much of a toll on our bodies,' how he often felt stranded between his African-American past and his African present, 'almost lost between two worlds.' But Pete also believed that Tanzania had offered him a shot at redemption. He regretted some elements of his Panther years but was much more troubled by his behavior before he joined that group, how as a young hustler in Kansas City he was 'destroying people's lives.' Their work helping impoverished African children 'is for my salvation.' 'Those kids,' remarked an observer from the US, 'are his life and he would go to any lengths to make them happy.'[86] For all of Pete's sense of cultural dislocation, he is socially embedded in his new home.

Black American women journalists have also found meaning with particular Africans rather than in the continent as a whole. Lynne Duke, who reported from Africa for the *Washington Post* in the late 1990s, recalled in her 2003 memoir *Mandela, Mobutu, and Me* that she at first felt 'grand' in Africa, surrounded by 'faces that looked like mine, in places that were ruled by my kind.' But she soon 'had to grapple with ugly Africa, the Africa of horror and unspeakable brutality,' of corrupt and repressive tyrants such as Mobutu and mayhem that prompted her to 'fear that maybe Africa would not, could not, right itself.' It was the spirit and courage of ordinary Africans that sustained her, such as the drummers who joyfully played music on a boat on the Congo River even as soldiers lurked. Likewise, National Public Radio's Charlayne Hunter-Gault in *New News out of Africa* (2006) reported on AIDS in South Africa not by dwelling on its many horrors but by presenting people such as Puseletso Takana, a young woman in Lesotho who 'was writing and performing' short plays 'aimed at educating her peers in the hopes of saving their lives.' The reporter who as a little girl had been drawn to Africa, who had run across Countee Cullen's classic 'Heritage' poem soon after she had begun to read, and who had found in her first trip to Africa the landscape of her childhood dream, found hope in particular African people.

AFRICA COSMOPOLITAN IN THE NEW MILLENNIUM

The Priscilla's Homecoming project, facilitated by US historian and former Peace Corps Volunteer Joseph Opala, was conceived to recover Pan-African history. But for many participants contemporary relationships trumped historical quests. Priscilla, who had been taken as a slave from West Africa in 1756, died in 1811 in South Carolina after bearing ten children. The homecoming project brought some of her descendants in 2005 back to Sierra Leone. But, as in *The Language you Cry In*, filmed in nearby Liberia, black American returnees were often more moved by modern West Africa than by the history of trans-Atlantic slavery. One remarked that what left him sobbing was not the tour to Bunce Island, the fortress in which captives were kept before being forced into slave ships, but rather the difficulties confronting modern residents of Freetown. By the same token, a representative of Sierra Leone's National Museum interpreted the homecoming through the lens of the recent, not distant, past: 'Priscilla's coming home has made up for all the horrors of the civil war.'[87]

The most famous black American who has struggled to work out the import of his African ancestry has been President Barack Obama in his aptly entitled *Dreams From My Father: A Story of Race and Inheritance*, first published in 1995. Raised by his liberal white mother and her parents, Obama barely knew his father, and Africa figured little in his struggle to forge a racial identity. With even his doting white grandparents standing at the other side of a racial chasm Obama himself could not grasp, he realized 'that I was utterly alone.' His solution in college was to cultivate an 'alienated' pose that began to crumble after graduation with the news of his long-absent father's death. A year later he had a vivid dream in which his father greeted him from a prison cell, told him that 'I always wanted to tell you how much I love you' then became small, like a boy, his face suffused by 'implacable sadness.' Obama awoke and realized that 'I needed to search for him.' He finally arrived in Kenya in his mid-twenties to find that his father's actual life fell far short of the image Barack had created in his own mind. There were many other racial complexities to negotiate. At a nice restaurant, his half-sister on his father's side was galled when the black waiters favored white customers. A relative dismissed his assertion that many black people struggled in the US. He was at first enthralled by the warm attentions of his extended family, 'reacted to all this attention like a child to its mother's bosom, full of simple, unquestioning gratitude.' But then he saw how upward mobility by one family member inevitably meant a sort of betrayal, provoked 'looks of unspoken hurt.' At his grandmother's village he felt that at last 'a circle was beginning to close, so that I might finally recognize myself as I was, here, now, in one place.' But that grandmother, like himself, is 'pained ... not to be able to speak to the son of her son.' 'A man can never be too busy to know his own people' she retorted when he explained, through an interpreter, that he did not have the time to learn her language. 'My life,' Obama realized, 'was neither tidy nor static,' nor ever would be. That is what Africa taught him: his father's life became tragic once he lost his capacity to abide with such painful paradoxes. As Smithers puts it in 'Challenging a Pan-African Identity,'

Obama's solution was more 'functionalist' than romantic.[88] He integrated his African heritage and experiences into a multi-faceted identity that he put forward as the quintessential American story.

Of course President Obama's African heritage was more immediate or grounded than Richard Wright's or Maya Angelou's had been. He did not need to go looking for family. His African quest was grounded in messy and complicated relationships; it was personal. Indeed, the happiest black African expats in Africa seem to be not those who are seeking for some sort of abstract ideal or to fill a void, but rather those who throw themselves into working alongside and befriending Africans and creating cosmopolitan Afrocentric identities that defy pat generalizations or abstract models.

COSMOPOLITANISM

Cosmopolitanism is the title of a 2007 book by Kwame Anthony Appiah, whose life expresses its thesis. Born in England and raised in Ghana, he received a PhD from Cambridge University, has taught philosophy at elite American universities, and in 2016 became the President of the Modern Languages Association. He married his long-time American partner in 2012, soon after gay marriage became legal in New York. Appiah's mother is English, and his father was the Ghanaian friend of George Padmore whose 'superstitious' religious beliefs discomfited Wright shortly before his unhappy sojourn in Ghana. Appiah has consistently argued against racial and cultural essentialism in its myriad forms, a recognition of hybridization in matters both academic and practical; cosmo-politanism should help us all to discern which values 'are, and should be universal.'[89]

Teju Cole, described on his website as a 'writer, art histo-rian, and photographer,' is perhaps the leading example of an African cosmopolitan, a cultural critic who refuses to be bound by or limited to Africa.[90] Born to Nigerian parents then living in the US, Cole's family returned to Nigeria when he was young. Cole went to the US and eventually the UK for college before settling in New York City. Cole contributed one of the most withering critiques of 'KONY 2012,' coining the term 'White Industrial Savior Complex,' and regularly comments on developments in and interpretations of Africa. But he also writes pieces such as a meditation on the film *Red* by Polish director Krzysztof Kie lowski.[91] Cole's cosmopoli-tanism is fully developed in the 2012 novel *Open City*, which features a bi-racial Nigerian named Austin who, like Cole, defies convenient categories. Cole's novel bears the mark of a quintessential American trope: 'alienation.'[92] With his father dead and estranged from his European mother, Austin is a consummate American individualist very much at home in New York City's anonymity, freed from the constraints of social obligations so that he can pursue his eclectic aesthetic and intellectual interests. He is irked by an African taxi driver who takes him to task for not offering him a proper African greeting: 'I was in no mood for people who tried to lay claims on me.' A black American postal worker irritates him by assuming that Austin is 'my brother ... from the Mother-land.' At a classical music concert he is 'annoyed' with himself for noticing that he is in a sea of elderly white people, for 'Mahler's music is not white, or black, not old or young.'

Cole's critique of African essentialism, then, is discomfiting to a wide range of Americans: old-fashioned racists confronted by a Nigerian with a sophisticated knowledge of western history and culture; white do-gooders who believe Africa's fate is in their hands; and Afrocentrists who presume a common point of view Cole and his characters do not share. Certainly it is no coincidence that in *Open City* when Austin is nettled by a black American postal worker's Afrocentrism he is there to mail a copy of Appiah's *Cosmopolitanism*.

Americans are more and more likely to meet Africans like Cole at home. More than half of the over 350,000 African-born people listed in the 1990 census had arrived during the previous decade, and the number of African-born rose more than four-fold in the next twenty years, reaching more than 1.6 million in 2010, or nearly 4% of the nation's foreign-born. Many of these immigrants, moreover, are highly educated; African-born people living in the US are more than 50% more likely to hold a graduate degree than are the rest of the nation's population. American college students are more and more likely to be learning about Africa, and other subjects, from Africans.[93]

Representations of Africa by Africans have become much more common outside as well as inside of academia. By the time South African comedian Trevor Noah succeeded Jon Stewart as host of the *Daily Show* in 2015 he already had a strong American following. Noah's satire is indiscriminate: the outsized ego of South African President Zuma ('that great man'); Oprah Winfrey's naïve South African philanthropy ('you won't spank these children, will you?'); 'Donald Trump: America's African President.'[94] YouTube commonly features less prominent Africans puncturing western assumptions about their continent. 'Africa for Norway,' a 2012 video in which Africans spoof 'We are the World' by emoting about the need for Africans to take care of their cold Norwegian brothers and sisters had more than 1.5 million YouTube hits by the end of 2015. 'African Men. Hollywood Stereotypes,' 2012, a slick compendium of violent movie clips narrated by four gentle young black Africans had more than 1 million. Other Americans have enjoyed the wit of African expat children from YouTube videos such as 'Sh*t African Parents Say' filmed in 2012 with over half a million hits by the end of 2015. African voices crop up in venues ranging from Disney's Animal Kingdom Lodge in Orlando, Florida, where African employees subtly push back against the very stereotypes that they are hired to reinforce by providing detailed cultural context on the structure's African art, to the Smithsonian, which consulted heavily with Africans to ensure that its 'African Voices' exhibit represented the continent as home to modern, individuated people.[95]

African art and literature has become ubiquitous. Chinua Achebe's novels have long been a staple of world literature courses in secondary schools and colleges across the US. More recently, many high school students have been required to read Ishmael Beah's 2007 *A Long Way Gone: Memoirs of a Boy Soldier*. Many others have read John Bul Dau's 2007 *God Grew Tired of Us*, about the so-called lost boys of Sudan, or at least have seen the 2006 film of the same name, or perhaps heard about or read the work of Nobel Peace Prize winner and Kenyan environmentalist Wangari Maathai. There are also luminous novels, many by Nigerian authors such as Chris Abani and Chimamanda Ngozi Adichie. Like Cole, these writers are cosmopolitan. Abani is a Board of Trustees Professor of English at Northwestern University whose 2014 novel is set in Las Vegas, 'really an African city.' Adichie regularly appears on National Public Radio and in 2006 published an op-ed in *The Washington Post* pointing out how well-meaning American celebrities from Madonna to Anderson Cooper contributed to malignant stereotypes about Africa. Kenya's Binyavanga Wainaina's many writings include the widely read 2005 satire 'How to Write About Africa.'[96] African photographers who have long treated their subjects much more sympathetically and richly than have their counterparts in *National Geographic* or *Life*, 'were showing themselves to themselves.'[97] By the millennium's turn, the work of Fazal Sheikh, born in 1965 to parents from Kenya, was widely dispersed through his many celebrated projects and depicted African refugees and survivors of hunger and rape with great dignity and respect. For educated Americans interested in African art, literature, politics, history, or culture, African voices can hardly be avoided.

That Africans are assuming a major slice of modern descriptions of Africa changes everything. As Wainaina observes, westerners have diverged on whether or not Africa was 'to be pitied, worshipped or dominated.' But they were in full agreement with each other 'that without your intervention and your important book, Africa is doomed.'[98] Hence one of the most subversive moments in modern African literature transpires when the only major white character in Adichie's *Half of a Yellow Sun*, 2007, surrenders his dream of writing a book about the Nigerian Civil War, since it 'isn't my story to tell, really.'

The Africa described by African novelists defies demonization, deification, or reification. Irele argues that African literature has moved from the colonial Romanticism of Negritude, an often simplistic 'process of self-affirmation,' to a more complicated, post-colonial lens he terms 'the new realism.'[99] Modern African literature is rife with corrupt public officials, crumbling infrastructure, and poverty. Many characters are desperate to escape to the West, to be, as Wainaina puts it in his 2011 memoir, 'Getting Somewhere People.' Nor is African culture idealized. In Taiye Selasi's 2013 *Ghana Must Go*, a *New York Times* bestseller, one character wonders if African parents 'so bully their children, through beatings and screaming, to lighten the load of post-colonial angst.' Wainaina excoriates Kenya's political culture, from the authoritarian Moi regime to the eruption of ethnic violence after Moi finally left office in 2002. Nigerian writers routinely describe Nigerians as grandiose and ruthless. In *A Bit of Difference* from 2013 Sefi Atta remarks: 'Nigerians made beggars out of child refugees from Niger and impregnated their mothers. Nigerians kicked out Ghanaians when Ghanaians became too efficient, taking over jobs Nigerians could do.' They 'aren't even sorry about the civil war. They are still blaming that on the British.'

Yet these authors also express a strong desire for and loyalty to Africa. Part of this is a reaction to America's pervasive racism toward and ignorance of Africans, the eclectic condescension of 'white people who liked Africa too much and those who liked Africa too little,' as Adichie puts it in a 2010 short story. But Africa is also simply part of who these characters are. An African immigrant in Doreen Baingana's 2005 short story 'Lost in Los Angeles' describes leaving Uganda as being 'torn from natural living chaos that wrapped itself strongly around our lives.' In Los Angeles 'I am alone and trapped in metal. I am lost.' A character in Atta's *A Bit of Difference* remarks that every Nigerian she knows who lives abroad 'is to some degree broken.' Zimbabwean NoViolet Bulawayo's *We Need New Names* of 2014 features a chapter, 'How They Lived,' strongly evocative of the melancholy dilemmas that confront poorer, undocumented African expats in the US, of not being able to visit familiar landscapes or dying parents, of putting their hopes in their own children, children who 'did not sound like us' and 'did not want to hear the stories our grandmothers had told to us around village fires,' children who will 'not beg us to stay with them' as they age, children who 'will not know how to wail' when they die.

Atta deftly captures African expats' ambivalence over their new home in her 'News from Home' from her 2010 collection of short stories by the same name. Her protagonist sometimes wants to scream at the Americans who trouble her: 'If not for the havoc your people have wreaked in my country, would I be here taking shit from you?!' But then she reflects on 'the guerrilla politicos' of Nigeria who 'treat the land and people ... like waste matter,' smells the New Jersey air 'that is supposedly polluted,' and then 'think, "Well, Gawd bless America."'

Yet these stories from modern Africans tend to end on hopeful notes, a hope often rooted in hybridity. *Measuring Time*, a 2007 novel by Helon Habila of Nigeria and George Mason University, features an idealistic Nigerian head-master, Iliya, who believes in the selective mining of tradition and outside ideas, of cosmopolitanism. And despite the poverty and the corruption that shuttered his school, he is, at the book's end, gathering signatures for a petition to get it re-opened. 'This is life,' he tells his nephew. 'There's nothing more. The trick is never to give up.' Life and African history, the younger man realizes 'was all about survival.' The US and the West offer technologies and techniques, but in African fiction Africans' long acquaintance with tragedy, resilience, and sociality are essential to fashioning a stronger culture, society, and identity. As in the American fiction of Paule Marshall, Gloria Naylor, and Toni Morrison, the past informs the present through a tradition of creative survival.

Peggielene Bartels is a real-life example of a modern, hybridized African/American. The title of *King Peggy: An American Secretary, Her Royal Destiny, and the Inspiring Story of How She Changed an African Village* of 2012, a condensed version of which appeared in *The Washington Post* magazine, suggests an American gal setting things right in Africa. The protagonist did exactly that, overcoming the sexism, super-stition, and corruption of local politicians through prayer, determination, the help of an American church, and 'all my advantages as an American citizen to help these people.' Upon hearing that wife beating is common in Otuam, she asserted: 'As a lady King, as an American, I will not tolerate any form of brutality against women.' Bartels had indeed left Ghana in her late twenties and was returning after a thirty-year absence. But she was also thoroughly Ghanaian in her belief in witchcraft and her deep commitment to sociality and her role as head of the town. Indeed, her return to the materially impoverished but socially rich Ghana prompted her to reflect on the subtle ways in which America is 'poor.' Bartels' cultural identity was difficult to pigeon-hole.

Ashesi University is a remarkable expression of institutional hybridity. It certainly bears the marks of founding President's Patrick Awuah's years as a student at Swarthmore College and an engineer at Microsoft. In some respects, Ashesi seems out of place in Ghana. The campus is meticulously clean, class sizes are small, and the faculty emphasize independent thinking. Students even refer to Awuah as 'Patrick.' But Ashesi is an African institution. Awuah repeatedly urges students to 'stay in Africa' and 'serve humanity.' Students are continuously required and urged to collaborate with each other both in classroom projects and in forming an astonishing array of organizations. Unlike Swarthmore, where in 2013 the Religious and Spiritual Life Adviser and Interfaith Coordinator reported that students 'feel it's not safe to share a religious view,' Ashesi students commonly emphasize their faith, particularly those who spend much of their time volunteering in organizations serving marginal Africans. Kpetermeni Siakor and his parents twice fled Liberia's civil wars, tragedies that left him 'bitter.' Then he realized that 'God had spared me' for a reason, so he devoted himself to acquiring computer skills to make free online education more widely available in West Africa and then, in 2014, to map the spread of ebola. Both *Forbes* and National Public Radio noted this Ashesi University student's contribution to halting ebola in Liberia.[100] Ashesi aspires to combine the best of African and American traditions.

Marriages between black Africans and white Americans appear to be both more common and hybridized than ever before. Kennedy Odede and Jessica Posner describe a highly collaborative marriage in *Find Me Unafraid: Love, Loss and Hope in an African Slum*, published in 2015. Posner was already a headstrong idealist when she met Odede in 2007 through a Wesleyan College study-abroad program in Kibera, Nairobi's massive slum. Indeed, she insisted on the highly unorthodox step of living in Kibera. Despite or because of its many dangers, she was energized by the intensity of life and relationships in Kenya, particularly her friendship and then romance with Odede, who had overcome great obstacles to become a community organizer. Odede was immediately drawn to her, and did not want her to be a traditional Kibera wife who would serve and defer to him. But he was also interested in puncturing her pretensions. When she objected to him spending money on her, he accused her of being a typical American who 'always think the rest of the world is just waiting for your money.' When she regretted her privileges, he asserted: 'Guilt is a luxury.'

Kibera and Odede brought complications to Posner's uncomplicated life. She wanted to mesh with Odede and his community, but her presence set her apart and at times burdened him. They came to love each other, but in a context in which, as Odede's father explained, 'people like you, they come here, use our people,' or 'disappear them,' take them away. There was a 'chasm between our worlds.'

Bridging the chasm required the sort of courage that Odede had already needed to survive a childhood of poverty and violence but that Posner was less familiar with. She returned to college bereft of the 'certainty' she had taken to Kenya. Her love for Odede and his community 'binds' rather than frees her and compelled her return even after the post-election violence that swept through Kibera. They married, and Posner joined Odede's community development work. A deep sense of belonging rewarded this vulnerability. As a resident explained to a visitor: 'You know she may not look like us, but she is one of us. She is married here.'

The account of another Jewish American, G. Pascal Zachary's 2009 *Married to Africa: A Love Story*, also describes how a relationship challenged and transformed bedrock American assumptions. Zachary is unusually candid about his perceptions of, and attraction to, Chizo's exoticism. Her facial scars made her seem 'special, otherworldly, like a heavenly creature.' 'She wore the face of her continent. She moved according to the rhythms of her place.' But Chizo continually imposed herself on his beliefs and habits. He set out to 'persuade her that god did not exist.' Her faith did not waver, but his atheism did. When they visited his mother in her Florida gated community he insisted that she allow them to stay with her, regardless of what her neighbors would say about an interracial couple. Chizo demurred: 'We stay in a hotel, we see your mother, we don't shove our marriage in her face. You do your duty.' And he did. Their visit to Ghana's Cape Coast Castle aroused his libido; he proposed a role play in which he, the white commander, would select her, the beautiful slave. But she scrambled history, made herself the black commander and he the white, defenseless piece of chattel, a role which turned his desire to grief, for he began to 'identify with the real slaves of the past, the women who suffered here … the violence done to them.'

Marriage to Chizo was a disruptive process of learning vulnerability through empathy. She broke open Zachary's assumptions of religion and family, freedom and obligation. He retained his white American privileges but because of his love for her started to fathom the deep historical implications of those privileges. His 'powerful and upsetting' wife 'has robbed me of my routine.' White Americans cloak their lives with 'fear, anxiety and the relentless drive for self-protection.' Marriage to Chizo brings Africa to him, a life of 'routine surprises' and 'humbling vulnerability.'

African friendship, too, can break open American lives, as the Songhay did over a period of decades for anthropologist Paul Stoller, who had first lived among them in Niger as a Peace Corps Volunteer. In *The Power of Between*, his 2009 meditation on the relationship between his personal and professional life, Stoller observes that the Songhay tended to be both more grateful to and less optimistic about their lives than Americans are. Life is 'a loan that can never fully be repaid,' and successfully negotiating it required many skills and characteristics, not least of which was 'humility.' Stoller makes no pretensions of actually being Songhay. Among some Songhay friends in Central Harlem he reflected that he could no more become African than a log could become a crocodile by floating in a river for a century. 'I am forever between' worlds. But, as he recounts in his 2004 *Stranger in the Village of the Sick*, his training in Songhay sorcery came to the fore when he was diagnosed with cancer, helping him to approach the disease with equanimity and skill, just as it had shaped his scholarship to focus on cultural nuances and complexities rather than global, all-encompassing theories. Americans' steadily increasing interactions with Africans on both sides of the Atlantic has led to unprecedented levels of cultural hybridity.

Two signal events in 2016 illustrate the reach of cosmopolitan Africa in the US: Yaa Gyasi's *New York Times* best-seller *Homegoing* and Disney's *Queen of Katwe*. Gyasi was born in Ghana and raised in the US by Ghanaian parents. A 2009 trip to Cape Coast during her sophomore year at Stanford inspired the novel. *Homegoing* features two eighteenth-century sisters, one in the slave dungeons, soon to be shipped to North America, and one living above, as in a different world, married to a white commander. The book then traces the descendants of each woman until two are drawn to each other in modern California.

Gyasi avoids simple moral tropes. The white officer is a loving husband and father while prosecuting a horrific business. Black Africans are deeply implicated in as well as reduced by the slave trade, a sin that blights both halves of the lineage for generations to come. But both halves also have in common a resilience and determination that bequeaths to the last generation the possibility of a rich and intermingled life.

Gyasi's first 'flash of recognition,' the first time she saw herself in literature, came when she read Toni Morrison's *Song of Solomon*. Like many African immigrants and their children, she had felt alienated from black Americans. *Homegoing* is a gesture toward identifying 'the things that connect us,' that bring black Americans and Africa together.[101] *Homegoing* expresses a sort of no-host Pan-Africanism in which the divides between black America and black Africa submerge and old lineages and continuities surface organically, as in the fiction of Marshall, Naylor, and Morrison.

Queen of Katwe is also a Pan-African enterprise. Based on a book by a white American sportswriter about an impoverished Ugandan girl who became a brilliant chess player, the film has benefited from a panoply of prominent African sponsors: Disney Executive Vice President of Production Tendo Nagenda, whose projects include *Cinderella*, is of Ugandan descent; Director Mira Nair, born and raised in India, has long been married to the prominent Ugandan academic Mahmood Mamdani and has lived and worked in Uganda for nearly three decades. The film's two adult leads are Nigerian David Oyelowo, who played Dr. Martin Luther King in *Selma*, and Mexican-born Kenyan actress Lupita Nyongo'o, who won the Academy Award for best supporting actress for her role in *12 Years a Slave*.

These powerful Africans are why Hollywood at last created a major film that has no major white characters and presents black African people and neighborhoods compellingly and respectfully. This is, to be sure, a Disney movie with a happy ending. But the characters are complex and complicated. Best of all, they are realistically rendered. Like the African city it is set in, the sound track is more influenced by hip hop's Africa than Paul Simon's. 'I wanted to evoke a world that pulsates with life,' remarks Nair. 'When do we see the joy and dignity of any African country onscreen? I live in it, and I haven't seen that yet.'[102] That wait is now over.

It has become more difficult to treat Africa as a place apart because it no longer is. Most of Africa is becoming more stable, prosperous, and educated. African literature, writers, and other opinion makers have spread across the US. They contest hackneyed accounts of Africa, and they are creating their own stories in which Africans emerge not as foils to sundry American quests but as complex and compelling people with their own agendas.

We are all the richer for it. For those willing to abide with complexity, and particularly for those willing to make common cause with actual Africans as friends and colleagues rather than tropes, Africa has provided, if not all the answers, a good many of them, and much better questions, too.

CONCLUSION

THE IN BETWEEN

Queen of Katwe is based on a 2012 book of the same name, and the book develops two major themes that the film neglects. First, the book has three significant white or *mzungu* characters, Americans who created and funded the organization for which Richard Katende, the Ugandan man who began the chess club, worked. Second, the film elides its main characters' religious life. The book describes all of the major actors as being transformed by a Christian 'born again' experience. Most North American moviegoers would be both surprised and offended to read that Katende's primary goal in working with Phiona was to 'see her life transformed through fear of the Lord.'

The two absences are defensible. The erasure of white protagonists, those heroic 'bridge characters' that white Americans love to relate to, leaves viewers with no choice but to empathize with the courageous resilience of black African protagonists, while requiring American audiences to also make sense of religious beliefs that so many of them associate with narrow-mindedness and self-righteousness would have been asking them to cross a cultural divide that reached too far.

But these absences obscure both the source of the actual Ugandan protagonists' courage and how Africans shaped the lives of the *mzungus* who supported Katende's ministry. 'I used to spend most of the time crying and worried before I got saved,' recalls Harriet, Philomena's struggling mother, in the book. 'Then I became strong and I gained hope and inner peace' and 'began to meditate on what God had done for us, somehow keeping us alive.' In the film, Philomena's resilience seems remarkable but natural. That is not how she describes the source of her strength. The book also features white visitors to Uganda motivated by Christian conviction. Rodney Suddith of Sports Outreach Institute, the organization sponsoring the chess club, told his wife upon returning from Uganda: *'I think God's calling me to this,'* to the 'in between' of the securities of America and the horrific challenges that so many children in Uganda faced. 'In between' seems to have several meanings for Suddith. He is between North America and Africa, the spiritual and the material, security and risk. A bereaved American couple, major funders to the Institute, also found in-between spaces in Katwe. Norm and Tricia Popp's world fell apart when their talented son committed suicide at the age of eighteen. The Institute's founder eventually drew them to Uganda, where they met Phiona and her family. 'As a Westerner we don't like to face death and we don't like to face loss,' reflects Tricia. Being in Uganda 'helped me understand death and life,' brought 'a sense of wholeness,' a capacity to 'live with the why' of her son's senseless death. Phiona became a model in how 'to embrace all the hardship' that life brings to people on both sides of the globe.

Queen of Katwe, the movie, reveals an Africa of shimmering resilience and courage. *The Queen of Katwe*, the book, shows Americans not simply contributing to their efforts, but learning from them. Africa is an invitation to occupy 'the in between,' a place in which dangers and challenges too stark to be obscured or elided are met through religious faith manifested through hope, love, and service in which Africans commonly inspired Americans.

Both the book and film are major historical departures. James Clark, a pupil and associate of Carl Akeley, remarked in 1928 that the typical safari-goer 'is not much interested' in black Africans. Teddy Roosevelt sought moments of sublime danger leavened by a constant stream of picturesque landscapes and subservient black 'boys.' W.E.B. Du Bois wished to validate racial equality through his visit to Liberia, but this entailed avoiding both indigenous Africans and evidence of their exploitation by the descendants of black Americans. This same pattern of eliding Africans in Africa persisted into the second half of the twentieth century. The white men represented in *The African Queen* or by Robert Ruark, Peter Beard, and William Harrison were desperate for Africa's timeless landscapes, but little interested in its indigenous peoples. Black Americans such as Richard Wright, Frank Yerby, and Stokely Carmichael/Ture focused on black Africans, but often as representatives of an abstract ideal.

Women have been more likely than men to seek out and befriend black Africans. Jean Kenyon Mackenzie and Eslanda Robeson encountered and described compelling and admirable people. Much later in the twentieth century the fiction of Florence Ladd and Maria Thomas featured women protagonists who found meaning in Africa by committing themselves to Africans.

Black Americans' search for home in Africa has suggested if not required sociality. But this quest has often proved problematic, has been easier to imagine as an abstraction than to accomplish on the ground. Saidiya Hartman went to Ghana 'to excavate a wound' but instead opened new ones. Her determination to trace the origin of African-American loss puzzled or offended Ghanaians. Black Americans' African quests have often entailed pain, the discovery that if America was not really home, neither was Africa. Yet black Americans, well acquainted with tragedy, have often adjusted. Visitors as diverse as Langston Hughes, Era Bell Thompson, and Maya Angelou were able to absorb the shock of alienation but still fold Africa into their black and American identities. The black Americans and Africans of *The Language You Cry In* detected their commonalities in Sierra Leone not simply in the cultural artifact of a shared song but through a thick history of suffering on both sides of the Atlantic Ocean.

White Americans, less acquainted with the tragic, have been tempted to withdraw when faced with an Africa that confounded their expectations. This was certainly true in the 1960s, when independent black Africa did not conform to American agendas, but later, too. Once enthusiastic visitors—

from Robert Ruark to Peter Beard to Martha Gellhorn to Bruce Wilkinson—have been disappointed by Africa, by Africans, in the end. White Americans tend to expect happy endings to their quests.

It is precisely this sense of entitlement that so often strikes modern Africans as peculiar. African writers commonly describe white Americans, in particular, not only as racist and rude but also as self-absorbed, incurious, and child-like—'adorned with certainty,' as the female protagonist in Adichie's 2013 novel *Americanah*, winner of the National Book Critics Circle Award, puts it. Our brashness and sense of privilege, our assumption that comfort and ease are our birthright, seem naïve. Americans, observes an Adichie character from a 2010 short story, 'think they had the right to protect their child from disappointment and want and failure.'

From the perspective of Africa, then, it is the modern US, not Africa, which has been exotic and peculiar, a place in which hundreds of millions of people have become unhinged from material scarcity, social obligations, and good manners. Its people seem at sea, unbounded.

Sustained contact with Africans has poked holes in white Americans' cocoons of certainty, privilege, and self-pre-occupation. For black Americans, it has both enriched and compounded the complexities of forging a more collective sense of self, of finding home. To white and black Americans increasingly drawn to Romantic quests of meaning and identity, respectively, Africa has countered with dense webs of sociality, of relationships and experiences entailing obligation, suffering, and contingency.

But if Africa and Africans have contested American quests and dreams they have also inspired deeper, more grounded ones. Mackenzie in 1917 remembered 'those black maternal hands upon the hair of lonely white women' in Kamerun. In Tanzania Pete O'Neal has felt marooned between two cultures, but that has not kept him from devoting himself to Tanzanian children. Emily Rabateou's Zion remained out of reach in Ethiopia and Ghana, but they bequeathed to her a determination to make a home at home.

Africans have increasingly challenged American adventurers to abide with uncertainty, to make their quests contingent upon or even subordinate to the needs of others. Since the American Dream of perfect freedom can easily become a nightmare of alienation and fragmentation, they have a point. What if the very self we go to Africa to perfect or define requires not transcendent experiences or insights but rather the touch of many hands, the weight of others' lives?

Encounters with Africans are upsetting old stories from university campuses to Disney movies. Even the letters that pass back and forth between Yo Ghana! students in the US and West African destabilize clichés. Ghanaian students accustomed to think of themselves as marginal in every way discern, as several of them have put it, 'that we are not less than them.' Their American friends discover that Africa is much more than a crucible of suffering, let alone a wildlife preserve. They realize that 'there are other kids in the world.' Given the contemporary political climate in the US, imagine the implications of that African discovery!

NOTES

PREFACE

1   A. Williams, 'Into Africa'. *New York Times*, 13 August 2006.
2   K. Mathers, *Travel, Humanitarianism, and Becoming American in Africa*. New York: Palgrave Macmillan, 2010, p.177.
3   W. Jordan, *White Over Black: American Attitudes toward the Negro, 1550–1812*. Chapel Hill: University of North Carolina Press, 1968, pp.257–258; A. Mbembe, *On the Postcolony*. Berkeley: University of California Press, 2001.
4   O. Bohlmann, *Conrad's Existentialism*. New York: St. Martin's, 1991, pp.95–103.
5   T. Adeleke, *UnAfrican Americans: Nineteenth-Century Black Nationalists and the Civilizing Mission*. Lexington: University Press of Kentucky, 1998, p.77.
6   J. Ciment, *Another America: The Story of Liberia and the Former Slaves Who Ruled It*. New York: Hill and Wang, 2013.
7   T.J.J. Lears, *No Place of Grace: Antimodernism and the Transformation of American Culture, 1880–1920*. New York: Pantheon, 1981.
8   D. Peterson del Mar, *The American Family: From Obligation to Freedom*. New York: Palgrave Macmillan, 2011, p.88.
9   I.T. Thomson, 'The Transformation of the Social Bond: Images of Individualism in the 1920s versus the 1970s'. *Social Forces*, Vol. 67, No. 4 (June 1989), p.862.
10 D.T. Rodgers, *Age of Fracture*. Cambridge, MA: Harvard University Press, 2011, pp.29–30; A. Giddens, *Modernity and Self-Identity: Self and Society in the Late Modern Age*. Stanford, CA: Stanford University Press, 1991.

11 J. Heath and A. Potter, *Nation of Rebels: Why Counterculture Became Consumer Culture*. New York: HarperCollins, 2004.

12 J.M. Twenge and W.K. Campell, *The Narcissism Epidemic: Living in the Age of Entitlement*. New York: Free Press, 2010.

13 G. Packer, *The Unwinding: An Inner History of the New America*. New York: Farrar, Straus and Giroux, 2013.

14 M. Torgovnick, *Primitive Passions: Men, Women, and the Quest for Ecstasy*. Chicago: University of Chicago Press, 1996, pp.62, 182–184, 158–165.

15 N. Chodorow, *The Reproduction of Mothering: Psychoanalysis and the Sociology of Gender*. Berkeley: University of California Press, 1978.

16 C. Keim, *Mistaking Africa: Curiosities and Inventions of the American Mind*, 2nd ed. Boulder, CO: Westview, 2009, p.83.

17 W.L. Belcher, 'Out of Africa'. *Salon*, 28 July 1999.

1 'BRIGHTEST AFRICA' IN THE EARLY TWENTIETH CENTURY

1 N.I. Huggins, *Harlem Renaissance*. New York: Oxford University Press, 2007 [orig. 1971], p.92.

2 M. Summers, *Manliness and Its Discontents: The Black Middle Class and the Transformation of Masculinity, 1900–1930*. Chapel Hill: University of North Carolina Press, 2004, pp.157–241.

3 C. Sears, 'Africa in the American Mind, 1870–1955: A Study in Mythology, Ideology and the Reconstruction of Race'. Unpublished PhD thesis, University of California, Berkeley, 1997.

4 E.B. Holtsmark, *Edgar Rice Burroughs*. Boston: Twayne, 1986; E.H. McKinley, *The Lure of Africa: American Interests in Tropical Africa, 1919–1939*. New York: Bobbs-Merrill, 1974, p.68.

5 G. Bederman, *Manliness and Civilization: A Cultural History of Gender and Race in the United States, 1880–1917*. Chicago: University of Chicago Press, 1995, pp.217–231; M. Torgovnick, *Gone Primitive: Savage Intellects, Modern Lives*. Chicago: University of Chicago Press, 1990, pp.45–62.

6 C. Grant, *Negro with a Hat: The Rise and Fall of Marcus Garvey*. Oxford: Oxford University Press, 2008, p.49.

7 Ibid., p.117.

8   Ibid., p.246.

9   M.G. Rolinson, *Grassroots Garveyism: The Universal Negro Improvement Association in the Rural South, 1920–1927.* Chapel Hill: University of North Carolina Press, 2007, pp.152, 17.

10 R.K. Burkett, *Black Redemption: Churchmen Speak for the Garvey Movement.* Philadelphia, PA: Temple University Press, 1978, pp.45, 47, 48, 137.

11 Grant, *Negro with a Hat*, p.265.

12 W.J. Moses, *Black Messiahs and Uncle Toms: Social and Literary Manipulations of a Religious Myth.* University Park: Pennsylvania State University Press, 1982, pp.132–133.

13 Grant, *Negro with a Hat*, pp.262–263.

14 C.N. Harold, *The Rise and Fall of the Garvey Movement in the Urban South, 1918–1942.* New York: Routledge, 2007, p.34.

15 J. Wagner, trans. K. Douglas, *Black Poets of the United States: From Paul Laurence Dunbar to Langston Hughes.* Urbana: University of Illinois Press, 1973, p.329.

16 A.R. Shucard, *Countee Cullen.* Boston, MA: Twayne, 1984, p.23; Wagner, *Black Poets*, p.329.

17 J.L. Gardner, *Departing Glory: Theodore Roosevelt as ex-President.* New York: Charles Scribner's Sons, 1973, pp.110–111, 120–123.

18 Bederman, *Manliness and Civilization*, pp.170–215.

19 J. Alter, *Stewart Edward White.* Boise, ID: Boise State University, 1975.

20 T.G. Dyer, *Theodore Roosevelt and the Idea of Race.* Baton Rouge: Louisiana State University Press, 1980; R.P. Neumann, 'Churchill and Roosevelt in Africa: Performing and Writing Landscapes of Race, Empire, and Nation'. *Annals of the Association of American Geographers*, Vol. 103, No. 6 (2013).

21 Sears, 'Africa in the American Mind', pp.136–178.

22 P. Bodry-Sanders, *Carl Akeley: Africa's Collector, Africa's Savior.* New York: Paragon House, 1991, p.138.

23 L.E. Meyer, *The Farther Frontier: Six Case Studies of Americans and Africa, 1848–1936.* Selinsgrove, PA: Susquehanna University Press, 1992, p.185.

24 D. Haraway, *Primate Visions: Gender, Race, and Nature in the World of Modern Science*. New York: Routledge, 1989, p.30.

25 J. Kirk, *Kingdom Under Glass: A Tale of Obsession, Adventure, and One Man's Quest to Preserve the World's Greatest Animals*. New York: Henry Holt, 2010, p.201.

26 Bodry-Sanders, *Carl Akeley*, pp.223, 224–225; Kirk, *Kingdom Under Glass*, p.201.

27 Kirk, *Kingdom Under Glass*, p.340.

28 A. Douglass, *Terrible Honesty: Mongrel Manhattan in the* 1920s. New York: Noonday Press, 1995, p.221.

29 S. del Gizzo, 'Going Home: Hemingway, Primitivism, and Identity'. *Modern Fiction Studies*, Vol. 49, No. 3 (Fall 2003): 503, 504.

30 J.M. Armengol-Carrera, 'Race-ing Hemingway: Revisions of Masculinity and/as Whiteness in Ernest Hemingway's *Green Hills of Africa* and *Under Kilimanjaro*'. *The Hemingway Review*, Vol. 31, No. 1 (Fall 2011): 46.

31 ibid.; O. Evans, '"The Snows of Kilimanjaro": A Reevaluation'. In J.M. Howell, ed., *Hemingway's African Stories: The Stories, their Sources, their Critics*, New York: Charles Scribner's Sons, 1969.

32 Bodry-Sanders, *Carl Akeley*, p.155.

33 E.F. Olds, *Women of the Four Winds*. Boston: Houghton Mifflin, p.115.

34 Bodry-Sanders, *Carl Akeley*, p.231.

35 Ibid., p.222.

36 P.J. Imperato and E. Imperato, *They Married Adventure: The Wandering Lives of Martin and Osa Johnson*. New Brunswick, NJ: Rutgers University Press, 1992, pp.112–113.

37 K. Enright, *Osa and Martin: For the Love of Adventure*. Guilford, CT: Lyons Press, 2011, p.177.

38 Imperato and Imperato, *They Married Adventure*, p.168.

39 Ibid., pp.207–210; Enright, *Osa and Martin*, pp.198–210.

40 W.R. Hutchinson, *Errand to the World: American Protestant Thought and Foreign Missions*. Chicago: University of Chicago Press, 1987, pp.91–95, 101–111.

41 P.R. Hill, *The World their Household: The American Women's Foreign Mission Movement and Cultural Transformation, 1870–1920.* Ann Arbor: University of Michigan Press, 1985, pp.23–60.

42 G.A. Wilder, 'Hindrances to Christianity in Africa'. *Missionary Review of the World*, October 1928, p.792.

43 E.M. Wilkinson, 'African Women in the New Day'. *Missionary Review of the World*, October 1928, p.809.

44 C.S. Jenkins, 'Hindrances to Mission Work in Africa'. *Missionary Review of the World*, November 1936, p.526.

45 J.E. Geil, 'African Leadership for Africa'. *Missionary Review of the World*, December 1928, p.978.

46 S.M. Jacobs, 'James Emman Kwegyir Aggrey: An African Intellectual in the United States'. *Journal of Negro History*, Vol. 81, No. 1/4 (Autumn/Winter 1996): 50.

47 'African Appraisals of Missions'. *Missionary Review of the World*, March 1933, p.129.

48 B. Molaba, 'What Christ Has Done for My People'. *Missionary Review of the World*, November 1936, pp.531–534; D.G.S. M'Timkulu, 'An African View of Indigenous African Religions'. *Missionary Review of the World*, October 1936, pp.462–464.

49 S.S. Tema, 'An African View of African Needs'. *Missionary Review of the World*, April 1937, p.196.

50 R.P. Harper, 'Jean Kenyon Mackenzie's *The Trader's Wife*: A Critical Edition'. Unpublished PhD thesis, University of Missouri, 2004, p.13.

51 Hill, *World their Household*, p.139.

52 Harper, 'Jean Kenyon Mackenzie's *The Trader's Wife*', p.73.

53 E.E. Prevost, *The Communion of Women: Missions and Gender in Colonial Africa and the British Metropole.* Oxford: Oxford University Press, 2010, p.4.

54 Ibid., p.204.

55 Ibid., p.85.

56 Hutchinson, *Errand to the World*, pp.138–145.

57 Hill, *World their Household*, pp.177, 178.

58 K.A. Appiah, *Lines of Descent: W.E.B. Du Bois and the Emergence of Identity.* Cambridge, MA: Harvard University Press, 2014, p.217.

59 J.T. Campbell, *Middle Passages: African American Journeys to Africa, 1787–2005*. New York: Penguin, 2007, p.233.

60 I. Sundiata, *Brothers and Strangers: Black Zion, Black Slavery, 1914–1940*. Durham, NC: Duke University Press, 2003, p.73.

61 Campbell, *Middle Passages*, p.241.

62 B. M'Baye, 'Africa, Race, and Culture in the Narratives of W.E.B. Du Bois'. *Philosophia Africana*, Vol. 7 (August 2004): 36.

63 K. Talalay, *Composition in Black and White: The Life of Philippa Schuyler*. New York: Oxford University Press, 1995, p.97.

64 O.R. Williams, *George S. Schuyler: Portrait of a Black Conservative*. Knoxville: University of Tennessee Press, 2007, p.43.

65 Ibid., p.32.

66 M.W. Peplow, *George S. Schuyler*. Boston, MA: Twayne, 1980, pp.88–97.

67 Campbell, *Middle Passages*, p.262.

68 Williams, *George S. Schuyler*, p.98; J.B. Ferguson, *The Sage of Sugar Hill: George S. Schuyler and the Harlem Renaissance*. New Haven, CT: Yale University Press, 2005, pp.21–22.

69 Campbell, *Middle Passages*, p.266.

70 Wagner, *Black Poets*, p.394.

71 F. Berry, *Langston Hughes: Before and Beyond Harlem*. Westport, CT: Lawrence Hill, 1983, p.38.

72 Wagner, *Black Poets*, p.396.

73 A. Rampersad, *The Life of Langston Hughes*, Vol. II. New York: Oxford University Press, 1988, pp.236–240, 292–293, 347–349.

74 K.A. Wilson, 'The Cosmopolitan Creative-Intellectual: The Creative Ideal of Paul Robeson'. *Journal of Black Studies*, Vol. 44, No. 7 (2013).

75 B. Rensby, *Eslanda: The Large and Unconventional Life of Mrs. Paul Robeson*. New Haven, CT: Yale University Press, 2013, p.99.

76 C. Musser, 'Presenting "a True Idea of the African of To-Day": Two Documentary Forays by Paul and Eslanda Robeson'. *Film History*, Vol. 18, No. 4 (2006): 433.

77 Rensby, *Eslanda*, p.174.

78 C.W. Counter, 'Problems Arising from Industrialization of Native Life in Central Africa'. *American Journal of Sociology*, Vol. 40, No. 5 (March 1935): 588.

79 Kirk, *Kingdom Under Glass*, pp.337–338.

2 POST-WAR AMERICA AND THE 'NEW AFRICA'

1 A. Petigny, *The Permissive Society: America, 1941–1965.* Cambridge: Cambridge University Press, 2009, p.244.

2 B. Ehrenreich, *The Hearts of Men: American Dreams and the Flight from Commitment.* New York: Anchor Press, 1983, p.44.

3 E.T. May, *Homeward Bound: American Families in the Cold War Era.* New York: Basic Books, 1988.

4 P. Ichac, 'The Carefree People of the Cameroons'. *National Geographic*, February 1947, p.247.

5 R. Carlson, 'Hollywood Safari'. *Reader's Digest*, October 1950, pp.48, 50, 51.

6 G. Gaskill, 'Liberia, a *New Frontier*'. *Reader's Digest*, October 1948.

7 W. Langewiesche, 'The Conqueror of the Congo'. *Saturday Evening Post*, 23 June 1951, p.128.

8 W.R. Moore, 'White Magic in the Belgian Congo'. *National Geographic*, March 1952.

9 E.M.B. Grosvenor, 'Safari Through Changing Africa'. *National Geographic*, August 1953, p.198.

10 'South African Racial Hatreds Erupt in Riots'. *Life*, 7 February 1949, p.27.

11 'South Africa and Its Problems'. *Life*, 18 September 1950, pp.111, 125.

12 'South African Racial Hatreds', p.27.

13 'Africa: A Continent in Ferment'. *Life*, 4 May 1953.

14 'Black Africa'. *Life*, 4 May 1953, p.91.

15 K.M. Cameron, *Africa on Film: Beyond Black and White.* New York: Continuum, 1994, p.203.

16 A.J. Staples, 'Safari Adventure: Forgotten Cinematic Journeys in Africa'. *Film History*, Vol. 18, No. 4 (2006): 405–406.

17 T. Gallagher, *John Ford: The Man and His Films.* Berkeley: University of California Press, 1986, p.308.

18 Cameron, *Africa on Film*, p.29.

19 L. Brill, '"The African Queen" and John Huston's Filmmaking', Cinema Journal, Vol. 34, No. 2 (1995): 17.

20 K. Hepburn, *The Making of "The African Queen", or, How I Went to Africa with Bogart, Bacall and Huston and Almost Lost My Mind*. New York: Alfred A. Knopf, 1987, p.25.

21 J. Meyers, *Bogart: A Life in Hollywood*. Boston, MA: Houghton-Mifflin, 1997, p.253.

22 P. Davis, *In Darkest Hollywood: Exploring the Jungles of Cinema's South Africa*. Athens: Ohio University Press, 1996, pp.149–152.

23 J. Gunther, *Inside Africa*. New York: Harper & Brothers, 1953.

24 D.E. Apter, 'Review of *Inside Africa*'. *The American Political Science Review*, Vol. 51 (March 1957): 240.

25 J. Gunther, 'Is the White Man Finished in Africa?' *Reader's Digest*, January 1954, p.91.

26 Gunther, 'Shadows Over South Africa'. *Reader's Digest*, December 1955, p.55.

27 Gunther, *Inside Africa*, p.775.

28 Gunther, 'Uganda: Land of Hope and Crisis'. *Reader's Digest*, March 1955, p.111.

29 T.F. Brady, 'American Showcase: The Gold Coast'. *Reader's Digest*, January 1957, pp.134–135.

30 C.B. Randall, 'I Saw the New Africa'. *Reader's Digest*, November 1958, p.162.

31 R.W. Wallace, 'How the Negro Came to Slavery in America'. *Life*, 3 September 1956, p.46.

32 'Proof of Progress'. *Life*, 18 March 1957, p.32.

33 'Ghana's Thanks and Advice'. *Life*, 4 August 1958, p.26.

34 E. Schulthess, 'Rich Surprises in Africa'. *Life*, 1 December 1958, p.88.

35 R. Coughlan, 'Black Africa Surges to Independence'. *Life*, 26 January, 1959, p.100; Coughlan, 'Stormy Future for Africa'. *Life*, 2 February 1959, p.83.

36 C.A. Lutz and J.L. Collins, *Reading National Geographic*. Chicago: University of Chicago Press, 1993, pp.89–93.

37 W.R. Moore, 'Progress and Pageantry in Changing Nigeria'. *National Geographic*, September 1956, p.342.

38 J. Fiévet and M. Fiévet, 'Beyond the Bight of Benin'. *National Geographic*, August 1959, p.221.

39 Cameron, *Africa on Film*, pp.133–134.

40 R. Ruark, *Something of Value*. Garden City, NY: Doubleday, 1955.

41 Cameron, *Africa on Film*, pp.119–121.

42 A. Goudsouzian, *Sidney Poitier: Man, Actor, Icon*. Chapel Hill: University of North Carolina Press, 2004, pp.127, 128.

43 R. Squires, *Frederic Prokosch*. New York: Twayne, 1964, p.131.

44 R.C. Carpenter, 'The Novels of Frederic Prokosch'. *College English*, Vol. 18 (February 1956): 262.

45 Squires, *Frederic Prokosch*, p.55.

46 Ibid., p.138.

47 Carpenter, 'Novels of Frederic Prokosch', p.262.

48 G. Horne, *Mau Mau in Harlem? The U.S. and the Liberation of Kenya*. New York: Palgrave Macmillan, 2009, p.221.

49 T. Wieland, *A View from a Tall Hill: Robert Ruark in Africa*. Prescott, WI: Thorn Tree Press, 2000, p.6.

50 R. Ruark, coll. and annot. M. McIntosh, *Robert Ruark's Africa*. New Albany, OH: Countryside Press, 1991, pp.29, 79; A. Ritchie, ed. J. Casada, *Ruark Remembered—By the Man Who Knew Him Best*. Np: Sporting Classics, 2006.

51 Ruark, *Robert Ruark's Africa*, p.75.

52 Wieland, *View from a Tall Hill*, p.184.

53 H.W. Foster, *Someone of Value: A Biography of Robert Ruark*. Agoura, CA: Trophy Room Books, 1992, p.292.

54 R. Ruark, 'My Last Safari'. *Saturday Evening Post*, 27 April 1963, p.80.

55 S. del Gizzo, 'Going Home: Hemingway, Primitivism, and Identity'. *Modern Fiction Studies*, Vol. 49, No. 3 (Fall 2003): 508; U.R. Bittner, 'Hemingway's Influence on the Life and Writings of Robert Ruark'. *The Hemingway Review*, Vol. 21, No. 2 (Spring 2002).

56 E. Hemingway, 'Safari'. *Look*, 26 January 1954, p.20.

57 Del Gizzo, 'Going Home', pp.514, 515.

58 Ibid., pp.519, 516.

59 Ibid., p.512.

60 G.L. Cronin, 'Henderson the Rain King: A Parodic Exposé of the Modern Novel'. In G.L. Cronin and L.H. Holdman, eds., *Saul Bellow in the 1980s: A Collection of Critical Essays*, East Lansing: Michigan State University Press, 1989, pp.192–193, 195.

61 Ibid., p.197.

62 J.P. Stout, *The Journey Narrative in American Literature: Patterns and Departures*. Westport, CT: Greenwood Press, 1983, pp.221, 226.

63 Cronin, 'Henderson the Rain King', p.198.

64 A.B. Tillery, Jr., *Between Homeland and Motherland: Africa, U.S. Foreign Policy, and Black Leadership in America*. Ithaca, NY: Cornell University Press, 2011, p.72.

65 P.M. Von Eschen, *Race against Empire: Black Americans and Anticolonialism, 1937–1957*. Ithaca, NY: Cornell University Press, 1997, pp.145–166; J.L. Roark, 'American Black Leaders: The Response to Colonialism and the Cold War, 1943–1953'. In M.L. Krenn, ed., *The African American Voice in U.S. Foreign Policy since World War II*, New York: Garland, 1998.

66 P. Wamba, *Kinship: A Family's Journey in Africa and America*. New York: Dutton, 1999, p.72.

67 'A Future in America, not Africa'. *Ebony*, 1 July 1947, p.40.

68 'Africa's New Medicine Men'. *Ebony*, 1 February 1947, p.23.

69 'U.S. Negroes Changing their Opinion of African Cousins'. *Ebony*, 1 June 1952, p.100.

70 'Brilliant Bishop Speaks Five Languages, 3 African Dialects'. *Ebony*, 1 August 1953.

71 'African Influence in Fashion'. *Ebony*, 1 June 1948, p.50.

72 'Africa's Greatest Artist'. *Ebony*, 1 March 1949.

73 'The World's Worst Slums'. *Ebony*, 1 November 1947.

74 'Black and Yellow Gold'. *Ebony*, 1 May 1947.

75 'Chocolate'. *Ebony*, 1 April 1949, p.31.

76 'All Africa Stirring with Native Cries for Self-Rule'. *Ebony*, 1 February 1951.

77 'How to Stop the Mau Mau'. *Ebony*, 1 March 1953, p.88.

78 B.I. Obichere, 'Afro-Americans in Africa: Recent Experiences'. In J. Drachler, ed., *Black Homeland, Black Diaspora: Cross-*

Currents of the African Relationship. Port Washington, NY: National University Publications, 1975, p.17; M. Clough, *Free At Last? U.S. Policy toward Africa at the End of the Cold War.* New York: Council on Foreign Relations Press, 1992, p.31; I. Sundiata, *Brothers and Strangers: Black Zion, Black Slavery, 1914–1940.* Durham, NC: Duke University Press, 2003, pp.334–335.

79 R.W. Walters, *Pan Africanism in the Africa Diaspora: An Analysis of Modern AfroCentric Political Movements.* Detroit, MI: Wayne State University Press, 1993, p.98.

80 Horne, *Mau Mau in Harlem?*, pp.171–175.

81 A. Cheney, *Lorraine Hansberry.* Boston: Twayne, 1984, pp.6–7, 9, 11-12, 58-60, 101-108; S.R. Carter, *Hansberry's Drama: Commitment and Complexity.* Urbana: University of Illinois Press, 1991, pp.34–40.

82 'Backstage'. *Ebony*, June 1957, p.33.

83 'Africa Rediscovered'. *Ebony*, February 1960, p.96; 'The Return of Saturday's Child.' *Ebony*, October 1958, p.17.

84 E.B. Thompson, 'Prime Minister Proves Ghana is Free', *Ebony*, February 1958, p.92.

85 J.T. Campbell, *Middle Passages: African American Journeys to Africa, 1787–2005.* New York: Penguin, 2007, p.310.

86 M. Walker, *Richard Wright, Daeomonic Genius: A Portrait of the Man, A Critical Look at His Work.* New York: Warner, 1988, p.310.

87 S. Shankar, 'Richard Wright's *Black Power*: Colonial Politics and the Travel Narrative'. In V.W. Smith, ed., *Richard Wright's Travel Writings: New Reflections*, Jackson: University Press of Mississippi, 2001, pp.10–11.

88 H. Rowley, *Richard Wright: The Life and Times.* New York: Henry Holt, 2001, p.418.

89 Campbell, *Middle Passages*, p.305.

90 M. Diawara, *In Search of Africa.* Cambridge, MA: Harvard University Press, 1998, p.74.

91 K.A. Appiah, 'A Long Way from Home: Wright in the Gold Coast'. In H. Bloom, ed., *Richard Wright*, New York: Chelsea House, 1987, p.188.

92 A.K. Hardison, *Writing through Jane Crow: Race and Gender Politics in African American Literature*. Charlottesville: University of Virginia Press, 2014, p.175.

93 J.M. Braxton, *Black Women Writing Autobiography: A Tradition Within a Tradition*. Philadelphia, PA: Temple University Press, 1989, p.178.

94 Campbell, *Middle Passages*, pp.300–301.

95 Rowley, *Richard Wright*, p.347.

96 Campbell, *Middle Passages*, p.312.

97 Thompson, 'Prime Minister Proves Ghana is Free'.

98 Campbell, *Middle Passages*, pp.288–295.

99 Ibid., pp.312–314; K.G. Zacharias, 'Era Bell Thompson: Reflections in the Mirror, Observations of an American Daughter on the American South and the African Congo'. Unpublished PhD thesis, University of Kansas, 2012, p.200.

100 K. Talalay, *Composition in Black and White: The Life of Philippa Schuyler*. New York: Oxford University Press, 1995, pp.159–167.

101 Ibid., pp.130, 192, 201–211.

102 Ibid., pp.191, 273.

103 Cameron, *Africa On Film*, p.137.

104 C.M. Geary, 'Pygmy Images and the Making of *Madami*, a Memoir by Anne Eisner Putnam and Allan Keller (1954)'. In C. McDonald, *Images of Congo: Anne Eisner's Art and Ethnography, 1946–1958*. Milan: 5 Continents, 2005, p.129.

105 C. McDonald, 'Anne Eisner's Art and Ethnology, 1946-58'. In McDonald, ed., *Images of Congo*.

106 E. Bowne, 'My Husband Crashed in the Jungle'. *Saturday Evening Post*, 30 April 1955.

107 Geary, 'Pygmy Images', p.132.

3 FROM POLITICAL TO PERSONAL

1 D.C. Dickerson, 'African American Religious Intellectuals and the Theological Foundations of the Civil Rights Movement, 1930–55'. *Church History*, Vol. 74, No. 2 (June 2005): 231; D.L. Chappell, *A Stone of Hope: Prophetic Religion and the Death of Jim Crow*. Chapel Hill: University of North Carolina Press, 2004.

2   H. Schuman and M. Krysan, 'A Historical Note on Whites' Beliefs about Racial Inequality'. *Sociological Review*, Vol. 64, No. 6 (December 1999): 88.

3   R.R. Kinder and L.M. Sanders, *Divided by Color: Racial Politics and Democratic Ideals*. Chicago: University of Chicago Press, 1996, p.101; M. Omi and H. Winant, *Racial Formation in the United States: From the 1960s to the 1980s*. New York: Routledge, 1986; R.N. Jacobs, *Race, Media, and the Crisis of Civil Society*. Cambridge: Cambridge University Press, 2000; H. Schuman, C. Stech and L. Bobo, *Racial Attitudes in America: Trends and Interpretations*. Cambridge, MA, Harvard University Press, 1985.

4   P. Clecak, *Radical Paradoxes: Dilemmas of the American Left: 1945–1970*. New York: Harper & Row, 1973, p.247.

5   D. Rossinow, *The Politics of Authenticity: Liberalism, Christianity, and the New Left in America*. New York: Columbia University Press, 1998; D. Savran, *Taking It Like a Man: White Masculinity, Masochism, and Contemporary American Culture*. Princeton, NJ: Princeton University Press, 1989, pp.109–122.

6   W.J. Moses, *The Wings of Ethiopia*. Ames: Iowa State University Press, 1990, p.38.

7   'That's Africa: Troubles Worse than Teething'. *Life*, 14 February 1964, p.4.

8   'Second Revolution'. *Time*, 11 March 1966.

9   'Harvest of Anarchy in the Congo'. *Life*, 17 February 1961, p.22.

10 R. Wallace, 'This is the Way it Came About: Greed and Then Blood'. *Life*, 15 December 1961, p.33; 'Lumumba's Legacy'. *Life*, 24 February 1961.

11 'Congo: Savagery Has No Excuse'. *Life*, 11 December 1964.

12 D. Reed, 'The Stanleyville Massacre'. *Reader's Digest*, September 1965, pp.234, 268, 272.

13 D. Reed, 'Africa's Man of Mystery'. *Reader's Digest*, December 1961, p.162.

14 D. Reed, 'Africa's River of Mystery'. *Reader's Digest*, September 1962, pp.196, 198.

15 S. Alsop, 'Will Africa Go Communist?' *Saturday Evening Post*, 18 February 1961, p.13.

16 S. Alsop, 'What Africa Is Really Like'. *Saturday Evening Post*, 25 March 1961, pp.71, 72.

17 F.V. Drake, 'Don't Decry Colonialism!' *Reader's Digest*, August 1960, p.67.

18 F. L. Howley, 'Behind the Terror in African Angola'. *Reader's Digest*, November 1961.

19 C.B. Randall, 'Why South Africa Needs More Time'. *Reader's Digest*, August 1963, pp.153, 155.

20 J. Morris, 'Long Live Imperialism'. *Saturday Evening Post*, 3 July, 1965, p.10.

21 A. Smith, 'Jambo: Gasbag Safari in Africa'. *Saturday Evening Post*, 9 November 1963, p.41; 'Diary of a Hitchhike across the Sahara'. *Life*, 17 April 1964; R. Bradbury, 'The Kilimanjaro Machine'. *Time*, 22 January 1965; H. Moffett, 'The White Wizard's 90th'. *Life*, 19 February 1965, pp.82–94; R. Chelminski, 'Goodbye at Lambarene'. *Life*, 17 September 1965, pp.90–94.

22 K. Drake, 'Africa's Garden of Eden'. *Reader's Digest*, January 1963, pp.182, 185.

23 C.A. Lindbergh, 'Is Civilization Progress?' *Reader's Digest*, July 1964, pp.67, 69, 71.

24 A.M. Lindbergh, 'Discovery and Renewal'. *Reader's Digest*, January 1967, p.40.

25 J.D. Ratcliff, 'A Day in the Life of a Bushman'. *Reader's Digest*, September 1967, pp.30, 34.

26 R.J. Granqvist, 'Photojournalism's White Mythologies: Eliot Elisofon and LIFE in Africa, 1959–1961'. *Research in African Literatures*, Vol. 43, No. 3 (Fall 2012): 94.

27 E. Elifson, 'Storied World of Africa'. *Life*, 13 October 1961, p.86.

28 N.T. Kenney, 'Africa: The Winds of Freedom Stir'. *National Geographic*, September 1960, pp.303, 332–333, 321, 324.

29 L.S.B. Leakey, 'Finding the World's Earliest Man'. *National Geographic*, September 1960, p.427.

30 V. Wentzel, 'Mozambique: Land of the Good People'. *National Geographic*, August 1964, pp.196–197, 201, 231.

31 A.C. Fisher, Jr., 'Kenya Says *Harambee!' National Geographic*, February 1969, pp.157, 205.

32 C.A. Lutz and J.L. Collins, *Reading National Geographic*. Chicago: University of Chicago Press, 1993, pp.39–40.

33 W. Attwood, *The Reds and the Blacks: A Personal Adventure*. New York: Harper & Row, 1967, pp.227–228.

34 D.L. Lewis, 'Khartoum'. In M.C. Carnes, ed., *Past Imperfect: History According to the Movies*. New York: Henry Holt, 1995, p.164.

35 S. Jeppie, 'From Khartoum to Kufrah: Filmic Narratives of Conquest and Resistance'. In V. Bickford-Smith and R. Mendelsohn, eds., *Black and White in Colour: African History on Screen*, Oxford: James Curry, 2007, pp.139–142.

36 K.M. Cameron, *Africa on Film: Beyond Black and White*. New York: Continuum, 1994, p.148.

37 T. McCarthy, *Howard Hawks: The Grey Fox of Hollywood*. New York: Grove Press, 1997, p.586.

38 R. Roberts and J.S. Olson, *John Wayne: American*. New York: Free Press, 1995, p.487.

39 C. Chris, *Watching Wildlife*. Minneapolis: University of Minnesota Press, 2006, p.60; G. Mitman, *Reel Nature: America's Romance with Wildlife on Film*. Cambridge, MA: Harvard University Press, 1999.

40 Cameron, *Africa on Film*, pp.203–204.

41 J. Bowermaster, *The Adventures and Misadventures of Peter Beard in Africa*. Boston: Little, Brown, 1993, p.viii.

42 J. Lee, 'The Mask of Form in *Out of Africa*'. In O.A. Pelensky, ed., *Isak Dinesen: Critical Views*. Athens: Ohio University Press, 1993, pp.278, 279.

43 Bowermaster, *Adventures and Misadventures*, p.61.

44 Ibid., pp.95, 132.

45 L. Bennetts, 'African Dreamer'. *Vanity Fair*, November 1996.

46 A. Larocca, 'Bwana Comes Home'. *New York Magazine*, 18 August 2003; R. Mayer, *Artificial Africas: Colonial Images in the Times of Globalization*. Hanover, NH: Dartmouth College, 2002, pp.90–97.

47 P. Theroux, 'Reminiscence: Malawi'. In M. Viorst, ed., *Making a Difference: The Peace Corps at Twenty-Five*. New York: Weidenfeld & Nicolson, 1986, pp.84–85.

48 J.C. Gruesser, *White on Black: Contemporary Literature about Africa*. Urbana: University of Illinois Press, 1992, pp.74–76.

49 Ibid., pp.76–81; D. Kuhne, *African Settings in Contemporary American Novels*. Westport, CT: Greenwood Press, 1999, pp.123–137.

50 P. Theroux, 'Over There'. In J. O'Reilly, L. Habegger and S. O'Reilly, eds., *The Best Travel Writing*. Palo Alto, CA: Travelers' Tales, 2007, pp.228, 230, 232.

51 P. Theroux and A. McCarthy, 'I Hate Vacations'. *The Atlantic*, September 2013, p.43.

52 C. Rollyson, *Nothing Ever Happens to the Brave: The Story of Martha Gellhorn*. New York: St. Martin's Press, 1990.

53 C. Moorehead, *Gellhorn: A Twentieth-Century Life*. New York: Henry Holt, 2003, p.366.

54 Ibid., p.378.

55 Gruesser, *White on Black*, pp.89–98.

56 W.L. Hansberry and E.H. Johnson, 'Africa's Golden Past'. *Ebony*, October 1964, January, February, March, April 1965.

57 'Brothers of the Skin'. *Ebony*, November 1961.

58 E.B. Thompson, 'African Safari'. *Ebony*, February 1969, p.120.

59 K. Woodard, *A Nation Within a Nation: Amiri Barka (LeRoi Jones) and Black Power Politics*. Chapel Hill: University of North Carolina Press, 1999.

60 A.J. Ratcliff, 'The Radical Evolution of Du Boisian Pan-Africanism'. *Journal of Pan African Studies*, Vol. 5, No. 9 (March 2013).

61 E. Dunbar, *The Black Expatriates: A Study of American Negroes in Exile*. New York: Pocket, 1970 [orig. 1968], pp.96, 97, 75.

62 K.K. Gaines, *American Africans in Ghana: Black Expatriates and the Civil Rights Era*. Chapel Hill: University of North Carolina Press, 2006.

63 J.C. Gruesser, 'Afro-American Travel Literature and Africanist Discourse'. *Black American Literature Forum*, Vol. 24, No. 1 (1990): 18.

64 J.M. Elliot, ed., *Conversations with Maya Angelou.* Jackson: University Press of Mississippi, 1989, p.40.

65 J.L. Hill, 'Anti-Heroic Perspectives: The Life and Works of Frank Yerby'. Unpublished PhD thesis, University of Iowa, 1976, p.43; R. Nye, *The Unembarrassed Muse: The Popular Arts in America.* New York: Dial Press, 1970, pp.47, 54; V.M. Crawford, 'Middle Ground: Frank Yerby's Novels in the African American Literary Tradition'. Unpublished PhD thesis, University of North Carolina, 1999; B.A. Glasrud and L. Champion, '"The Fishes and the Poet's Hands": Frank Yerby, a Black Author in White America'. *Journal of American and Comparative Cultures*, Vol. 23, No. 4 (2000); J.L. Hill, 'An Interview with Frank Garvin Yerby'. *Resources for American Literary Study* Vol. 21, No. 2 (1995).

66 D.T. Turner, 'Frank Yerby as Debunker'. In R. Hemenway, ed., *The Black Novelist*, Columbus, OH: Charles E. Merrill, 1970, p.70.

67 G. Breitman, ed., *Malcolm X Speaks.* New York: Grove Press, 1990, pp.61, 73; A. Austin, *Achieving Blackness: Race, Black Nationalism, and Afrocentrism in the Twentieth Century.* New York: New York University Press, 2006, pp.39–46; J.O.G. Ogbar, *Black Power: Radical Politics and African American Identity.* Baltimore, MD: Johns Hopkins University Press, 2004, pp.23–35.

68 P. Goldman, *The Death and Life of Malcolm X.* Urbana: University of Illinois Press, 1973, p.176.

69 S. Brown, *Fighting for US: Maulana Karenga, the US Organization, and Black Cultural Nationalism.* New York : New York University Press, 2003; J. Jones, *Labor of Love, Labor of Sorrow: Black Women, Work, and the Family from Slavery to the Present.* New York: Vintage, 1985, pp.310–318; M. Dubey, *Black Women Novelists and the Nationalist Aesthetic.* Bloomington: Indiana University Press, 1994, pp.16–20.

70 Woodard, *Nation Within a Nation*, pp.222, 169.

71 T.L. Liyong, 'Negroes are not Africans'. In J. Drachler, ed., *Black Homeland, Black Diaspora: Cross-Currents of the African Relationship.* Port Washington, NY: National University Publications, 1975, p.260.

72 T. Mboya, 'Africa and Afro-America'. In J. Drachler, ed., *Black Homeland, Black Diaspora: Cross-Currents of the African Relationship*. Port Washington, NY: National University Publications, 1975, pp.251–252, 253.

73 P.E. Joseph, 'Revolution in Babylon: Stokely Carmichael and America in the 1960s'. *Souls: A Critical Journal of Black Politics, Culture, and Society*, Vol. 9, No. 4, 2007: 296.

74 W.L. Van Deburg, *New Day In Babylon: The Black Power Movement and American Culture, 1965–1976*. Chicago, IL: University of Chicago Press, 1992, p.306; R.G. Weisbord, *Ebony Kinship: Africa, Africans, and the Afro-American*. Westport, CT: Greenwood Press, 1973, pp.187–211.

75 K. Schwarz, *What You Can Do for Your Country: An Oral History of the Peace Corps*. New York: William Morrow, 1991, p.27.

76 E.C. Hoffman, *All You Need Is Love: The Peace Corps and the Spirit of the 1960s*. Cambridge, MA: Harvard University Press, 1998; R. Fischer, *Making Them Like Us: Peace Corps Volunteers in the 1960s*. Washington, DC: Smithsonian Institution Press, 1998; G.T. Rice, *The Bold Experiment: JFK's Peace Corps*. Notre Dame, IN: University of Notre Dame Press, 1985.

77 R. Klein, 'Being First: A Memoir of Ghana I', Peace Corps Writers, 2003, http://www.peacecorpswriters.org/pages/2003/0301/301pchist.html.

78 J. Coyne, 'But No Postcards'. In J. Coyne et al., eds., *To Touch the World: The Peace Corps Experience*. Washington, DC: Peace Corps, 1985, p.157.

79 Schwarz, *What You Can Do*, pp.37, 38.

80 G. May, 'Passing the Torch and Lighting the Fire: The Peace Corps'. In T.G. Paterson, ed., *Kennedy's Quest for Victory: American Foreign Policy, 1961–1963*. New York: Oxford University Press, 1989, p.287.

81 M. Mead, 'Foreword'. In R.B. Textor, ed., *Cultural Frontiers of the Peace Corps*. Cambridge, MA: MIT Press, 1966, p.ix.

82 E. Fox, G. Nicolau and H. Wofford, eds., *Citizen In a Time of Change: The Returned Peace Corps Volunteer*. Washington, DC: Peace Corps, 1965, p.46.

83 'Second Thoughts'. *The Volunteer*, August 1962, p.1.

84 D. Robinson, 'Ivory Coast'. *Peace Corps Volunteer,* April 1967, p.16.

85 D.M. Warren, 'The Road Toward Cross-Cultural Understanding'. In B.E. Schwimmer and D.M. Warren, eds., *Anthropology and the Peace Corps: Case Studies in Career Preparation.* Ames: Iowa State University Press, 1993, p.70.

86 I. Luce, ed., *Letters from the Peace Corps.* Washington, DC: Robert B. Luce, 1964, p.4.

87 W. Siegel, 'Hanging On (and Hanging Out) in Boston'. Peace Corps Writers, 2005, http://www.peacecorpswriters.org/pages/2005/0503/503wrwrsiegel.html.

88 Rice, *Bold Experiment,* p.168; M.B. Smith, 'Explorations in Competence: A Study of Peace Corps Teachers in Ghana'. *American Psychologist,* Vol. 21, No. 6, 1966.

89 J.A. Amin, *The Peace Corps in Cameroon.* Kent, OH: The Kent State University Press, 1992, p.99.

90 R.A. Randall, 'Similarities Between Peace Corps and Anthropological Experience'. In B.E. Schwimmer and D.M. Warren, eds., *Anthropology and the Peace Corps: Case Studies In Career Preparation.* Ames: Iowa State University Press, 1993, pp.91–92.

91 T. Zurlo, 'Becoming a Man in the Sixties: The Peace Corps and the Army'. Peace Corps Writers, 2005, http://www.peacecorpswriters.org/pages/2005/0501/501warpeace.html.

92 F.J. Mahony, 'Success in Somalie'. In R.B. Textor, ed., *Cultural Frontiers of the Peace Corps.* Cambridge, MA: MIT Press, 1966, pp.131–132.

93 V.R. Dorjahn, 'Transcultural Perceptions and Misperceptions in Sierra Leone'. In Textor, ed., *Cultural Frontiers,* p.177.

94 A. Zeitlin, *To the Peace Corps with Love.* Garden City, NY: Doubleday, 1965, p.16.

95 Schwarz, *What You Can Do,* p.36.

96 Siegel, 'Hanging On'.

97 J. Demos, 'Ghana'. *The Volunteer,* March 1962, p.4.

98 'Volunteer Life Called "Unsentimental Education"'. *Peace Corps Volunteer* September 1963, p.2; Smith, 'Explorations in Competence'.

99 J. Zimmerman, 'Beyond Double Consciousness: Black Peace Corps Volunteers in Africa, 1961–1971'. *American Historical Review*, Vol. 82, No. 3, 1995: 1020, 1024, 1023.

100 D. Schickele, 'When the Right Hand Washes the Left', Peace Corps Writers, 2003, http://www.peacecorpswriters.org/pages/2003/ 0303/prntvrs303/pv303all.html#pchist303.

101 P. Stevens, Jr. 'An Ethnographer without Portfolio'. In Schwimmer and Warren, eds., *Anthropology and the Peace Corps*, p.31.

102 Warren, 'Road Toward Cross-Cultural Understanding', pp.70, 74.

103 K. Moore, 'Returning'. In K. Coskran and C.W. Truesdale, eds., *An Inn Near Kyoto: Writing by American Women Abroad*. Minneapolis, MN: New Rivers Press, 1998, p.51.

104 T. Peyton, 'A Personal Experience'. *Peace Corps Volunteer*, August 1963, p.15.

105 T. Heidlebaugh, 'First Lion Hunt'. In G. Kennedy, ed., *From the Center of the Earth: Stories Out of the Peace Corps*. Santa Monica, CA: Clover Park Press, 1991, p.56.

106 D. Dearborn, 'Times Affect Motives'. *Peace Corps Volunteer*, March 1968, p.23.

107 V.L. Washington, 'Building "self-hood"'. *Peace Corps Volunteer*, June 1969, p.32.

108 D. Douglas, '"A Good Place to Live"'. *The Peace Corps Volunteer*, August 1969, p.22.

109 G. Chuzi, 'The Passive Idealists'. *The Peace Corps Volunteer*, 1967, p.4.

110 G.T. Rice, *Peace Corps in the '80s*. Washington, DC: Peace Corps, 1986, pp.3, 33.

111 R.G. Carey, *The Peace Corps*. New York: Praeger, 1970, p.200.

112 Siegel, 'Hanging On'.

113 M. Stanisland, *American Intellectuals and African Nationalists, 1955–1970*. New Haven, CT: Yale University Press, 1991.

4 GENDERED AMERICAN QUESTS IN 'TIMELESS AFRICA'

1 P. Bourdieu, *Distinction: A Social Critique of the Judgement of Taste*, trans. R. Nice. Cambridge, MA: Harvard University Press, 1984, p.367.

2   J. Cowie, *Stayin' Alive: The 1970s and the Last Days of the Working Class*. New York: Free Press, 2010, p.310.

3   D.E. Miller, *Reinventing American Protestantism: Christianity in the New Millennium*. Berkeley: University of California Press, 1997; E. Omri, 'Faith Beyond Belief; Evangelical Protestant Conceptions of Faith and the Resonance of Anti-Humanism'. *Social Analysis*, Vol. 52, No. 1, Spring 2008; D. Frum, *How We Got Here*. New York: Basic Books, 2000.

4   P. Lester and R. Smith, 'African-American Photo Coverage in *Life*, *Newsweek* and *Time*, 1937–1988'. *Journalism Quarterly*, Vol. 67, No. 1, Spring 1990: 133–134.

5   S. Crouch, *The Artificial White Man: Essays on Authenticity*. New York: Basic Books, 2004, p.85; L.E. Wynter, *American Skin: Pop Culture, Big Business, and the End of White America*. New York: Crown, 2002, pp.99–130; T. Boyd, *Young, Black, Rich and Famous: The Rise of the NBA, the Hip Hop Invasion, and the Transformation of American Culture*. New York: Doubleday, pp.19–22, 97, 103–104, 117–118; B. Kitwana, *Why White Kids Love Hip-Hop: Wankstas, Wiggers, Wannabes, and the New Reality of Race in America*. New York: Basic, 2005.

6   E. Bonilla-Silva, *Racism without Racists: Color-Blind Racism and the Persistence of Racial Inequality in the United States*. Lanham, MD: Rowman & Littlefield, 2003.

7   O. Patterson, 'A Poverty of the Mind'. *New York Times*, 26 March 2006; T. Boyd, *Am I Black Enough for You? Popular Culture from the 'Hood and Beyond*. Bloomington: Indiana University Press, 1997; B. Landry, *The New Black Middle Class*. Berkeley: University of California Press, 1987.

8   A. Hacker, *Mismatch: The Growing Gulf Between Women and Men*. New York: Scribner, 2003, p.97; F. Pfeil, 'From Pillar to Postmodern: Race, Class and Gender in Male Rampage Film'. In J.L. Lewis, ed., *The New American Cinema*, Durham, NC: Duke University Press, 1998: pp.146–186; W.P. Hammond, 'Being a Man About It: Manhood Meaning Among African Men'. *Psychology of Men and Masculinity*, Vol. 6, No. 2, 2005.

9   L. Morrow, 'Africa: The Scramble for Existence'. *Time*, 7 September 1992, pp.40–46.

10 J.E. Fair, 'War, Famine, and Poverty: Race in the Construction of Africa's Media Image'. *Journal of Communication Inquiry*, Vol. 17, No. 5, Summer 1993; J.E. Fair 'The Body Politic, the Bodies of Women, and the Politics of Famine in U.S. Television Coverage of Famine in the Horn of Africa'. *Journalism and Mass Communication*, Vol. 158, 1996; L.H. Malkki, 'Speechless Emissaries: Refugees, Humanitarianism, and Dehistoricization'. *Cultural* Anthropology, Vol. 11, No. 3, August 1996; M. Allimadi, *The Hearts of Darkness: How White Writers Created the Racist Image of Africa*. New York: Black Star Books, 2002.

11 G. Myers, T. Klak and T. Koehl, 'The Inscription of Difference: News Coverage of the Conflicts in Rwanda and Bosnia'. *Political Geography*, Vol. 15, No. 1, 1995: 33, 37–38.

12 S. Fabian, 'Journey Out of Darkness? Images of Africa in American Travelogues at the Turn of the Millennium'. *Continuum: Journal of Media and Cultural Studies*, Vol. 27, No. 1, 2013.

13 R.D. Kaplan, 'The Coming Anarchy'. *The Atlantic Monthly*, February 1994, pp.44–45, 46, 54.

14 K.C. Dunn, 'Fear of a Black Planet: Anarchy Anxieties and Postcolonial Travel to Africa'. *Third World Quarterly*, Vol. 25, No. 3, 2004.

15 D. Ibert, '"The Man Who Gave Us Courage"'. *Reader's Digest*, August 1992; M. McConnell, 'Escape from Terror'. *Reader's Digest*, October 1994; M. Vollers, 'A Life in the Wild'. *Reader's Digest*, August 1991; D. Owens and M. Owens, 'The Ivory War'. *Reader's Digest*, October 1992; J. Domatob, 'Coverage of Africa in American Popular Magazines'. *Issue: A Journal of Opinion*, Vol. 22, No. 1, Winter/Spring 1994; J.E. Fair and P. Chakravartty, 'Touring Disaster: American Television Coverage of Famine in the Horn of Africa'. In K. Nordenstreng and M. Griffin, eds., *International Media Monitoring*. Cresskill, NJ: Hampton, NJ, 1999; S.D. Moeller, *Compassion Fatigue: How the Media Sell Disease, Famine, War and Death*. New York: Routledge, 1999, pp.98–111; G. Berger, *USA for Africa: Rock Aid in the Eighties*. New York: Franklin Watts, 1987, pp.51–59.

[16] 'A Continent's Slow Suicide'. *Reader's Digest*, May 1993.

[17] M.D. Leakey, 'Footprints in the Ashes of Time'. *National Geographic*, April 1979, p.457.

[18] V. Englebert, 'Drought Threatens the Tuareg World'. *National Geographic*, April 1974, pp.544–545.

[19] N. Sobania, 'But Where Are the Cattle? Popular Images of Maasai and Zulu across the Twentieth Century'. *Visual Anthropology*, Vol. 15, No. 3, 2002, p.319; J. Kambites and S. Kambites, 'Return to Uganda'. *National Geographic*, July 1980; A. Fisher, 'Africa Adorned'. *National Geographic*, November 1984.

[20] G. Gerster, 'Tsetse', *National Geographic*. December 1986, pp.816–817, 822–823, 832–833.

[21] C.E. Cobb, Jr., 'The Twilight of Apartheid'. *National Geographic*, August 1993; P. Caputo, 'Tragedy Stalks the Horn of Africa'. *National Geographic*, February 1993.

[22] G.B. Schaller, 'Gentle Gorillas, Turbulent Times'. *National Geographic*, October 1995; P. Miller, 'Jane Goodall'. *National Geographic*, December 1995.

[23] S. Montgomery, *Walking with the Great Apes: Jane Goodall, Dian Fossey, Biruté Galdikas*. Boston: Houghton Mifflin, 1991, p.216.

[24] J.S. Adams and T.O. McShane, *The Myth of Wild Africa: Conservation Without Illusion*. Berkeley: University of California Press, 1996, p.184.

[25] J. Goldberg, 'The Hunted'. *New Yorker*, 5 April 2010, pp.43, 53, 62; Adams and McShane, *Myth of Wild Africa*, pp.143–152.

[26] J.M. McClary, 'A Glimpse of Eden on Safari in Zaire'. *New York Times*, 11 August 1985.

[27] R. Mayer, *Artificial Africas: Colonial Images in the Times of Globalization*. Hanover, NH: Dartmouth College, 2002, p.64.

[28] R.G. Gooding, 'Disney in Africa and the Inner City: On Race and Space in *The Lion King*'. *Social Identities*, Vol. 1, No. 2, 1995.

[29] S.J. May, *Michener: A Writer's Journey*. Norman: University of Oklahoma Press, 2005, pp.249–250.

[30] Ibid., p.244.

[31] 'Africa', 1982. http://www.songfacts.com/detail.php?id=3009.

32 D. Hickey and K.C. Wylie, *An Enchanting Darkness: The American Vision of Africa in the Twentieth Century*. East Lansing: Michigan State University Press, 1993, pp.229–231.

33 B. Cooper, *Weary Sons of Conrad: White Fiction against the Grain of Africa's Dark Heart*. New York: Bern, 2002.

34 Ibid., pp.35–68; D. Buchbinder, 'Enter the Schlemiel: The Emergence of Inadequate or Incompetent Masculinities in Recent Film and Television'. *Canadian Review of American Studies*, Vol. 38, No. 2, 2008.

35 K.A. Koza, 'The Africa of Two Western Women Writers: Barbara Kingsolver and Margaret Laurence'. *Critique*, Vol. 44, No. 3, Spring 2003: 293.

36 D. Kunz, 'White Men in Africa: On Barbara Kingsolver's *The Poisonwood Bible*'. In M.C. Carnes, ed., *Novel History: Historians and Novelists Confront America's Past (and Each Other)*. New York: Simon & Schuster, 2004, p.287; S.E. Ruble, *The Gospel of Freedom and Power: Protestant Missionaries in American Culture after World War II*. Chapel Hill: University of North Carolina Press, 2012, pp.153–157; W.F. Purcell, 'Barbara Kingsolver's *The Poisonwood Bible* and the Essentializing of Africa: A Critical Double Standard?' *Notes on Contemporary Literature*, Vol. 37, No. 5, November 2007.

37 P.H. Demory, 'Into the Heart of Light: Barbara Kingsolver Rereads Heart of Darkness'. *Conradiana*, Vol. 34, No. 3, Fall 2002.

38 M. Thomas, 'I Never Quite Felt at Home in America', *Chicago Tribune*, 28 June 1987.

39 Hickey and Wylie, *Enchanting Darkness*, p.233.

40 K. Heron, 'Longing for Blackness'. *New York Times*, 11 October 1987.

41 Thomas, 'I Never Felt Quite at Home'.

42 Heron, 'Longing for Blackness'.

43 Thomas, 'I Never Felt Quite at Home'.

44 M.M. Schmidt, 'Interview with John Coyne'. Peace Corps Writers, 2005, http://www.peacecorpswriters.org/pages/2005/0509/509talkschmidt.html.

45 J. Swiller, 'Talking with Josh Swiller'. Peace Corps Writers, 2007, http://www.peacecorpswriters.org/pages/2007/0709/709talk-swiller.html.

46 Ibid.

47 T. D'Souza, 'Talking with Tony D'Souza'. Peace Corps Writers, 2006, http://www.peacecorpswriters.org/pages/2006/0603/603 talkdsouza.html.

48 M. Sullivan, 'Better Remember This'. Peace Corps Worldwide, 23 May 2009, http://peacecorpsworldwide.org/better-remember-this-2/.

49 M. Szumowski, 'Falling in Love with Africa'. Peace Corps Writers, 2003, http://www.peacecorpswriters.org/pages/2003/0309/prntvrs309/pv309wrwr.html.

50 K. Holloway, 'Talking with Kris Holloway'. Peace Corps Writers, 2006, http://www.peacecorpswriters.org/pages/2006/0609/prntvrs609/pv609talk-holloway.html.

51 A.F. Fitzpatrick, 'Letter Home'. Peace Corps Writers, 2001, http://www.peacecorpswriters.org/pages/2001/0107/107letbots.html.

52 S. Junger, *Tribe: On Homecoming and Belonging*. London: Fourth Estate, 2016, pp.94, 90.

53 D.C. Moore, 'Routes: Alex Haley's *Roots* and the Rhetoric of Geneaology'. *Transition*, Vol. 64, 1994, p.14; K. Cartwright, *Reading Africa into American Literature: Epics, Fables, and Gothic Tales*. Lexington: University of Kentucky, 2002, pp.72–80.

54 Hickey and Wylie, *Enchanting Darkness*, pp.202–204.

55 A. Austin, Achieving Blackness: *Race, Black Nationalism, and Afrocentrism in the Twentieth Century*. New York: NYU Press, 2006, pp.170, 193.

56 E. Pleck, 'Kwanzaa: The Making of a Black Nationalist Tradition, 1966–1990'. *Journal of American Ethnic History*, Vol. 20, Vol. 4, Summer 2001, p.18.

57 A. Ducille, *Skin Trade*. Cambridge, MA: Harvard University Press, 1996, p.133; C.E. Walker, *We Can't Go Home Again: An Argument about Afrocentrism*. Oxford: Oxford University Press, 2001; P.M. Sniderman and T. Piazza, *Black Pride and*

Black Prejudice. Princeton, NJ: Princeton University Press, 2002, pp.35–37, 112–119, 154–155, 176–178.

58 "'I Thee Wed'". *Essence*, April 1973.

59 J.B. Woodard and T. Mastin, 'Black Womanhood: *Essence* and its Treatment of Stereotypical Images of Black Women'. *Journal of Black Studies*, Vol. 36, No. 2, November 2005: p.278; 'A Touch of Africa'. *Essence*, July 1980 ; A.P. Gumbs, 'Black (Buying) Power: The Story of *Essence* Magazine'. In L.W. Hill and J. Rabig, eds., *The Business of Black Power: Community Development, Capitalism, and Corporate Responsibility in Postwar America.* Rochester, NY: University of Rochester Press, 2012.

60 W. Intelligent, 'Interview'. In J.D. Eure and J.G. Spady, eds., *Nation Conscious Rap.* New York: PC International Press, 1991.

61 S. Soujah. In Eure and Spady, eds., *Nation Conscious Rap*, p.257.

62 V. Yenika-Agbaw, *Representing Africa In Children's Literature: Old and New Ways of Seeing.* New York: Routledge, 2008; B. Bader, 'How the Little House Gave Ground: The Beginnings of Multiculturalism in a New, Black Children's Literature'. *Horn Book Magazine*, November/December 2002.

63 V. Yenika-Agbaw, 'Images of West Africa in Children's Books: Replacing Old Stereotypes with New Ones?' In D.L. Fox and K.G. Short, eds., *Stories Matter; The Complexity of Cultural Authenticity in Children's Literature.* Urbana, IL: National Council of Teachers of English, 2003; M. Markman, *The Path: An Adventure in African History.* Brooklyn, NY: A&B, 1977.

64 K. Woodard, *Nation within a Nation: Amiri Barka (LeRoi Jones) and Black Power Politics.* Chapel Hill: University of North Carolina Press, 1999, pp.173–180; B.G. Plummer, *Rising Wind: Black Americans and U.S. Foreign Affairs, 1935–1960.* Chapel Hill: University of North Carolina Press, 1996, p.323 ; B.G. Plummer, *In Search of Power: African Americans in the Era of Decolonization, 1956–1976.* Cambridge University Press, New York, 2013.

65 T. Adeleke, 'The Color Line as a Confining and Restraining Paradigm: Keith Richburg and his Critiques Analyzed'. *Western Journal of Black Studies*, Vol. 23, No. 2, 1999: p.107.

66 N.M. Rooks, *Ladies' Pages: African American Women's Magazines and the Culture that Made Them*. New Brunswick, NJ: Rutgers University Press, 2004, p.144.

67 K. Fufuka, 'Bringing It Down Front'. *Essence*, August 1971, p.8.

68 O. Okore, 'The Mermaid'. *Essence*, September 1976; B. Rubens, 'The Gold Widows'. *Essence*, November 1978; H. Boyd, '"Roots" ... The Selling of a People'. *Essence*, August 1977; K. Quaye, 'The African Stereotype'. *Essence*, December 1982.

69 G. Simpson, 'Kiss the Ground'. *Essence*, July 1979, p.66; L. Payne, 'Dada: When Africa Bleeds'. *Essence*, July 1980; D. O'Connor, 'When the Gods and Heroes Are Black'. *Essence*, July 1980; M. Chabaku, '"Guts and the Will to Keep on": A Woman of South Africa Speaks Out'. *Ebony*, January 1985; M. Ogundipe-Leslie, 'Sisterhood is Global'. *Essence*, February 1985; A.A. Aidoo, 'Sisterhood is Global'. *Essence*, March 1985.

70 B. Golden Kayode, 'African Afro-American Marriages: Do They Work?' *Essence*, July 1979, p.127.

71 O. Lake, 'Diaspora African Repatriation: The Place of Diaspora Women in the Pan-African Nexus'. In M. Grosz-Ngaté and O.H. Kokole, eds., *Gendered Encounters: Challenging Cultural Boundaries and Social Hierarchies in Africa*. New York: Routledge, 1997.

72 E. Julien, 'The Romance of Africa: Three Narratives by African-American Women'. In E. Mudimbe-Boyi, ed., *Beyond Dichotomies: Histories, Identities, Cultures, and the Challenge of Globalization*. Albany: State University of New York Press, 2002, p.145.

73 Ibid., p.142.

74 J. McLaren, 'Alice Walker and the Legacy of African American Discourse on Africa'. In I. Okpewho, C.B. Davies and A.A. Mazrui, eds., *The African Diaspora: African Origins and New World Identities*. Bloomington: Indiana University Press, 1999.

75 K. Kanneh, *African Identities: Race, Nation and Culture in Ethnography, Pan-Africanism and Black Literatures*. London: Routledge, 1998, p.114; M. Kieti, 'Homesick and Eurocentric? Alice Walker's Africa'. In F. Ojo-Ade, ed., *Of Dreams Deferred,*

Dead or Alive: African Perspectives on African-American Writers.
Westport, CT: Greenwood Press, 1996.

76 V. Pollard, 'Cultural Connections in Paule Marshall's *Praisesong for the Widow'. Caribbean Quarterly*, Vol. 34, No. 1/2, March/June 1988: p.58.

77 D.H. Denniston, *The Fiction of Paule Marshall: Reconstructions of History, Culture, and Gender.* Knoxville: University of Tennessee Press, 1983; E.C. DeLamotte, *Places of Silence, Journeys of Freedom: The Fiction of Paule Marshall.* Philadelphia: University of Pennsylvania Press, 1998; C. Thorsson, 'Dancing up a Nation: Paule Marshall's *Praisesong for the Widow'. Callaloo*, Vol. 30, No. 2, Spring 2007; A.P.A. Busia, 'What Is Your Nation? Reconnecting Africa and Her Diaspora through Paule Marshall's *Praisesong for the Widow'.* In C.A. Wall, ed., *Changing Our Own Words: Essays on Criticism, Theory, and Writing by Black Women.* New Brunswick, NJ: Rutgers University Press, 1987.

78 M.D. Kubitschek, 'Paule Marshall's Women on Quest'. *Black American Literature Forum*, Vol. 21, No. 1/2, Spring/Summer 1987: p.59; J. Olmsted, 'The Pull to Memory and the Language of Place in Paule Marshall's *The Chosen Place, the Timeless People* and *Praisesong for the Widow'. African American Review*, Vol. 31, No. 2, Summer 1997.

79 M.A. Kelley, *Gloria Naylor's Early Novels.* Gainesville: University Press of Florida, 1999, p.98.

80 V.C. Fowler, *Gloria Naylor: In Search of Sanctuary.* New York: Twayne, 1996, pp.92–93, 115–116, 120; A.K. Levin, *Africanism and Authenticity in African-American Women's Novels.* Gainesville: University Press of Florida, 2003, pp.1–5, 27–46.

81 T.E. Higgins, *Religiosity, Cosmology, and Folklore: The African Influence in the Novels of Toni Morrison.* New York: Routledge, 2001, pp.29–44; L.V.D. Jennings, *Toni Morrison and the Idea of Africa.* Cambridge: Cambridge University Press, 2008, pp.4–7; Levin, *Africanism and Authenticity*, pp.47–77; R.A. York, *The Extension of Life: Fiction and History in the American Novel.* London: Associated University Press, London, 2003,

pp.89–100; K. Zuaditu-Selassie, *African Spiritual Traditions in the Novels of Toni Morrison*. Gainesville: University Press of Florida, 2009.

82 J.-H. Kai, 'The African-Americans' Quest for Identity in Toni Morrison's *Song of Solomon*: Humanistic Geographic Perspectives'. In A.J.M. Pérez, ed., *Restless Travelers: Quests for Identity across European and American Time and Space*. Newcastle upon Tyne: Cambridge Scholars, 2011.

83 M. Dubey, *Black Women Novelists and the Nationalist Aesthetic*. Bloomington: Indiana University Press, 1994, pp.16–29; Kanneh, *African Identities*, pp.116–134; C. Thorsson, *Women's Work: Nationalism and Contemporary African American Women's Novels*. Charlottesville: University of Virginia Press, 2013, pp.14–24.

5 AFRICA COSMOPOLITAN IN THE NEW MILLENNIUM

1 R.R. Tomes, 'American Exceptionalism in the Twenty-First Century'. *Survival: Global Politics and Strategy*, Vol. 56, No. 1, 2014, p.28; G. Hodgson, *The Myth of American Exceptionalism*. New Haven, CT: Yale University Press, 2009, pp.115–127; J. Margulies, *What Changed When Everything Changed: 9/11 and the Making of National Identity*. New Haven, CT: Yale University Press, 2013.

2 A. Lieven, *America Right or Wrong: An Anatomy of American Nationalism*, 2nd ed. Oxford: Oxford University Press, 2012, p.14.

3 J.L. Jackson, Jr., *Harlemworld: Doing Race and Class in Contemporary Black America*. Chicago: University of Chicago Press, 2001, pp.43–44; E. Robinson, *Disintegration: The Splintering of Black America*. New York: Doubleday, 2010; T.J. Sugrue, *Not Even Past: Barack Obama and the Burden of Race*. Princeton, NJ: Princeton University Press, 2010.

4 L. Grubbs, *Secular Missionaries: Americans and African Development in the 1960s*. Amherst: University of Massachusetts Press, 2009, p.186.

5 A. Williams, 'Into Africa'. *New York Times*, 13 August 2006; K. Mathers, 'Mr. Kristof, I Presume?' *Transition*, Vol. 107, 2012.

6   A. Hess, 'The White Knight'. *Slate*, 18 June 2014, http://www.
     slate.com/articles/double_x/doublex/2014/06/nicholas_
     kristof_wants_to_save_the_world_with_his_new_york_
     times_columns.html.

7   A. Deaton, *The Great Escape: Health, Wealth, and the Origins
     of Inequality*. Princeton, NJ: Princeton University Press, 2013,
     p.283.

8   A. Huffman, *Mississippi in Africa*. New York: Gotham Books,
     2005, p.256; M.B. Robins, '"Lost Boys" and the Promised
     Land: U.S. Newspaper Coverage of Sudanese Refugees'.
     Journalism, Vol. 4, No. 1, 2003; A. Wilkinson and M. Leach,
     'Briefing: Ebola—Myths, Realties, and Structural Violence'.
     African Affairs, Vol. 114, No. 454, 2014; Y. Kalyango, Jr.,
     and U. Onyebadi, 'Thirty Years of Broadcasting Africa on
     U.S. Network Television News'. *Journal of Broadcasting and
     Electronic Media*, Vol. 56, No. 4, 2012.

9   H. Härting, 'Global Humanitarianism, Race, and the Spectacle
     of the African Corpse in Current Western Representations of
     the Rwandan Genocide'. *Comparative Studies of South Asia,
     Africa and the Middle East*, Vol. 28, No. 1, 2008.

10   K. Gabbard, *Black Magic: White Hollywood and African
     American Culture*. New Brunswick, NJ: Rutgers University
     Press, 2004, pp.143–176.

11   L. Hubbard and K. Mathers, 'Surviving American Empire in
     Africa: The Anthropology of Reality Television'. *International
     Journal of Cultural Studies*, Vol. 7, No. 4, 2004: p.452; H.L.
     Steeves, 'Commodifying Africa on U.S. Network Reality
     Television'. *Communication, Culture and Critique*, Vol. 1, No. 4,
     2008: pp.428–429; I.R. Roy, 'Worlds Apart: Nation-Branding
     on the National Geographic Channel'. *Media, Culture and Society*,
     Vol. 29, No. 4, 2007.

12   D. Quammen, 'Megatransect'. *National Geographic*, October
     2000, pp.2–3, 10; Quammen, 'The Green Abyss'. *National
     Geographic*, March 2001, pp.4, 5; D. Quammen, 'End of the
     Line'. *National Geographic*, August 2001, p.103.

13   G. Packer, *The Unwinding: An Inner History of the New America*.
     New York: Farrar, Straus and Giroux, 2013: p.4; F. Furedi,

'Celebrity Culture'. *Society*, Vol. 47, 2010: p.495; 'Making the Scene'. *New York Times*, 13 August 2006.

14 H.L. Talley and M.J. Casper, 'Oprah Goes to Africa: Philanthropic Consumption and Political (Dis)Engagement'. In T.T. Cotton and K. Springer, eds., *Stories of Oprah: The Oprahfication of American Culture*. Jackson: University Press of Mississippi, 2010, p.107; Williams, 'Into Africa'.

15 R. Barnard, 'Oprah's Paton; or, South Africa and the Globalization of Suffering'. *English Studies in Africa: A Journal of the Humanities*, Vol. 47, No. 1, 2004.

16 A. Samuels, 'Oprah Goes to School'. *Newsweek*, 8 January 2007.

17 R. Traister, 'What Oprah Can't Forget', *Salon*, 13 January 2007, http://www.salon.com/2007/01/13/oprah_school/.

18 N. Paris, 'Paris Hilton to Visit Rwanda to "Leave her Mark"', *Telegraph*, 16 October 2007, http://www.telegraph.co.uk/news/worldnews/1566366/Paris-Hilton-to-visit-Rwanda-to-leave-her-mark.html; 'Paris Hilton Arrested for Allegedly Possessing Marijuana', *Guardian*, 2 July 2010, https://www.theguardian.com/lifeandstyle/2010/jul/02/paris-hilton-arrest-marijuana.

19 D. MacCannell, 'Staged Authenticity: Arrangements of Social Space in Tourist Settings'. *American Journal of Sociology*, Vol. 79, No. 3, November 1973, p.590; K. Mathers, *Travel, Human-itarianism, and Becoming American in Africa*. New York: Palgrave McMillan, 2010, pp.23–24; C.M. Rogerson, 'Adventure Tourism in Africa: The Case of Livingstone, Zambia'. *Geography*, Vol. 89, No. 2, 2004.

20 K. Mathers and L. Hubbard, 'Doing Africa: Travelers, Adventurers, and American Conquest of Africa'. In L.A. Vivanco and R.J. Gordon, eds., *Tarzan was an Eco-Tourist ... and Other Tales in the Anthropology of Adventure*. New York: Berghahn, 2006, pp.202, 204.

21 R. Trillo and J. Hudgens, *The Rough Guide to West Africa*, 5th ed. New York: Rough Guides, 2009, p.12.

22 T. Neville, 'A Walk on the Wild Coast'. *Outside*, 17 November 2003.

23 Mathers, *Travel, Humanitarianism, and Becoming American*, p.168; M. Rolfes, 'Poverty Tourism: Theoretical Reflections and Empirical Findings Regarding an Extraordinary Form of Tourism'. *GeoJournal*, Vol. 75, No. 5, 2010; P.L. Pearce, 'Tourists' Written Reactions to Poverty in Southern Africa'. *Journal of Travel Research*, Vol. 51, No. 2, 2012.

24 D. Hammett and N. Jayawardane, 'Performing the Primitive in the Postcolony: Nyoni's Kraal in Cape Town'. *Urban Forum*, Vol. 20, No. 2, 2009: pp.218, 221, 228; E.M. Bruner and B. Kirshenblatt-Gimblett, 'Maasai on the Lawn: Tourist Realism in East Africa'. *Cultural Anthropology*, Vol. 9, No. 4, November 1994; E.M. Bruner, 'The Maasai and the Lion King: Authenticity, Nationalism, and Globalization in African Tourism'. *American Ethnologist*, Vol. 28, No. 4, November 2001; M. Mkono, 'African and Western Tourists: Object Authenticity Quest?' *Annals of Tourism Research*, Vol. 41, 2013.

25 S. Boer et al., *Mutation: Rem Koolhaas Harvard Project on the City*. [Barcelona]: Actar, 2001, p.718.

26 T. Hecker, 'The Slum Pastoral: Helicopter Visuality and Koolhaas's Lagos'. *Space and Culture*, Vol. 13, No. 3, 2010, p.257.

27 B. Charbonneau, 'Where I Am'. In J. O'Reilly, L. Habegger and S. O'Reilly, eds., *The Best Traveler's Tales, 2004*. San Francisco, CA: Travelers' Tales, 2004, pp.113–118.

28 D. Fryer, 'Cause for Alarm'. In J. O'Reilly, L. Habegger and S. O'Reilly, eds., *The Best Travel Writing, 2005*. San Francisco, CA: Travelers' Tales, 2005, pp.5, 6, 8.

29 K. Fedarko, 'High in Hell'. In S. Orlean, ed., *The Best American Travel Writing, 2007*. Boston: Houghton Mifflin, 2007, pp.40–42; Mathers, *Travel, Humanitarianism, and Becoming American*, pp.160–162.

30 Mathers, *Travel, Humanitarianism, and Becoming American*, pp.170, 59.

31 M.A. Wall, 'Africa on YouTube: Musicians, Tourists, Missionaries and Aid Workers'. *International Communication Gazette*, Vol. 71, No. 5, 2009: p.405.

32 Bruner, 'Maasai and the Lion King', p.901.

33 K. Salak, 'Mungo Made Me Do It'. In I. Frazier, ed., *The Best American Travel Writing, 2003*. Boston: Houghton Mifflin, 2003, pp.238, 247, 252, 253.

34 J.W. Egerton, 'The New Missionary'. *Christian Century*, 8 December 1965, pp.1509, 1508; W.R. Hutchinson, *Errand to the World: American Protestant Thought and Foreign Missions*. Chicago: University of Chicago Press, 1987, pp.188–202; S.E. Ruble, *The Gospel of Freedom and Power: Protestant Missionaries in American Culture after World War II*. Chapel Hill: University of North Carolina Press, 2012, pp.63–75.

35 R. Wuthnow, *Boundless Faith: The Global Outreach of American Churches*. Berkeley: University of California Press, Berkeley, 2009, pp.162–175.

36 'Falwell Raises a Stir by Opposing Sanctions against South Africa'. *Christianity Today*, 4 October 1985; R.J. Sider, *Rich Christians in an Age of Hunger: Moving from Affluence to Generosity*. New York: Paulist Press, 1977.

37 R. Stearns, 'We Are Not Commanded to Be a Docent in the Art Museum. We Are Commanded to Love the Poor'. *Christianity Today Online*, 12 June 2009, http://www.christianitytoday.com/ct/2009/juneweb-only/richard-stearns-on-americans-biggest-gospel-compromise.html.

38 D. Worth, 'Don't Forget Us'. *A Common Place*, September 2003; S. Dicklitch and H. Rice, 'The Mennonite Central Committee (MCC) and Faith-Based NGO Aid to Africa'. *Development in Practice*, Vol. 14, No. 5, August 2004; S. Corbett and B. Fikkert, *When Helping Hurts: How to Alleviate Poverty without Hurting the Poor ... and Yourself*. Chicago: Moody, 2009; D.A. Livermore, *Serving with Eyes Wide Open: Doing Short-Term Missions with Cultural Intelligence*. Grand Rapids: BakerBooks, 2006; J.F. Engel and W.A. Dyrness, *Changing the Mind of Missions: Where Have We Gone Wrong?* Downers Grove, IL: InterVarsity Press, 2000; D. Elmer, *Cross-Cultural Servanthood: Serving the World in Christlike Humility*. Downers Grove, IL: IVP Books, 2006; S. Wunderink, 'What to Do about Polygamy'. *Christianity Today*, July 2009.

39 W.R. Shenk, 'Recasting Theology of Mission: Impulses from the Non-Western World'. *International Bulletin of Missionary Research*, July 2001, p.105.

40 T. Stafford, 'Historian Ahead of His Time'. *Christianity Today*, February 2007, p.87.

41 M. Galli, 'Making the Local Church a Hero'. *Christianity Today*, March 2009.

42 E. Katongole, 'From Tower-Dwellers to Travelers'. *Christianity Today*, July 2007, pp.38, 39; J.L. Allen, Jr., 'Africa and Catholicism'. *National Catholic Reporter*, 10 March 2006, pp.12–15; F.A. Oborji, 'Poverty and the Mission-Charity Trend: A Perspective from Matthew'. *International Review of Mission*, Vol. 91, No. 360, 2002.

43 T.C. Morgan, 'Purpose Driven in Rwanda'. *Christianity Today*, October 2005, p.34.

44 A. Paquin, 'Politically Driven Injustice'. *Christianity Today*, February 2006; J. Michaelson, 'Rick Warren's Troubling Africa Mission'. *The Daily Beast*, 14 September 2014, http://www.thedailybeast.com/articles/2014/09/14/rick-warren-s-troubling-africa-mission.html ; B. Allen, 'Ugandan Pastors Blast Rick Warren for Opposing Anti-Gay Law'. *The Baptist Standard*, 21 December 2009.

45 Morgan, 'Purpose Driven', p.34.

46 M.M. Phillips, 'Unanswered Prayers'. *Wall Street Journal*, 19 December 2005.

47 'The Lessons of Jabez'. *Christianity Today*, March 2006.

48 M. Moring, '"Machine Gun Preacher" Under Heavy Fire'. *Christianity Today* online, 22 September 2011, http://www.christianitytoday.com/ct/2011/septemberweb-only/machinegunpreacher.html.

49 J. Donnelly, *A Twist of Faith: An American Christian's Quest to Help Orphans in Africa*. Boston: Beacon, 2012.

50 M. Mamdani, *Saviors and Survivors: Darfur, Politics, and the War on Terror*. New York: Pantheon, 2009, p.6; R. Hamilton, *Fighting for Darfur: Public Action and the Struggle to Stop Genocide*. New York: Palgrave Macmillan, 2011.

51 N. Munk, *The Idealist: Jeffrey Sachs and the Quest to End Poverty*. New York: Doubleday, 2013, p.37.

52 D. Moyo, *Dead Aid: Why Aid Is Not Working and How There Is a Better Way for Africa*. New York: Farrar, Straus and Giroux, 2009; A. Perry, *Lifeblood: How to Change the World One Dead Mosquito at a Time*. New York: PublicAffairs, 2011; W. Easterly, *The White Man's Burden: Why the West's Efforts to Aid the Rest Have Done So Much Ill and So Little Good*. New York: Penguin, 2007 ; M. Maren, *The Road to Hell: The Ravaging Effects of Foreign Aid and International Charity*. New York: Free Press, 1997.

53 E. Meehan, 'The Humanitarian's Dilemma'. *Slate*, June 2010, http://www.slate.com/articles/news_and_politics/dispatches/features/2010/the_humanitarians_dilemma/meet_aim.html.

54 A.C. Finnegan, 'The White Girl's Burden'. *Contexts*, Vol. 12, No. 1, Winter 2013: p.31; A.C. Finnegan, 'Beneath Kony 2012: Americans Aligning with Arms and Aiding Others'. *Africa Today*, Vol. 59, No. 1, Spring 2013.

55 E. Ross, 'The Invisible Christians of #Kony2012'. Africa is a Country, 13 March 2012. http://africasacountry.com/2012/03/the-invisible-christians-of-kony2012/.

56 V. Ochen, 'A War Victim's Opinion on Invisible Children's KONY 2012'. African Youth Initiative Network, 10 March 2012.

57 R. Anywar, 'KONY 2012: A View from Northern Uganda', National Geographic, 9 March 2012, http://voices.nationalgeographic.com/2012/03/09/kony-2012-a-view-from- northern-uganda/.

58 P. Curtis and T. McCarthy, 'Kony 2012: What's the Real Story?' *The Guardian*, 8 March 2012.

59 'Africa: KONY 2012, Selected Reflections', 14 March 2012, http://www.africafocus.org/docs12/kon1203a.php.

60 N. Egbunike, 'Great Story, Pity about the Movie.' MercatorNet, 16 March 2012, http://www.mercatornet.com/articles/view/great_story_pity_about_the_movie.

61 T. Cole, 'The White-Savior Industrial Complex'. *The Atlantic*, March 2012.

62 R. Murray, '"Kony 2102" Disappoints Ugandan Audience at Public Screening in Lira'. *New York Daily News*, 14 March 2012.

63 J. Russell, 'On KONY 2012', 2013, http://www.cbc.ca/player/play/2351973074.

64 http://africasacountry.com/; https://twitter.com/hashtag/TheAfricaTheMediaNeverShowsYou?src=hash; http://thisisafrica.me/.

65 R.L. Stirrat, 'Mercenaries, Missionaries and Misfits: Representations of Development Personnel'. *Critique of Anthropology*, Vol. 28, No. 4, 2008: pp.414–415.

66 L.J. Rice, 'Michael's Return & Spotlight on Africa'. *Ebony*, December, 2007.

67 S. Monroe, 'The Africa You Don't Know'. *Ebony*, December 2007, p.115.

68 '40 Fierce & Fabulous'. *Essence*, September 2010.

69 J. Hasty, 'Rites of Passage, Routes of Redemption: Emancipation Tourism and the Wealth of Culture'. *Africa Today*, Vol. 49, No. 3, Autumn 2002: p.60.

70 B. Holsey, *Routes of Remembrance: Refashioning the Slave Trade in Ghana*. Chicago: University of Chicago Press, 2008, p.165.

71 K. Schramm, 'Pan-Africanism as a Resource: The W.E.B. Du Bois Memorial Centre for Pan-African Culture in Ghana'. *African Identities*, Vol. 2, No. 2, 2004: p.161; A. Reed, *Pilgrimage Tourism of Diaspora Africans to Ghana*, New York: Routledge, 2015.

72 S.L. Richards, '"What Is to Be Remembered?" Tourism to Ghana's Slave Castle-Dungeons'. *Theatre Journal*, Vol. 57, No. 4, December 2005: p.631.

73 J. Pierre, *Predicament of Blackness: Postcolonial Ghana and the Politics of Race*. Chicago: University of Chicago Press, 2013, p.154.

74 C. Phillips, *The Atlantic Sound*. New York: Alfred A. Knopf, 2000, p.149.

75 A. Benton and K.Z. Shabazz, '"Find their Level": African American Roots Tourism in Sierra Leone and Ghana'. *Cahiers d'Études africaines*, Vol. 49, No. 102, 2009: p.498.

76 B. Holsey, 'Black Atlantic Visions: History, Race, and Trans-nationalism in Ghana'. *Cultural Anthropology,* Vol. 28, No. 3, 2013: p.514.

77 J.W. Shipley, 'Aesthetic of the Entrepreneur: Afro-Cosmopolitan Rap and Moral Circulation in Accra, Ghana'. *Anthropological Quarterly*, Vol. 82, No. 3, Summer 2009: pp.647, 651.

78 Phillips, *Atlantic Sound*, p.221.

79 J.C. Miller, 'The Wonders of My Africa: An Africanist Historian's View of Henry Louis Gates Jr.'s *Wonders of the African World*'. *Perspectives*, May 2000.

80 A.A. Mazrui, 'A Preliminary Critique of the TV Series by Henry Louis Gates, Jr.'. *The Black Scholar*, Vol. 30, No. 1, 2000: p.5.

81 F. Ojo-Ade, '"Wonders of the African World": Another Wake-Up Call for Africans'. In N. Afolabi, ed., *Marvel of the African World: African Cultural Patrimony, New World Connections, and Identities.* Asmara, Eritrea: Africa World Press, 2003; Z. Magubane, '"Call Me America": The Construction of Race, Identity, and History in Henry Louis Gates Jr.'s *Wonders of the African World*'. *Cultural Studies óCritical Methodologies*, Vol. 3, No. 3, 2003.

82 Phillips, *Atlantic Sound*, p.154.

83 J.T. Campbell, *Middle Passages: African American Journeys to Africa, 1787–2005*. New York: Penguin, 2007: p.364.

84 'President Mills Informed of Death and Funeral of Dr. Robert Lee'. *Modern Ghana News, 2010*, http://www.modernghana.com/news/285336/president-mills-informed-of-death-and-funeral-of-dr-rober.html.

85 Reed, *Pilgrimage Tourism*, p.193.

86 S. Penn, *Case for a Pardon: The Pete O'Neal Story*. Np: Pembooks, 2013, p.194.

87 M. Shetterly, 'Priscilla's Homecoming'. *Madison Magazine*, Spring 2006, p.46; Campbell, *Middle Passages*, p.436.

88 G.D. Smithers, 'Challenging a Pan-African Identity: The Autobiographical Writings of Maya Angelou, Barack Obama, and Caryl Phillips'. *Journal of American Studies*, Vol. 45, No. 3, 2011: p.496.

89 K.A. Appiah, *Cosmopolitanism: Ethics in a World of Strangers.* New York: W.W. Norton, 2007, p.xxi.

90 T. Cole, 'Teju Cole', 2016, http://www.tejucole.com/about-2/.

91 T. Cole, 'Home'. *New Yorker*, 22/29 December 2014, p.95.

92 J. Wood, 'The Arrival of Enigmas'. *The New Yorker*, 28 February 2011.

93 J.A. Arthur, *Invisible Sojourners: African Immigrant Diaspora in the United States.* Westport, CT: Praeger, 2000, p.43; 'African Immigrants in America: A Demographic Overview'. Immigration Policy Center, 2012, http://immigrationpolicy. org/just-facts/african-immigrants-america-demographic-overview; Robinson, *Disintegration*, pp.165–176.

94 T. Noah, 2016, http://www.trevornoah.com/videos/.

95 C. Magee, *Africa in the American Imagination: Popular Culture, Racialized Identities, and African Visual Culture.* Jackson: University Press of Mississippi, 2012, pp.168–169; M.J. Arnoldi, C.M. Kreamer and M.A. Mason, 'Reflections on "African Voices" at the Smithsonian's National Museum of Natural History', *African Arts*, Vol. 34, No. 2, 2011.

96 B. Wainaina, 'How to Write About Africa'. *Granta*, Vol. 92, 2005; C.N. Adichie, 'Our "Africa" Lenses'. *Washington Post*, 13 November 2006.

97 F. Vanhaecke, *A Useful Dream: African Photography, 1960–2010.* Milano: Silvana Editoriale, 2010, p.18; E. Haney, *Photography and Africa.* London: Reaktion Books, 2010.

98 Wainaina, 'How to Write About Africa'.

99 F.A. Irele, *African Imagination: Literature in Africa and the Black Diaspora.* New York: Oxford University Press, 2001, p.213.

100 D. Peterson del Mar, '*Sankofa* at Ashesi: African and Western Motifs at a Model University'. Forthcoming in K. Akyeampong, ed., *Education Access and Opportunity in Africa: Aspirations and Realities.* London: Edward Elgar Publishing, 2017.

101 H. Wabuke, 'Meet Yaa Gyasi'. *The Root*, 30 June 2016, http:// www.theroot.com/articles/culture/2016/06/meet-yaa-gyasi-the-author-of-the-slavery-novel-everyone-is-talking-about/; I. Chotiner, '"I Was Thinking About Blackness in America'. *Slate*, 6 June 2016, http://www.slate.com/articles/

arts/books/2016/06/yaa_gyasi_on_her_debut_novel_ homegoing_and_getting_blurbed_by_ta_nehisi.html.

102 R. Sulcas, '"Queen of Katwe" Makes a Move on a Ugandan Chessboard'. *New York Times*, 11 September 2016; A. Wilkinson, 'Queen of Katwe is the Exact Opposite of a White Savior Movie'. *Vox*, 30 September 2016, http://www.vox. com/2016/9/23/13007894/queen-katwe-movie-review-phiona-mutesi-white-savior.

PRIMARY SOURCES: BOOKS

Abani, C. (2014) *The Secret History of Las Vegas*, Penguin, New York.

Adichie, C.N. (2007) *Half of a Yellow Sun*, Anchor Books, New York.

Adichie, C.N. (2010) *The Thing Around Your Neck*, Anchor Books, New York.

Adichie, C.N. (2013) *Americanah*, Anchor, New York.

Akeley, C.E. (1925) *In Brightest Africa*, Garden City Publishing, Garden City, NY.

Akeley, C. and M.L.J. Akeley (1953) *Adventures in the African Jungle*, Dodd, Mead & Company, New York [orig. 1936].

Akeley, D.J. (1928) *'J.T., Jr.': The Biography of an African Monkey*, Macmillan, New York.

Akeley, D. (1933) *Jungle Portraits*, Robert M. McBride, New York.

Akeley, M.L.J. (1929) *Carl Akeley's Africa*, Blue Ribbon, New York.

Akeley, M.L.J. (1940) *The Wilderness Lives Again: Carl Akeley and the Great Adventure*, Dodd, Mead & Company, New York.

Angelou, M. (1981) *The Heart of a Woman*, Random House, New York.

Angelou, M. (1986) *All God's Children Need Traveling Shoes*, Random House, New York.

Angelou, M. (2002) *A Song Flung Up to Heaven*, Random House, New York.

Appiah, K.A. (2007) *Cosmopolitanism: Ethics in a World of Strangers*, W.W. Norton, New York.

Atta, S. (2010) *News from Home: Stories*, Interlink, Northampton, MA: Interlink.

Atta, S. (2013) *A Bit of Difference*, Interlink, Northampton, MA.

Baingana, B. (2005) *Tropical Fish: Tales from Entebbe*, Harlem Moon, New York.

Bartels, P. and E. Herman (2012) *King Peggy: An American Secretary, Her Royal Destiny, and the Inspiring Story of How She Changed an African Village*, Doubleday, New York.

Beah, I. (2007) *A Long Way Gone: Memoirs of a Boy Soldier*, Farrar, Straus and Giroux, New York.

Beard, P.H. (1965) *The End of the Game*, Viking, New York.

Beard, P. (2004) *Zara's Tales from Hog Ranch: Perilous Escapades in Equatorial Africa*, Alfred Knopf, New York.

Belafonte, H. with M. Shnayerson (2001) *My Song: A Memoir*, Alfred A. Knopf, New York.

Belcher, W.L. (1988) *Honey from the Lion: An African Journey*, E.P. Dutton, New York.

Bellow, S. (1944) *Dangling Man*, Vanguard, New York.

Bellow, S. (1996) *Henderson the Rain King*, Penguin, New York, [orig. 1959].

Blixen, K. (2001) *Out of Africa*, Penguin, London, [orig. 1937].

Boone, C.C. (1927) *Congo as I Saw It*, J.J. Little and Ives, New York.

Boone, C.C. (1970) *Liberia as I Knew It*, Negro Universities Press, Westport, CT [orig. 1929].

Bowne, E. (1961) *Gift from the African Heart*, Dodd, Mead, New York [orig. 1960].

Boyle, T.C. (2006) *Water Music*, Penguin, New York [orig. 1981].

Bronson, E.B. (1910) *In Closed Territory*, A.C. McClurg, Chicago.

Bulawayo, N. (2014) *We Need New Names*, Back Bay Books, New York.

Burroughs, E.R. (1969) *The Return of Tarzan*, Ballantine, New York [orig. 1913].

Burroughs, E.R. (1969) *The Beasts of Tarzan*, Ballantine, New York [orig. 1914].

Burroughs, E.R. (2008) *Tarzan of the Apes*, Signet, New York [orig. 1912].

Caputo, P. (2002) *Horn of Africa*, Vintage, New York [orig. 1980].

Carmichael, S. (1971) *Stokely Speaks: Black Power Back to Pan-Africanism*, Vintage, New York.

Chernoff, J.M. (1979) *African Rhythm and African Sensibility: Aesthetics and Social Action in African Musical Idioms*, University of Chicago Press, Chicago.

Chernoff, J.M. (2003) *Hustling Is Not Stealing: Stories of an African Bar Girl*, University of Chicago Press, Chicago.

Childers, S. (2009) *Another Man's War: The True Story of One Man's Battle to Save Children in the Sudan*, Thomas Nelson, Nashville, TN.

Chilson, P. (1999) *Riding the Demon: On the Road in West Africa*, University of Georgia Press, Athens.

Crichton, M. (2009) *Congo*, Harper, New York [orig. 1980].

Clark, J.L. (1928) *Trails of the Hunted*, Little, Brown, and Company, Boston.

Cole, T. (2012) *Open City*, Random House, New York.

Conrad, J. (1950) *Heart of Darkness and Secret Sharer*, Signet, New York.

Crothers, T. (2016) *The Queen of Katwe*, Scribner, New York [orig. 2012].

Dau, J.B. with M.S. Sweenjer (2007) *God Grew Tired of Us*, National Geographic, Washington, DC.

Davis, K. with B. Clark (2011) *Kisses from Katie: A Story of Relentless Love and Redemption*, Howard, New York.

D'Haim, J. (1997) *The Last Camel: True Stories of Somalia*, Red Sea Press, Lawrenceville, NJ.

Drew, E. (1989) *Blue Taxis: Stories about Africa*, Milkweed, Minneapolis, MN.

Drew, E. (1996) *The Ivory Crocodile*, Coffee House Press, Minneapolis, MN.

D'Souza, T. (2006) *Whiteman*, Harcourt, Orlando, FL.

Du Bois, W.E.B. (1975) *Dusk of Dawn*, Kraus-Thomson, Millwood, NY [orig. 1940].

Duke, L. (2003) *Mandela, Mobutu, and Me: A Newswoman's African Journey*, Doubleday, New York.

Erdman, S. (2003) *Nine Hills to Nambonkaha: Two Years in the Heart of an African Village*, Henry Holt, New York.

Forman, J. (1972) *The Making of Black Revolutionaries*, Macmillan, New York.

Fossey, D. (1983) *Gorillas in the Mist*, Houghton Mifflin, Boston.

French, H.W. (2005) *A Continent for the Taking: The Tragedy and Hope of Africa*, Vintage, New York.

Gates, Jr., H.L. (1999) *Wonders of the African World*, Alfred A. Knopf, New York.

Gellhorn, M. (1979) *Travels with Myself and Another*, Dodd, Mead, New York.

Gellhorn, M. (2006) *The Weather in Africa: Three Novellas*, Eland, London [orig. 1978].

Golden, M. (1983) *Migrations of the Heart*, Anchor Press, Garden City, NY.

Golden, M. (1986) *A Woman's Place*, Doubleday, Garden City, NY.

Greenfield, E., illust. C. Byard (1977) *Africa Dream*, John Day, New York.

Gyasi, Y. (2016) *Homegoing*, Knopf, New York.

Habila, H. (2007) *Measuring Time*, W.W. Norton, New York.

Haley, A. (1976) *Roots*, Dell, New York.

Hansberry, L. (1994) *A Raisin in the Sun*, Vintage, New York [orig. 1959].

Hansberry, L. (1972) *Les Blancs: The Collected Last Plays of Lorraine Hansberry*. Random House, New York.

Harris, E.L. (1993) *Native Stranger: A Black American's Journey into the Heart of Africa*, Vintage, New York.

Harrison, W. (1977) *Africana*, William Morrow, New York.

Harrison, W. (1981) *Savannah Blue*, Richard Marek, New York.

Harrison. W. (1982) *Burton and Speke*, St. Martin's, New York.

Hartman, S. (2007) *Lose Your Mother: A Journey along the Atlantic Slave Route*, Farrar, Straus and Giroux, New York.

Haugen, G.A. (2008) *Just Courage: God's Great Expedition for the Restless Christian*, InterVarsity Press, Downers Grove, IL [orig. 2002].

Helser, A.D. (1940) *The Glory of the Impossible: Demonstrations of Divine Power in the Sudan*, Evangelical Publishers, Toronto.

Hemingway, E. (1963) *Green Hills of Africa*, Scribner, New York [orig. 1935].

Hemingway, E. (1995) *The Snows of Kilimanjaro and Other Stories*, Scribner, New York.

Hemingway, E. (1999) *True at First Light*, Scribner, New York.

Hemingway, E. (2005) *Under Kilimanjaro*, Kent State University Press, Kent, OH.

Hemingway, M.W. (1976) *How It Was*, Alfred A. Knopf, New York.

Higgins, C., Jr., *Feeling the Spirit: Searching the World for the People of Africa*, Bantam, New York, 1994.

Holloway, K. (2007) *Monique and the Mango Rains: Two Years with a Midwife in Mali*, Waveland Press, Long Grove, IL.

Hughes, L. (1968) *The Big Sea*, Hill and Wang, New York [orig. 1940].

Hulme, K. (1956) *The Nun's Story*, Little, Brown, Boston [orig. 1955].

Hunter-Gault, C. (2006) *New News out of Africa: Uncovering Africa's Renaissance*, Oxford University Press, Oxford.

Javins, M. (2006) *Stalking the Wild Dik-Dik: One Woman's Solo Misadventures across Africa*, Seal Press, Emeryville, CA.

Jeske, C. (2010) *Into the Mud: Inspiration for Everyday Activists*, Moody, Chicago.

Johnson, M. (1924) *Camera Trails in Africa*, Century, New York.

Johnson, M. (1928) *Safari: A Saga of African Adventure*, Grosset and Dunlap, New York.

Johnson, Mrs. M. (1930) *Jungle Babies*, G.P. Putnam's Sons, New York.

Johnson, Mrs. M. (1939) *Osa Johnson's Jungle Friends*, J.B. Lippincott, Philadelphia, PA.

Johnson, O. (1997) *I Married Adventure: The Lives of Martin and Osa Johnson*, Kodansha International, New York [orig. 1940].

Kaplan, R.D. (1997) *The Ends of the Earth: From Togo to Turkmenistan, from Iran to Cambodia—a Journey to the Frontiers of Anarchy*, Vintage, New York.

Kellersberger, J.L. (1936) *Congo Crosses: A Study of Congo Womanhood*, The Central Committee of the United Study of Foreign Missions, Boston, MA.

Kingsolver, B. (1999) *The Poisonwood Bible*, Harper Perennial, New York [orig. 1998].

Knight, M.B. and M. Melnicove, illust. A.S. O'Brien (2000) *Africa is Not a Country*, Millbrook Press, Brookfield, CT.

Lacy, L.A. (1970) *The Rise and Fall of a Proper Negro*, Macmillan, New York.

Ladd, F. (1997) *Sarah's Psalm*, Scribner, New York.

Lamb, D. (1987) *The Africans*, Vintage, New York [orig. 1983].

Latham, A. (1991) *The Frozen Leopard: Hunting My Dark Heart in Africa*, Prentice-Hall, New York.

Lowerre, S. (1991) *Under the Neem Tree*, Permanent Press, Sag Harbor, NY.

Maathai, W. (2006) *Unbowed*, Knopf, New York.

Maathai, W. (2009) *The Challenge for Africa*, Pantheon, New York.

Mackenzie, J.K. (1917) *An African Trail*, Central Committee on the United Study of Foreign Missions, West Medford, MA.

Mackenzie, J.K. (1917) *African Adventures*, Central Committee of the United Study of Foreign Missions, West Medford, MA.

Mackenzie, J.K. (1924) *African Clearings*, Houghton Mifflin, Boston.

Mackenzie, J.K. (1930) *The Trader's Wife*, Coward-McCann, New York.

Mackenzie, J.K. (1969) *Black Sheep: Adventures in West Africa*, Negro Universities Press, New York [orig. 1916].

Mackenzie, J.K., A.R.R. Fraser, C.D. Bridgman and J.H. Oldham (1928) *Friends of Africa*, Central Committee on the United States Study of Foreign Missions, Cambridge, MA.

Marshall, P. (1983) *Praisesong for the Widow*, Penguin, New York.

Marshall, P. (1992) *The Chosen Place, the Timeless People*, Vintage, New York [orig. 1969].

Michener, J.A. (1987) *The Covenant*, Fawcett Crest, New York [orig. 1980].

Morrison, T. (2004) *Song of Solomon*, Vintage, New York [orig. 1977].

Morrison, T. (2004) *Beloved*, Vintage [orig. 1987].

Murray, P. (1987) *Song in a Weary Throat: An American Pilgrimage*, Harper & Row, New York.

Naylor, G. (1989) *Mama Day*, Vintage, NY.

Naylor, W.S. (1905) *Daybreak in the Dark Continent*, Eaton & Mains, New York.

Obama, B. (2004) *Dreams from My Father: A Story of Race and Inheritance*, Three Rivers Press, New York [orig. 1995].

Odede, K. and J. Posner (2015) *Find Me Unafraid: Love, Loss and Hope in an African Slum*, HarperCollins, New York.

Packer, G. (2000) *Blood of the Liberals*, Straus and Giroux, New York.

Packer, G. (2001) *The Village of Waiting*, Farrar, Straus and Giroux, New York [orig. 1988].

Powers, W. (2006) *Blue Clay People: Seasons on Africa's Fragile Edge*, Bloomsbury, New York.

Preston, R. (1994) *The Hot Zone*, Anchor, New York.

Prokosch, F. (1948) *Storm and Echo*, Doubleday, New York.

Putnam, A.E., with A. Keller (1954) *Madami: My Eight Years of Adventure with the Congo Pigmies*, Prentice-Hall, New York.

Raboteau, E. (2013) *Searching for Zion*, Grove, New York.

Richburg, K.B. (1997) *Out of America: A Black Man Confronts Africa*, BasicBooks, New York.

Robeson, E.G. (1945) *African Journey*, John Day, New York.

Roosevelt, T. (1988) *African Game Trails*, St. Martin's Press, New York [orig. 1910].

Ruark, R. (1953) *Horn of the Hunter*, Doubleday, Garden City, NY.

Ruark, R. (1955) *Something of Value*, Doubleday, Garden City, NY.

Ruark, R. (1969) *Uhuru*, Corgi Books, London [orig. 1962].

Rush, N. (1992) *Whites*, Vintage, New York.

Rush, N. (1992) *Mating*, Vintage, New York.

Sanders, L. (2000) *Three Complete Novels*, G.P. Putnam's Sons, New York.

Schmidt, M.M. (2005) *Last Moon Dancing: A Memoir of Love and Real Life in Africa*, Clover Park Press, Santa Monica, CA.

Schuyler, P.D. (1960) *Adventures in Black and White*, R. Speller, New York.

Schuyler, P. (1962) *Who Killed the Congo?*, Devin-Adair, New York.

Schuyler, G.S. (1966) *Black and Conservative: The Autobiography of George S. Schuyler*, Arlington House, New Rochelle, NY.

Schuyler, G.S. (1969) *Slaves Today: A Story of Liberia*, McGrath, College Park, MD [orig. 1931].

Scieszka C. and S. Weinberg (2011) *To Timbuktu*, Roaring Brook Press, New York.

Selasi, T. (2013) *Ghana Must Go*, Penguin, New York.

Shannon, L.J. (2010) *A Thousand Sisters: My Journey into the Worst Place on Earth to be a Woman*, Seal Press, Berkeley, CA.

Sheikhk, F. (2001) *A Camel for the Son*, n.p., n.p.

Skelton, Jr., J.W. (1991) *Volunteering in Ethiopia: A Peace Corps Odyssey*, Beaumont, Denver, CO.

Smith, E. (1967) *Where To, Black Man?* Quadrangle, Chicago.

Smith, J. (2010) *Crossing the Heart of Africa: An Odyssey of Love and Adventure*, Harper Perennial, New York.

Smith, W.G. (1967) *Return to Black America*, Prentice-Hall, Englewood Cliffs.

Stinetorf, L.A. (1950) *White Witch Doctor*, Westminster Press, Philadelphia, PA.

Stinetorf, L.A. (1954) *Beyond the Hungry Country*, J.B. Lippincott, Philadelphia, PA.

Stinetorf, L.A. (1956) *Elephant Outlaw*, J.B. Lippincott, Philadelphia, PA.

Stoller, P. (2004) *Stranger in the Village of the Sick: A Memoir of Cancer, Sorcery, and Healing*, Beacon, Boston.

Stoller, P. (2009) *The Power of Between: An Anthropological Odyssey*, University of Chicago Press, Chicago.

Swiller, J. (2007) *The Unheard: A Memoir of Deafness and Africa*, Henry Holt, New York.

Tayler, J. (2000) *Facing the Congo: A Modern-Day Journey into the Heart of Darkness*, Three Rivers Press, New York.

Tayler, J. (2005) *Angry Wind: Through Muslim Black Africa by Truck, Bus, Boat, and Camel*, Houghton Mifflin, Boston.

Theroux, P. (1983) *Girls at Play*, Penguin, Harmondsworth [orig. 1969].

Theroux, P. (1985) *Sunrise with Seamonsters: Travels and Discoveries, 1974–1984*, Houghton Mifflin, Boston.

Theroux, P. (1992) *Fong and the Indians*, Penguin, London [orig. 1968].

Theroux, P. (1996) *My Secret History*, Fawcett Columbine, New York [orig. 1989].

Theroux, P. (2004) *Dark Star Safari: Overland from Cairo to Cape Town*, Houghton Mifflin, Boston.

Theroux, P. (2012) *The Lower River*, Houghton Mifflin Harcourt, Boston.

Theroux, P. (2013) *The Last Train to Zona Verde: Overland from Cape Town to Angola*, Hamish Hamilton, London.

Thomas, M. (1987) *Come to Africa and Save Your Marriage and Other Stories*, Soho Press, New York.

Thomas, M. (1991) *African Visas: A Novella and Stories*, Soho, New York.

Thomas, M. (2007) *Antonia Saw the Oryx First*, Soho Press, New York [orig. 1987].

Thompson, E.B. (1946) *American Daughter*, University of Chicago Press, Chicago.

Thompson, E.B. (1954) *Africa: Land of My Fathers*, Doubleday, New York.

Tidwell, M. (1990) *The Ponds of Kalambayi: An African Sojourn*, Lyons & Burford, New York.

Wainaina, B. (2011) *One Day I Will Write About This Place: A Memoir*, Graywolf Press, Minneapolis, MN.

Walker, A. (1967) *In Love & Trouble: Stories of Black Women*, Harcourt Brace Jovanovich, New York.

Walker, A. (1985) *The Color Purple*, Pocket, New York [orig. 1982].

Walker, A. (1989) *The Temple of My Familiar*, Harcourt Brace Jovanovich, San Diego, CA.

Walker, A. (1992) *Possessing the Secret of Joy*, Harcourt Brace Jovanovich, New York.

Wheeler, W.F. (2008) *Alive in Africa: My Journeys on Foot in the Sahara, Rift Valley, and Rain Forest*, Lyons Press, Guilford, CT.

White, S.E. (1913) *The Land of Footprints*, Doubleday, Page & Co., New York.

White, S.E. (1913) *African Camp Fires*, Doubleday, Page & Co., New York.

White, S.E. (1915) *The Rediscovered Country*, Doubleday, Page & Co., New York.

White, S.E. (1926) *Lions in the Path*, Doubleday, Page & Co., Garden City, NY.

Williams-Garcia, R. (2004) *No Laughter Here*, HarperCollins, New York.

Wilson, B. (2006) *Dead Men Don't Leave Tips: Adventures X Africa*, Pilgrim's Tales, Paia, HI.

Wilson, J.R. (1935) *Men and Woman of Far Horizons*, Friendship Press, New York.

Wright, R. (1940) *Native Son*, Harper, New York.

Wright, R. (1954) *Black Power: A Record of Reactions in a Land of Pathos*, Harper, New York.

Wright, R. (1963) *Black Boy: A Record of Childhood and Youth*, Signet, New York [orig. 1945].

Wright, R. (1995) *White Man, Listen!* Harper, New York [orig. 1957].

Yerby, F. (1971) *The Dahomean*, Dial Press, New York.

Zachary, G.P. (2009) *Married to Africa: A Love Story*, Scribner, New York.

PRIMARY SOURCES: FILMS

Africa Extreme (2001) USA, National Geographic Channel.

'Africa for Norway' (2012) https://www.youtube.com/watch?v=oJ Lqyuxm96k.

'African Men. Hollywood Stereotypes' (2012) https://www.youtube.com/watch?v=qSElmEmEjb4&nohtml5=False.

The African Queen (1951) USA, Romulus Films.

Africa: The Serengeti (1994) USA, Graphic Films.

Black Hawk Down (2001) USA, Revolution Studios.

Blood Diamond (2006) USA, Warner Brothers.

Born Free (1966) UK, Open Road Films.

Bwana Devil (1952) USA, Gulu Productions.

Cheetah (1989) USA, Silver Screen Partners.

Clarence the Cross-Eyed Lion (1965) USA, Ivan Tors Production.

The Color Purple (1985) USA, Amblin Entertainment.

Congorilla (1932) USA, Fox Film Corporation.

Daktari (1966–1969).

Dark of the Sun (1968) USA, MGM.

Drums of Africa (1963) USA, MGM.

A Far Off Place (1993) USA, Walt Disney Pictures.

The Four Feathers (2002) USA, Paramount Pictures.

The Ghost and the Darkness (1996) USA, Constellation Entertainment.

God Grew Tired of Us (2006) USA, Lost Boys of Sudan.

The Gods Must Be Crazy (1980) South Africa, CAT Films.

Hatari (1962) USA, Malabar.

Hotel Rwanda (2004) USA, United Artists.

I Dreamed of Africa (2000) USA, Columbia Pictures Corporation.

Khartoum (1966) UK, Julian Blaustein Productions.

King Solomon's Mines (1950) USA, MGM.

'KONY 2012' (2012) https://www.youtube.com/watch?v=Y4 MnpzG5Sqc.

The Language You Cry In (1998) Sierra Leone, Inko Producciones.

The Last Safari (1967) UK, Paramount.

The Legend of Tarzan (2016) USA, Dark Horse Entertainment.

Lion King (1994) USA, Walt Disney Pictures.

Lord of War (2005) USA, Entertainment Manufacturing Company.

Machine Gun Preacher (2011) USA, Relativity Media.

The Macomber Affair (1947) USA, Benedict Bogeaus Production.

Mama C: Urban Warrior in the African Bush (2013) USA, Perennial Films.

Mogambo (1953) USA, MGM.

Mutual of Omaha's Wild Kingdom (1963–2011).

The New Adventures of Tarzan (1938) USA, Burroughs-Tarzan Enterprises.

The Nun's Story (1959) USA, Warner Brothers.

Out of Africa (1985) USA, Mirage Enterprises.

Outbreak (1995) USA, Warner Brothers.

A Panther in Africa (2004) USA, Independent Television Service.

Queen of Katwe (2016) USA, Walt Disney Pictures.

Red Scorpion (1988) USA, Abramoff Production.

Roots (1977).

The Roots of Heaven (1958) USA, Darryl F. Zanuck Productions.

Savage Splendor (1949) USA, Armand Denis Productions.

'Sh*t African Parents Say' (2012) https://www.youtube.com/ watch?v=EUennrxksM4&nohtml5=False.

The Snows of Kilimanjaro (1952) USA, Twentieth Century Fox.

Something of Value (1957) USA, MGM.

Sometimes in April (2005) France, CINEFACTO.

A Study of Peter Beard (1996) https://www.youtube.com/watch?v= _Y6w3elcz6U.

Tarzan (1999) USA, Walt Disney Pictures.

Tarzan and His Mate (1934) USA, MGM.

Tarzan and the Golden Lion (1927) USA, Robertson-Cole Pictures.

Tarzan and the Huntress (1947) USA, Sol Lesser Productions.

Tarzan and the Jungle Boy (1968) USA, Banner Productions.

Tarzan and the Lost Safari (1957) USA, Solar Films.

Tarzan and the She Devil (1953) USA, Sol Lesser Productions.

Tarzan and the Slave Girl (1950) USA, Sol Lesser Productions.

Tarzan Escapes (1936) USA, MGM.

Tarzan Finds a Son (1939) USA, MGM.

Tarzan of the Apes (1918) USA, National Film Corporation of America.

Tarzan the Magnificent (1960) UK, Solar Films.

Tarzan's Fight for Life (1958) USA, Sol Lesser Productions.

Tarzan's Greatest Adventure (1959) USA, Solar Films.

Tarzan's Magic Fountain (1949) USA, Sol Lesser Productions.

Tarzan's Savage Fury (1952) USA, Sol Lesser Productions.

Tears of the Sun (2003) USA, Cheyenne Enterprises.

Untamed (1955) USA, Twentieth Century Fox.

White Witch Doctor (1953) USA, Twentieth Century Fox.

Wonders of the African World (1999).

MAJOR SECONDARY SOURCES

Adams, J.S. and T.O. McShane (1996) *The Myth of Wild Africa: Conservation Without Illusion*, University of California Press, Berkeley.

Adeleke, T. (1998) *UnAfrican Americans: Nineteenth-Century Black Nationalists and the Civilizing Mission*, University Press of Kentucky, Lexington.

Allimadi, M. (2002) *The Hearts of Darkness: How White Writers Created the Racist Image of Africa*, Black Star Books, New York.

Austin, A. (2006) *Achieving Blackness: Race, Black Nationalism, and Afrocentrism in the Twentieth Century*, NYU Press, New York.

Berry, F. (1983) *Langston Hughes: Before and Beyond Harlem*, Lawrence Hill, Westport, CT.

Bodry-Sanders, P. (1991) *Carl Akeley: Africa's Collector, Africa's Savior*, Paragon House, New York.

Bowermaster, J. (1993) *The Adventures and Misadventures of Peter Beard in Africa*, Little, Brown, Boston.

Cameron, K.M. (1994) *Africa on Film: Beyond Black and White*, Continuum, New York.

Campbell, J.T. (2006) *Middle Passages: African American Journeys to Africa, 1787–2005*, Penguin, New York.

Carmichael, S. with E.M. Thelwell (2003) *Ready for Revolution: The Life and Struggles of Stokely Carmichael (Kwame Ture)*, Scribner, New York: Scribner.

Carter, S.R. (1991) *Hansberry's Drama: Commitment and Complexity*, University of Illinois Press, Urbana.

Cartwright, K. (2002) *Reading Africa into American Literature:*

Epics, Fables, and Gothic Tales, University of Kentucky, Lexington.

Cheney, A. (1984) *Lorraine Hansberry*, Twayne, Boston.

Ciment, J. (2013) *Another America: The Story of Liberia and the Former Slaves Who Ruled It*, Hill and Wang, New York.

Cooper, B. (2002) *Weary Sons of Conrad: White Fiction against the Grain of Africa's Dark Heart*, Bern, New York.

Davis, P. (1996) *In Darkest Hollywood: Exploring the Jungles of Cinema's South Africa*, Ohio University Press, Athens.

DeLamotte, E.C. (1998) *Places of Silence, Journeys of Freedom: The Fiction of Paule Marshall*, University of Pennsylvania Press, Philadelphia.

Denniston, D.H. (1983) *The Fiction of Paule Marshall: Reconstructions of History, Culture, and Gender*, University of Tennessee Press, Knoxville.

Diawara, M. (1998) *In Search of Africa*, Harvard University Press, Cambridge, MA.

Donnelly, J. (2012) *A Twist of Faith: An American Christian's Quest to Help Orphans in Africa*, Beacon, Boston.

Dubey, M. (1994) *Black Women Novelists and the Nationalist Aesthetic*, Indiana University Press, Bloomington.

Ducille, A. (1996) *Skin Trade*, Harvard University Press, Cambridge, MA.

Easterly, W. (2007) *The White Man's Burden: Why the West's Efforts to Aid the Rest Have Done So Much Ill and So Little Good*, Penguin, New York.

Enright, K. (2011) *Osa and Martin: For the Love of Adventure*, Lyons Press, Guilford, CT.

Ferguson, J.B. (2005) *The Sage of Sugar Hill: George S. Schuyler and the Harlem Renaissance*, Yale University Press, New Haven, CT.

Fischer, R. (1998) *Making Them Like Us: Peace Corps Volunteers in the 1960s*, Smithsonian Institution Press, Washington, DC.

Foster, H.W. (1992) *Someone of Value: A Biography of Robert Ruark*, Trophy Room Books, Agoura, CA.

Fowler, V.C. (1996) *Gloria Naylor: In Search of Sanctuary*, Twayne, New York.

Gabbard, K. (2004) *Black Magic: White Hollywood and African American Culture*, Rutgers University Press, New Brunswick, NJ.

Gaines, K.K. (2006) *American Africans in Ghana: Black Expatriates and the Civil Rights Era*, University of North Carolina Press, Chapel Hill.

Gardner, J.L. (1973) *Departing Glory: Theodore Roosevelt as ex-President*, Charles Scribner's Sons, New York.

Goldman, P. (1979) *The Death and Life of Malcolm X*, University of Illinois Press, Urbana.

Goudsouzian, A. (2004) *Sidney Poitier: Man, Actor, Icon*, University of North Carolina Press, Chapel Hill.

Grant, C. (2008) *Negro with a Hat: The Rise and Fall of Marcus Garvey*, Oxford University Press, Oxford.

Grubbs, L. (2009) *Secular Missionaries: Americans and African Devel-opment in the 1960s*, University of Massachusetts Press, Amherst.

Gruesser, J.C. (1992) *White on Black: Contemporary Literature about Africa*, University of Illinois Press, Urbana.

Hamilton, R. (2011) *Fighting for Darfur: Public Action and the Struggle to Stop Genocide*, Palgrave Macmillan, New York.

Haraway, D. (1989) *Primate Visions: Gender, Race, and Nature in the World of Modern Science*, Routledge, New York.

Hardison, A.K. (2014) *Writing through Jane Crow: Race and Gender Politics in African American Literature*, University of Virginia Press, Charlottesville.

Harold, C.N. (2007) *The Rise and Fall of the Garvey Movement in the Urban South, 1918–1942*, Routledge, New York.

Hickey, D. and K.C. Wylie (1993) *An Enchanting Darkness: The American Vision of Africa in the Twentieth Century*, Michigan State University Press, East Lansing.

Higgins, T.E. (2001) *Religiosity, Cosmology, and Folklore: The African Influence in the Novels of Toni Morrison*, Routledge, New York.

Hill, P.R. (1985) *The World their Household: The American Women's Foreign Mission Movement and Cultural Transformation, 1870–1920*, University of Michigan Press, Ann Arbor.

Hoffman, E.C. (1998) *All You Need Is Love: The Peace Corps and the Spirit of the 1960s,* Harvard University Press, Cambridge, MA.

Holsey, B. (2008) *Routes of Remembrance: Refashioning the Slave Trade in Ghana,* University of Chicago Press, Chicago.

Holtsmark, E.B. (1986) *Edgar Rice Burroughs,* Twanye, Boston.

Horne, G. (2009) *Mau Mau in Harlem? The U.S. and the Liberation of Kenya,* Palgrave Macmillan, New York.

Hutchinson, W.R. (1987) *Errand to the World: American Protestant Thought and Foreign Missions,* University of Chicago Press, Chicago.

Imperato, P.J. and E. Imperato (1992) *They Married Adventure: The Wandering Lives of Martin and Osa Johnson,* Rutgers University Press, New Brunswick, NJ.

Irele, F.A. (2001) *African Imagination: Literature in Africa and the Black Diaspora,* Oxford University Press, New York.

Jennings, L.V.D. (2008) *Toni Morrison and the Idea of Africa,* Cambridge University Press, Cambridge.

Kanneh, K. (1998) *African Identities: Race, Nation and Culture in Ethnography, Pan-Africanism and Black Literatures,* Routledge, London.

Keim, C. (2009) *Mistaking Africa: Curiosities and Inventions of the American Mind,* 2nd ed., Westview, Boulder, CO.

Kelley, M.A. (1999) *Gloria Naylor's Early Novels,* University Press of Florida, Gainesville.

Kirk, J. (2010) *Kingdom Under Glass: A Tale of Obsession, Adventure, and One Man's Quest to Preserve the World's Greatest Animals,* Henry Holt, New York.

Kuhne, D. (1999) *African Settings in Contemporary American Novels,* Greenwood Press, Westport, CT.

Levin, A.K. (2003) *Africanism and Authenticity in African-American Women's Novels,* University Press of Florida, Gaineseville.

Lutz, C.A. and J.L. Collins (1993) *Reading National Geographic,* University of Chicago Press, Chicago.

Magee, C. (2012) *Africa in the American Imagination: Popular Culture, Racialized Identities, and African Visual Culture,* University Press of Mississippi, Jackson.

Mamdani, M. (2009) *Saviors and Survivors: Darfur, Politics, and the War on Terror*, Pantheon, New York.

Maren, M. (1997) *The Road to Hell: The Ravaging Effects of Foreign Aid and International Charity*, Free Press, New York.

Mathers, K. (2010) *Travel, Humanitarianism, and Becoming American in Africa*, Palgrave Macmillan, New York.

May, S.J. (2005) *Michener: A Writer's Journey*, University of Oklahoma Press, Norman.

Mayer, R. (2002) *Artificial Africas: Colonial Images in the Times of Globalization*, Dartmouth College, Hanover, NH.

McCarthy, T. (1997) *Howard Hawks: The Grey Fox of Hollywood*, Grove Press, New York.

McDonald, C., ed. (2005) *Images of Congo: Anne Eisner's Art and Ethnography, 1946–1958*, Five Continents, Milan.

McKinley, E.H. (1974) *The Lure of Africa: American Interests in Tropical Africa, 1919–1939*, Bobbs-Merrill, New York.

Meriwether, J.H. (2002) *Proudly We Can Be Africans, 1935–1962*, University of North Carolina Press, Chapel Hill.

Meyer, L.E. (1992) *The Farther Frontier: Six Case Studies of Americans and Africa, 1848–1936*, Susquehanna University Press, Selinsgrove, PA.

Meyers, J. (1997) *Bogart: A Life in Hollywood*, Houghton-Mifflin, Boston, MA.

Mitman, G. (1999) *Reel Nature: America's Romance with Wildlife on Film*, Harvard University Press, Cambridge, MA.

Moeller, S.D. (1999) *Compassion Fatigue: How the Media Sell Disease, Famine, War and Death*, Routledge, New York.

Moorehead, C. (2003) *Gellhorn: A Twentieth-Century Life*, Henry Holt, New York.

Moses, W.J. (1990) *The Wings of Ethiopia*, Iowa State University Press, Ames.

Moyo, D. (2009) *Dead Aid: Why Aid Is Not Working and How There Is a Better Way for Africa*, Farrar, Straus and Giroux, New York.

Munk, N. (2013) *The Idealist: Jeffrey Sachs and the Quest to End Poverty*, Doubleday, New York.

Nesbitt, F.N. (2004) *Race for Sanctions: African Americans against Apartheid, 1946–1994*, Indiana University Press, Bloomington.

Olds, E.F. (1985) *Women of the Four Winds*, Houghton Mifflin, Boston.

Penn, S. (2013) *Case for a Pardon: The Pete O'Neal Story*, Pembooks, n.p.

Peplow, M.W. (1980) *George S. Schuyler*, Twayne, Boston, MA.

Phillips, C. (2000) *The Atlantic Sound*, Alfred A. Knopf, New York.

Phillips, C. (2001) *A New World Order*, Secker & Warburg, London.

Pierre, J. (2013) *Predicament of Blackness: Postcolonial Ghana and the Politics of Race*, University of Chicago Press, Chicago.

Plummer, B.G. (1996) *Rising Wind: Black Americans and U.S. Foreign Affairs, 1935–1960*, University of North Carolina Press, Chapel Hill.

Plummer, B.G. (2013) *In Search of Power: African Americans in the Era of Decolonization, 1956–1976*, Cambridge University Press, New York.

Prevost, E.E. (2010) *The Communion of Women: Missions and Gender in Colonial Africa and the British Metropole*, Oxford University Press, Oxford.

Rampersad, A. (1988) *The Life of Langston Hughes*, Vol. II, Oxford University Press, New York.

Reed, A. (2015) *Pilgrimage Tourism of Diaspora Africans to Ghana*, Routledge, New York.

Rensby, B. (2013) *Eslanda: The Large and Unconventional Life of Mrs. Paul Robeson*, Yale University Press, New Haven, CT.

Ritchie, A., ed. J. Casada (2006) *Ruark Remembered—By the Man Who Knew Him Best*, Sporting Classics, n.p.

Roberts, R. and J.S. Olson (1995) *John Wayne: American*, Free Press, New York.

Rollyson, C. (1990) *Nothing Ever Happens to the Brave: The Story of Martha Gellhorn*, St. Martin's Press, New York.

Rolinson, M.G. (2007) *Grassroots Garveyism: The Universal Negro Improvement Association in the Rural South, 1920–1927*, University of North Carolina Press, Chapel Hill.

Rowley, H. (2001) *Richard Wright: The Life and Times*, Henry Holt, New York.

Schwimmer, B.E. and D.M. Warren, eds., *Anthropology and the Peace Corps: Case Studies in Career Preparation*, Iowa State University Press, Ames.

Shucard, A.R. (1984) *Countee Cullen*, Twayne, Boston, MA.

Squires, R. (1964) *Frederic Prokosch*, Twayne, New York.

Stanisland, M. (1991) *American Intellectuals and African Nationalists, 1955–1970*, Yale University Press, New Haven, CT.

Sugrue, T.J. (2010) *Not Even Past: Barack Obama and the Burden of Race*, Princeton University Press, Princeton, NJ.

Sundiata, I. (2003) *Brothers and Strangers: Black Zion, Black Slavery, 1914–1940*, Duke University Press, Durham, NC.

Talalay, K. (1995) *Composition in Black and White: The Life of Philippa Schuyler*, Oxford University Press, New York.

Thorsson, C. (2013) *Women's Work: Nationalism and Contemporary African American Women's Novels*, University of Virginia Press, Charlottesville.

Thurman, J. (1983) *Isak Dinesen: The Life of a Storyteller*, St. Martin's Press, New York.

Tillery, Jr., A.B. (2011) *Between Homeland and Motherland: Africa, U.S. Foreign Policy, and Black Leadership in America*, Cornell University Press, Ithaca, NY.

Tillet, S. (2012) *Sites of Slavery: Citizenship and Racial Democracy in the Post-Civil Rights Imagination*, Duke University Press, Durham, NC.

Van Deburg, W.L. (1992) *New Day In Babylon: The Black Power Movement and American Culture, 1965–1976*, University of Chicago Press, Chicago.

Vanhaecke, F. (2010) *A Useful Dream: African Photography, 1960–2010*, Silvana Editoriale, Milano.

Von Eschen, P.M. (1997) *Race against Empire: Black Americans and Anticolonialism, 1937–1957*, Cornell University Press, Ithaca, NY.

Walker, C.E. (2001) *We Can't Go Home Again: An Argument about Afrocentrism*, Oxford University Press, Oxford.

Walters, R.W. (1993) *Pan Africanism in the Africa Diaspora: An Analysis of Modern AfroCentric Political Movements*, Wayne State University Press, Detroit, MI.

Weisbord, R.G. (1973) *Ebony Kinship: Africa, Africans, and the Afro-American*, Greenwood Press, Westport, CT.

Wieland, T. (2000) *A View from a Tall Hill: Robert Ruark in Africa*, Thorn Tree Press, Prescott, WI.

Williams, O.R. (2007) *George S. Schuyler: Portrait of a Black Conservative*, University of Tennessee Press, Knoxville.

Wuthnow, R. (2009) *Boundless Faith: The Global Outreach of American Churches*, University of California Press, Berkeley.

Yenika-Agbaw, V. (2008) *Representing Africa in Children's Literature: Old and New Ways of Seeing*, Routledge, New York.

Zuaditu-Selassie, K. (2009) *African Spiritual Traditions in the Novels of Toni Morrison*, University Press of Florida, Gainesville.

INDEX

Helser, Albert, 45
Hemingway, Ernest, 5, 86,
    88, 106, 137, 138, 150, 158,
    194; fiction of, 33–4, 93,
    95, 97; and film, 75–6; and
    misogyny, 33–4; nonfiction
    of, 32–3, 92–3, 94
Henderson the Rain King, 95–8,
    208
Homegoing, 307–8
Horn of Africa, 205–8, 212
Hotel Rwanda, 252–3, 277
Hughes, Langston, 5, 8, 14,
    60–1, 62, 63, 102, 314
Hulme, Kathryn, 6, 82, 122

In Brightest Africa, 29, 31
In Closed Territory, 24
individualism, 110, 232, 296;
    versus community, 133,
    166, 174; development of,
    4–5, 133, 185, 187; and
    masculinity, 4, 6, 97, 106,
    127, 169, 186, 187; and the
    Peace Corps, 180–1
Invisible Children, 280, 281,
    282, 283

Jane, 16, 17, 72, 82
Jeske, Christine, 276
Jobe, Mary, 37–8
Johnson, John H., 99, 104
Johnson, Martin, 5, 14, 38–42,
    43, 64
Johnson, Osa, 6, 38–40, 41,
    42, 43
Jones, LeRoi, 171

Jungle Babies, 42

Kaplan, Robert D., 190–1
Karenga, Maulana, 171, 231
Kayode, Marita Golden, 237,
    238–9, 240
Kennedy, John F., 174, 175,
    177
Kenney, Nathaniel, 139, 140
Kenyatta, Jomo, 135
Khartoum, 143–4, 145
Kinch, Emily Christmas, 19
Kingsolver, Barbara, 6, 210,
    211
Kirk, Jay, 31
KONY 2012, 280–1, 282–3,
    296
Kony, Joseph, 280, 281, 282
Kurtz, 2, 86, 156, 222

Lacy, Leslie Alexander, 163–4
Ladd, Florence, 239, 240, 314
Language You Cry In, The, 247,
    293, 314
Last Safari, The, 142–3, 145
Last Train to Zona Verde, The,
    156–7
Latham, Aron, 194–5
Liberia, 2, 113, 189, 211, 215,
    241, 280, 290, 293, 303;
    depicted in the American
    media, 70, 99, 125–7, 190,
    252, 304; and George
    Schuyler, 56, 57–8, 59, 60,
    63; missionaries in, 19, 20,
    21; and W.E.B. Du Bois,
    55–6, 59, 60, 63, 313

and the Huntress, 73; *Tarzan and the Jungle Boy*, 147–8; *Tarzan and the Lost Safari*, 81; *Tarzan and the She Devil*, 73; *Tarzan and the Slave Girl*, 73; *Tarzan Escapes*, 17; *Tarzan Finds a Son*, 17; *Tarzan's Fight for Life*, 81; *Tarzan's Greatest Adventure*, 81; *Tarzan of the Apes*, 15, 16; *Tarzan's Magic Fountain*, 73; *Tarzan's Savage Fury*, 73; *Tarzan the Magnificent*, 82
Tayler, Jeffrey, 261, 267–9
Tears of the Sun, 253–4
Tema, S.S., 47
Theroux, Paul, 6, 149, 156–8, 160, 182, 228, 261; fiction of, 153–5, 157; and *My Secret History*, 153, 155
Thomas, Maria, 6, 9, 215, 219, 229, 314; and *Antonia Saw the Oryx First*, 211–12, 213, 214
Thompson, Era Bell, 6, 104, 105,114, 116, 161; and identity, 110–11, 112, 113, 314
Thomson, Irene Taviss, 4
Tidwell, Mike, 223
Torgovnick, Marianna, 6
tourism, 260–5, 266, 267, 269, 285–6
Trump, Donald, 5, 298
Ture, Kwame, 170, 172, 173, 313 (see also Carmichael, Stokeley)

Uhuru, 91–2
United Negro Improvement Association (UNIA), 18, 19–20, 99, 230
Untamed, 78–9

Wainaina, Binyavanga, 299, 300
Walker, Alice, 6, 240, 241, 242
Warren, Rick, 6, 272–3
Warrick, Roberta, 211, 212–13 (see also Maria Thomas)
Water Music, 208
Whiteman, 225–6
White, Stuart Edward, 24, 26, 27, 28, 31, 32, 45, 64, 90
White Witch Doctor, 117–18
White Witch Doctor (film), 127–8
Wilkinson, Bruce, 273–4, 315
Winfrey, Oprah, 6, 186, 258, 259, 275, 298
World War II, 7, 8, 17, 38, 54, 65, 69, 84, 89, 98, 111
Wright, Richard, 5, 111, 113, 114, 116, 162, 168, 295, 313; childhood of, 105–6, 108, 110; politics of, 105, 106, 112; views on Ghana, 107–8, 109

Yerby, Frank, 6, 168, 169, 313
Yo Ghana!, 11, 12, 316

Zachary, G. Pascal, 305–6

ABOUT THE AUTHOR

David Peterson del Mar is an associate professor at Portland State University and the president and co-founder of Yo Ghana!, a non-profit dedicated to helping students in Ghana and the US learn about and from each other first hand. *African, American* is his seventh book. He lives in Portland, Oregon with his wife and son and is an usher at Portland International Church.